Helping People Through Grief

Helping People Through Grief

DELORES KUENNING

BETHANY HOUSE PUBLISHERS
MINNEAPOLIS, MINNESOTA 55438
A Division of Bethany Fellowship, Inc.

Manuscript edited by Penelope J. Stokes.

Verses marked TLB are taken from *The Living Bible*, copyright 1971 by Tyndale House Publishers, Wheaton, IL. Used by permission.

Scripture quotations marked NIV are from *The Holy Bible, New International Version*. Copyright © 1973, 1978, 1984 by International Bible Society.

Scripture quotations marked RSV are from the Revised Standard Version Bible, copyright 1946, 1952, 1971 by the Division of Christian Education of the National Council of the Churches of Christ in the USA, and are used by permission.

Scripture quotations from *The New English Bible*, copyright 1961, 1970 by Oxford University Press. Used by permission.

Published by Bethany House Publishers
A Division of Bethany Fellowship, Inc.
6820 Auto Club Road, Minneapolis, Minnesota 55438

Printed in the United States of America

Library of Congress Cataloging-in-Publication Data

Kuenning, Delores.
    Helping people through grief.

    Bibliography: p.
    1. Bereavement—Religious aspects—Christianity.
2. Consolation.   I. Title.
BV4905.2.K8   1987   259'.6   87-20870
ISBN 0-87123-921-3 (pbk.)

TO
hurting hearts everywhere
in the hope that loving arms will embrace them
and willing hearts will listen to their pain,
giving them permission to grieve,
and
to our son,
Paul John Kuenning

DELORES KUENNING (Ken´-ning) has been a freelance writer for over 19 years. From 1977 to 1985 she wrote professionally as director of public relations for a medical center in Illinois. The wife of a pastor and mother of four grown children, she has been very active in her church and is a speaker for workshops and retreats. Twelve years of working closely with medical professionals on all levels helped prepare her for writing this book.

FOREWORD

Congregations are becoming increasingly aware how important a role their members can play in assisting one another in times of grief and despair.

Delores Kuenning's book is a remarkable "textbook" to recommend for teaching caring people how to help helpfully. It is the most comprehensive treatment of "How to Care" I have ever come across.

It is an encyclopedia of information on every conceivable form of grief. But more than that, it describes simply and directly how to respond to these griefs. All of the suggestions are based upon the accumulated wisdom of the Scriptures, church tradition and the experiences of present-day Christians.

The author's sensitivity to the power of emotions is enhanced by her knowledge in the fields of both theology and the social sciences, which are evident on every page. She is a lay person's theologian.

> Granger E. Westberg
> Author of *Good Grief*
> Retired Clinical Professor of
> Preventive Medicine,
> University of Illinois

ACKNOWLEDGMENTS

In the publication of this book, I am indebted to the many, many individuals who have entrusted me with their pain. Often we cried together as their stories unfolded. Yet without exception, they were motivated to relive those life-shattering experiences so that others might be helped, and they shared my view that there is a special need for a book for caregivers. With their consent, their real names, unless otherwise noted, are used in the chapters.

A special word of appreciation is also due those professionals whose lectures or private interviews gave me additional insight into the nature of grief as it pertained to their specialized fields: Lucia Auman, S.W.; Kathy Demma; Beth Erickson, Ph.D.; Naomi Feil, A.C.S.W.; the Rev. Dr. Robert L. Frank; Rabbi Dr. Earl A. Grollman; John and Noreen Gosch; Chaplain Ron Hasley; Mary Hoffman, M.S.W.; Jo Lindquist; Father Michael Mannion; Marv Miller, Ph.D.; Pat Mieszela, R.N.; Kenneth Moses, Ph.D.; Patrick Doherty M.R.C.; Sister John Cecile; Father Eugene Gould; Mary Anne Hughes; Vickie Lannie, R.N., B.S.; Mary Jane McCorkle; Chris McCormick-Pries, A.R.N.P.; David W. McEchron, Ph.D.; Jeri Miller, R.N.; Carol Paper, B.S.W.; Vicky Thorn; Berlinda Tyler-Jamison, M.S.W.; and Chaplain Marlin Whitmer.

Heartfelt thanks to my Pen Women friends who painstakingly critiqued the manuscript: Judie Gulley, Connie Heckert, Betty Klaas, and Chris Walkowicz.

Thanks to my husband, Ken, who was supportive in all ways possible; and to Nathan Unseth and Carol Johnson of Bethany House Publishers who shared my vision and helped this book become a reality.

CONTENTS

PREFACE

The earth has been called a vale of tears. In the United States alone, statistics would verify that fact. Each year in this country, two million people die. On the average, one person dies every five minutes due to accidental injury; 462,000 die from cancer; 120,000 die from Alzheimer's disease. One out of every 21 babies dies during the first year of life.

But human suffering is not confined to death grief. Pain also comes with the birth of babies with handicaps, with abortions, with divorce, with missing children, and with debilitating illnesses and injuries. Approximately 2 million people will be directly involved with burns each year; 70,000 will be hospitalized; 12,000 people will die from burns. Each year there are an estimated 2 million stroke victims; 125,000 victims of spinal cord injury; and 140,000 brain-injured persons in rehabilitation programs.

During the four years I researched this book, I discovered marvelous outpourings of sympathy from persons who seemed to intuitively do the right thing to comfort the bereaved, usually in quiet, simple ways. I also became aware of just how much unspoken pain lies buried in the hearts of people. At times, as persons opened the doors of their hearts and let me see in, I felt like I was standing on "holy ground," for I was allowed to look into the innermost chambers of their souls where God alone dwells—and where they hurt the most.

I have also discovered anew the wisdom in the Scriptures, which tells us to "bear one another's burdens, and so fulfill the law of Christ" (Gal. 6:2, RSV). When tragedy occurs, we desperately need someone to care about what happens to us; from caring relatives and friends we draw added strength to survive.

I believe followers of Christ have a unique gift they can share with the bereaved. Through intercessory prayer, Christians can be in tune, through the work of the Holy Spirit, to the special needs of the bereaved. Frank Laubach once wrote, "Vital prayers always suggest things to be done."

If we care about others, we can learn how to help people through the grief process.

Delores A. Kuenning
Rock Island, Illinois
April, 1987

How to Use This Book

This is a handbook designed to help when you have a special need to know about a particular kind of grief. Each chapter is based on the true experiences of persons and the tragedies they endured. Though all people grieve in their own way, there are commonalities in the grief process. Their suggestions and advice to caregivers comes from knowing firsthand what proves to be most helpful to the grieving person. Appropriate scripture passages are listed for spiritual comfort and reflection.

After reading the stories giving you insight into "the head and the household" of those who have gone through the experience, and then reading the *Advice to Caregivers*, you can avoid the common blunders in communication so often made by well-meaning relatives, friends, and acquaintances. You may wish to give this book to your grieving friend, or share with him or her the list of suggestions for persons going through the crisis.

For professionals such as the clergy, chaplains, directors of Christian education and church-school teachers, funeral directors, Christian psychologists, social workers, counselors, hospital and hospice volunteers, support-group leaders, nurses, doctors, teachers, and insurance claim adjusters, this book can be a resource book, as well as a book you can give or recommend to your parishioner, pupil, patient, client, support-group member, or friend. The book may also be used for church school discussions or as a training guide for lay visitors.

At the end of each chapter, recommended books, films, and support groups or organizations are listed for you to recommend to your friend or loved one. Some books will be available in public libraries or through interlibrary loan; others may be found in Christian bookstores. Some you may need to special order through your local bookstore or from the publisher. A reference librarian in your public library should be able to give you the publisher's address.

◇ **1** ◇

NO EASY ANSWERS

My Introduction to Grief

We live our lives in a world marked by assumptions. We wake up in the morning and *assume* that life will be much as it was yesterday. We go to bed and wake up expecting the sun to rise. Our children go off to school and come home again at the end of the school day. We go to work and return at the end of our work day expecting our home and our possessions to be there when we return. We *assume* our good health, daily interactions with loved ones, co-workers and friends, and the business-as-usual routine in our job and community.

When illness, tragedy, or catastrophic events happen to us or to someone we care about, our world of assumption is threatened, if not shattered. According to Harold Kushner, author of *When Bad Things Happen to Good People*, "We find life's disasters upsetting not only because they are painful but because they are exceptional."[1]

When disaster strikes, we search for answers. We question "Why?" We blame others, often God himself. If it happens to us personally, we experience a whole gamut of emotions: numbness, disbelief, denial, outrage, confusion, emptiness, depression, guilt, fear, abandonment, and isolation. When it happens to someone else, we find ourselves groping for words to express the deep concern and sadness we feel for them. To some extent, we share their pain. Because we care, we want to say or do something meaningful and helpful in an attempt to offer comfort. Our intentions are well-meaning. But because we live in a death-denying society, Dr. Elisabeth Kubler-Ross, pioneer in the field of thanatology, claims that most of us lack the social skills required to communicate effectively with persons in the psychic, emotional, and spiritual pain associated with loss.

My first experience with grief came when our fourth child was born with a serious birth defect. I was introduced, without warning or prepa-

---

[1] Harold Kushner, *When Bad Things Happen to Good People* (New York: Schocken Books, 1981), p. 139. Used by permission.

ration, to the heartache and pain of having to face rearing a handicapped child. This experience sensitized me to grace on the part of some, and awkwardness on the part of others, as they responded to our son's malady and our sadness.

I was awake during the birth of our son. The bright surgical lights beamed down from above while the nurses talked in casual tones as they assisted Doctor Hawkins in what appeared to be a normal delivery.

As my baby emerged into the world, silence fell like a heavy curtain in the delivery room. Neither the doctor nor the nurse said anything more.

A resounding cry burst forth.

"What is it?" I asked anxiously.

"It's a boy," said Doctor Hawkins, his voice now guarded. The nurse promptly placed my baby in the isolette and wheeled him by me without stopping to let me see him. Still, no conversation. I was frightened by their silence.

"I'm going to put you under for the rest," the doctor said as the nurse promptly held the mask over my face.

But what's wrong? The scream inside my mind died as I succumbed to the drug-induced sleep.

Our baby had a fluid-filled sac the size of an orange on the back of his neck, a "cervical meningocele," which had to be removed surgically right away. Risk factors involved damage to the nerves in the spinal cord which could cause paralysis from the waist down, or the possibility of hydrocephalus, an abnormal amount of fluid in the brain causing enlargement of the head and atrophy of the brain.

Bill and Berniece Stiegemier, members of the 400-member congregation my husband pastored in the small southern Illinois town of Staunton, volunteered to go with us to the specialist in St. Louis. To this day, I cannot remember a thing our friends said to us. I just remember they were there with us, helping us, allowing us to grieve, and looking after our physical needs. I was weak, physically exhausted from the birth and the stress we were now experiencing. Their assistance was invaluable, something we would never have thought to ask for. Our dear friend, Edna Kinnikin, cared for our three small daughters, relieving us of yet another worry.

As the news about our baby, whom we had named Paul John, spread throughout our parish, a steady flow of cards and briefly worded letters began arriving. Others called and said they were praying for us. I felt enveloped in a God-given calm, as though we were being lifted up. We were not alone; the simple kindnesses our friends were voicing to us were tangible expressions of God's love.

Immediately following surgery, Ken and I stood on each side of our baby's crib and lovingly stroked his legs and watched for some response. As he moved his legs, we both breathed a sigh that released much of our pent-up tension. Within twenty-four hours, however, his condition worsened. His head increased in size one and one-half inches; fluid buildup or swelling was occurring. Four consulting physicians on his case agreed his prognosis was not good.

"We will just have to wait and see," said the neurosurgeon. He gave us a single ray of hope, which we clung to during the next six months.

While I waited, a war was raging inside me. I wanted answers to questions for which there apparently were no answers. Why had this happened to our son? What caused it? I remembered having a twenty-four hour virus my second month of pregnancy, but doctors would neither confirm nor deny the virus being a probable cause.

Seeing other healthy, normal babies aroused jealousy and bitterness within me. *What was wrong with me?* My feelings astonished me.

I projected our son's future over and over again in my mind. I struggled with projections of *my* future. Would all my time be consumed in his care as he grew older? Would I be confined to our home because of him? How would we bear the financial burden imposed by medical expenses? We were barely making it on our meager salary. Could we withstand the added stress on our family? A handicapped baby would be added to the pressures of the ministry, my husband's needs and those of our three growing daughters. I felt totally inadequate and overwhelmed, as well as guilty about the concerns for my future.

I felt so guilty about those feelings that I kept them locked in my heart. I didn't want another living soul to know my thoughts and feelings. *Something had to be wrong with me to have such self-centered feelings,* I thought. Years later, I learned this self-absorption is all part of a normal grief reaction.

Acceptance came hard. One day, under the weight of all my guilt and worry, I dropped to my knees and spilled out my tortured feelings to God. I had even tried to keep them hidden from Him.

"O God, help me love enough to accept my child just as he is!" I prayed long and hard. Finally exhausted, I lay on the bed in silence a long time. Gradually, I felt an increasing awareness of an outpouring of warmth and peace. His love penetrated like warm light rays. As if a floodgate had opened, His love was filling all the cold, despairing, empty corners of my aching heart. I sensed God saying, "He will require a *special* kind of love from you, Dee."

Acceptance had begun.

Though I had found my own inner peace, I was disturbed by some of the comments people made to me. Religious people—people who had been in the church most of their lives—indicated they felt this was God's will for our son, Paul.

"How could God possibly do this to an innocent baby?" I wanted to argue. It did not seem true to the nature of the God of love I knew. It just didn't seem logical to me that God, our heavenly Father, would intentionally will or cause a child to have a serious birth defect or be handicapped.

I was also puzzled and surprised at the awkwardness and difficulty some persons had in talking with us. A fellow pastor whom Ken and I both loved and respected got up and left the room because tears streamed down our faces as we talked with him about Paul's condition. We made him uncomfortable, so he fled our presence. I was embarrassed at first, then dismayed that he could not minister to our spiritual needs.

Fortunately, the hydrocephalic condition did not continue. But Paul's growing up years were not problem-free. He had minimal brain dysfunction caused by the rapid swelling after surgery, and he was slow maturing. His coordination and gross motor skills were so poor that he could not ride a bicycle until he was nine years old. He was dyslexic (learning disabled with letter reversal) and hyperactive.

Two persons in particular helped me by what they said during those difficult years when Paul was going through endless frustrations. During a battery of tests, a psychologist gave Paul a sign to wear that read, "GET OFF MY BACK!" Of course the message was intended for Ken and me. We had unrealistic expectations of him at times.

The second was a comment made by Dr. Eugene Wehrli, president of Eden Theological Seminary in St. Louis. "It is God who gives the growth," he said. "If we as parents don't mess things up too much and allow God to give the growth, our children will mature and become the persons God intends them to be." His advice allowed me to relax and trust that God was at work in our son's life, and that He played an important role in Paul's growth and development.

These problems over the years diminished. Paul has only slight dysfunction in the fingers of one hand. He is now in his twenties, and has a college degree in health care administration—despite the fact that psychologists said years ago he would never be "college material." In fact, during his junior and senior years in college, he was on the dean's list and was named one of ten outstanding students in his graduating class. He is presently a nursing home administrator and married to a wonderful woman named Charlotte.

Our life with Paul turned out to be somewhat of a "success story." But for many families, the birth of a child with a handicap or retardation is the beginning of a lifetime of pain mixed with only rare occasions of joy, and demands extraordinary caring and coping with one problem or crisis after another.

According to the statistics quoted in the Preface—and my experience with Paul—I realized the need for a resource book—a handbook for caregivers—as they attempt to comfort and communicate with persons in crisis and pain. To find out what is helpful and what is hurtful, I have gone to the experts—the people who, like myself, have "walked through the valley"—for they are the true teachers. They have willingly told me their stories so that others might be helped.

I have also interviewed those in the helping professions—pastors, hospital chaplains, physicians, psychologists, nurses, social workers, grief family therapists, and rehabilitation counselors—those who have special expertise in crisis and grief counseling.

One thing I learned from both lay persons and professionals: when tragedy happens to us personally, or to those we care about, ready-made answers, pious platitudes, and threadbare clichés do not help. Life and its profound mysteries are not that simple. There are no easy answers. But mourners are not looking for answers. They're looking for and needing comfort that sometimes only you and I can give. This book will teach caregivers how, in quiet, simple ways, to show they care.

But before we recount the personal narratives of those who have experienced grief, we need to look at the subject most often called into question when tragedy occurs: God's will. A discussion of God's will lays the groundwork necessary to understand many of the questions asked by victims. And it provides an understanding of many of the suggestions given to caregivers. Most importantly, it helps to deepen our understanding of the loving, caring God who grieves with us in life's darkest hours.

◊ **2** ◊

CLEAR THINKING ABOUT GOD'S WILL

Does God Cause Tragedies? What Does God Promise?

It's hard to believe in the goodness of God when a personal disaster strikes: a precious baby dies; a young person on the threshold of life is injured in an accident and paralyzed for life; a young mother of small children dies of cancer. Tragedies are common to the human experience. Every day they happen all around us. At such times, life seems cruel and unfair.

Even persons of faith express their whys to God when they are forced to face such tragedies. The will of God is called into question then more than at any other time. Is God punishing them? Does God have a plan so all-important that He intentionally causes the baby's death, the accident, the cancer? Is this God's will for that individual? Does God cause such things so that He can teach lessons that can be learned only through pain and suffering? These are the most common allegations made against God when crises and tragedy occur. Unfortunately, saying, "It's God's will," is much easier than thinking through the issue.

It is extremely important to think clearly and to develop a belief structure that incorporates some understanding of God's will *before* disaster befalls us. When the worst happens to us, "it is too late to talk about the anchor that should have been put down before the storm began."[1] Nor can we suddenly draw from deep reservoirs of faith within ourselves if nothing has been done to nurture our spiritual lives in the past.

There is much confusion and misunderstanding, as well as differing doctrinal views, about the subject of God's will.

---

[1]Leslie D. Weatherhead, *The Will of God* (Nashville: Abingdon, 1944, 1972), p. 16. Used by permission.

An Imperfect World

As human beings made of flesh and blood and bone rather than rubber, steel, or plastic, our reasoning tells us that generally deaths are caused by: errors in human judgment or planning; diseases (some of which are self-imposed); genetic disorders; the evil action of others; violence against self; acts of nature such as earthquake, wind, fire, and flood; and unbending natural laws such as the force of gravity.

Our reasoning also tells us that when we violate the God-given commandments—which are really positive statements designed to help us live a healthy, uncomplicated life—we create the conditions that can wreak havoc with our personal lives. When we disobey God's laws of health, for example, we can expect sickness and the suffering that goes with it. Our bodies are designed by God and require healthful living habits to function properly.

Who Is in Control?

But knowing *how* death or disease occurs does not answer the question of *why* it occurs. For the answer to that question, we ask God, "Why is this happening to me?" or "Why my loved one?"

Behind the many questions raised about God's will is the more basic question: Who is in control? Most of the time we feel relatively confident that we, as individuals, are in control of our lives. Those who teach and preach "success philosophies" claim we control our own destiny. In large measure, that may be true. We control our attitudes and how we look at life, how we spend our money, and the use of our time.

But when a crisis or tragedy occurs in our lives, we feel as though we have totally lost control. Indeed, circumstances are often beyond our control; death makes evident *how little we control life*. It would seem logical, then, to conclude that *if we are not in control, God must be in control!* Haven't we been taught that God is all powerful?

Dr. Richard Rice, professor of Theology at Loma Linda University in California, challenges this belief: "God maintains ultimate sovereignty over history. But He does not exercise absolute control."[2] In other words, God does control the final outcome of history, but on earth—by allowing human beings freedom—His control is not absolute.

If we believe that God is in total control or that He planned or predestined tragedy to befall certain individuals, then that conclusion leads us to the next question of *causality*. Does God willfully cause death, disease, and suffering? Swiss psychologist Jean Piaget explains why we do this: "The mind needs an explanation of how the world operates."

---

[2]Richard Rice, *God's Foreknowledge and Man's Free Will* (Minneapolis: Bethany House Publishers, 1985), p. 67. Used by permission of author.

There are various accounts in the Bible where God meted out justice and dealt a death blow for humanity's wickedness.[3] The story of the flood in Genesis 6–9 is an example. The Lord saw the wickedness of man was great, and He was sorry He had made man. "I will destroy man whom I have created" (Gen. 5:7), said the Lord, "and all flesh died that moved upon the earth" (Gen. 7:19, 21). The whole race, except Noah and his family, was destroyed. After the flood, God made a new covenant with Noah and said He would never again send a flood to destroy His creation, sending the rainbow as a symbol of that promise.

The New Testament reveals the depth of God's mercy and compassion for His creation. God's new covenant with humanity was made real in the person of Jesus Christ who dwelt on this earth to teach humankind the importance of obedience to God. By submitting to death on a cross, Jesus assumed the sins of humanity, thus reconciling God and humankind once and for all.

The New Testament, therefore, reflects a new image of God—an image of a heavenly Father who cares deeply for His children, revealing a fuller dimension to our understanding of God as revealed in the Old Testament. Christ has given us, through His teachings, a new understanding of the nature of God's love.

So when questions such as the following are raised, the answers we hear reflect the teachings in the New Testament and convey the image of a loving Father.

Tricia Horst, the young mother in Chapter 4, says that people often tell grieving parents, "God takes babies to heaven to be His little angels." To "take" a life means that God has willfully caused the baby's death. Would God deliberately take a child from its parents or kill the life He created?

Leslie Weatherhead, noted English author and preacher of this century, answers that question with a story.

In the throes of a cholera epidemic in India, his friend had lost a little son. Now he was concerned for his daughter, his only remaining child. She slept in a room nearby on a cot covered with mosquito net while the two men paced, the father agonizing over his son's death and worrying that his daughter also might die. "It is the will of God. That's all there is to it," said the grief-stricken father.

Not accepting the father's statement as truth, Weatherhead replied:

> "Supposing someone crept up the steps onto the veranda tonight, while you all slept, and deliberately put a wad of cotton soaked in cholera germ culture over your little girl's mouth? What would you think about that?"
>
> "My God," said the father, "What would I think? Nobody would do such a damnable thing. If he attempted it and I caught him, I would

---

[3]See Ex. 12, 14; Lev. 20; Num. 16; 1 Kings 17; 2 Sam. 12:14–18; Acts 5.

kill him with as little compunction as I would a snake, and throw him over the veranda. What do you mean by suggesting such a thing?"

"Isn't that what you have accused God of doing when you said it was His will? Call your little boy's death the result of mass ignorance, call it mass folly, call it mass sin, if you like, call it bad drains or communal carelessness, but don't call it the will of God. Surely we cannot identify as the will of God something for which a man would be locked up in jail, or put in a criminal lunatic asylum."[4]

Weatherhead concludes, "People get a lot of comfort from supposing that their tragedies are the will of God. One can bear a thing if it is God's will. It is hard to bear it if it is a ghastly mistake and not the will of God at all."[5]

But the God who would willfully inflict a child with cholera hardly fits the image of God who is kind and loving. Nor does it reflect the loving and kind spirit of our Lord Jesus Christ.

Moreover, it is extremely important that we think carefully before we casually attribute the death of a friend or loved one, or tragedy to God's will—a common practice today.

William Sloane Coffin, senior pastor at Riverside Church in New York, lost his son, Alex, when the car he was driving went off the road into the Boston harbor. In his book, *The Courage to Love*, Coffin says, "The one thing that should never be said when someone dies is, 'It is the will of God.' Never do we know enough to say that. My own consolation lies in knowing that it was *not* the will of God that Alex die; that when the waves closed over the sinking car, God's heart was the first of all our hearts to break."[6]

Calling a tragic loss the will of God can have devastating effects on our own faith and the faith of others—especially children—for it distorts the image of God.

Dorothy Manning, a member of our own congregation, tells her story: "When I was nine years old, my mother died and I was very sad. I refused to say my prayers in parochial school. Noticing that I was not participating in class, the Sister called me aside and asked what was wrong. I told her my mother had died and I missed her; to which she replied, 'God needs your mother in heaven.' But I felt I needed my mother far more than God needed her. I was angry at God for years because I felt he took her from me."

What we think of God and how we respond to Him are closely related. An inaccurate view of God can have disastrous effects on personal religious experience.[7]

---

[4]Weatherhead, op. cit., pp. 10, 11.

[5]Ibid., p. 16.

[6]William Sloane Coffin, *The Courage to Love* (San Francisco: Harper & Row, Publishers, 1984), pp. 94, 95.

[7]Rice, op. cit., p. 10.

Does God Permit Tragedy to Punish Us?

Another common question asked when injury, illness, or death touches our lives is, "Is God punishing me?"

This common reaction is often rooted in fear, unconfessed sin in our lives, a faulty image of God, and our insecurity about God's love for us.

Scripture gives us the following assurances to quell our fears: "We need have no fear if someone [God] loves us perfectly; his perfect love for us eliminates all dread of what he might do to us. If we are afraid, it is for fear of what he might do to us, and shows that we are not fully convinced that he really loves us" (1 John 4:18–19, TLB). "There is no fear in love. But perfect love drives out fear, because fear has to do with punishment" (1 John 4:18, NIV).

Does God Cause Disease or Death?

Jesus always regarded disease as part of the kingdom of evil, and with all His powers He fought it and instructed His disciples to do the same. He commissioned them to "heal the sick, raise the dead, cleanse lepers, cast out demons" (Matt. 10:8, RSV). If disease were part of God's plan, would Jesus have gone about healing the sick and every infirmity possible? The Book of Wisdom in the Apocrypha, says, "God did not make death, and he does not delight in the death of the living. For he created all things that they might exist."[8]

Our bodies are not meant to live forever. God's plan for humanity incorporates a life cycle, a "time to live and a time to die." But Scripture implies that God intends us to live long full adult lives. The Psalmist gives an estimate of our intended lifespan. "The length of our days is seventy years—or eighty, if we have the strength" (Ps. 90:10, NIV).

Denominational viewpoints differ in their beliefs regarding whether God causes, permits or allows tragedies, or interrupts life. There are also differing views with regard to the timing of each person's death. For example, Billy Graham believes "that God takes each Christian at the perfect time—the time when he can choose to make the biggest impact."[9]

In contrast, Belgian author, Louis Evely, believes that "God no more determined the end of our lives than he established the beginning. God has made man free."[10]

---

[8]The New Oxford Annotated Bible with the Apocrypha.
[9]Leighton, Ford, *Sandy—A Heart for God* (Downers Grove, Ill.: InterVarsity Press, 1985), p. 116.
[10]Louis Evely, *In the Face of Death* (New York: The Seabury Press, 1979), p. 100.

Suffering Is Universal

Suffering is the one experience that is universal. Each person will ultimately experience pain and loss. Jesus was no exception. When his friend Lazarus died, he wept.

Jesus was abandoned, rejected, despised, and verbally and physically abused. He died on a cross, a horribly painful and humiliating death. God's own Son was not spared pain and suffering. The Bible is filled with stories of human tragedy and suffering. "The good man [person] does not escape all troubles—he has them too" (Ps. 34:19, TLB).

The question of why good people suffer and experience catastrophe has puzzled humankind throughout the centuries. The Book of Job poses the age-old question: "Why do the righteous suffer?" Job was a patriarch whose faith was tested [by Satan] and nearly crushed with a number of overwhelming losses. The message we learn from Job is not an explanation of "why," but of how the person faithful to God responds.

Anger Is a Common Response

It is not uncommon during the grief process to feel anger toward God. Tricia Horst says, in counseling parents who have lost a child, there is always some mention of God. "God usually gets the blame."

These feelings against God usually add to the problem because we then feel guilty for our anger. Pierre Wolff, author of *May I Hate God?*, helps put guilt to rest, assuring us that God is big enough to handle our anger. He can take it. I would strongly recommend this book to those who are angry with God.

God put within our bodies two healing processes: one for healing the body; the other for healing the spirit—we call this second process grief. Anger is one of grief's normal reactions.

Anger toward God, if prolonged, however, does shut us off from God. "Being angry at God erects a barrier between us and all the sustaining, comforting resources of religion that are there to help us in such times,"[11] says Harold Kushner. In this state of mind, we feel lost and empty. Warren Wiersbe warns, "Bitterness only makes suffering worse and closes the spiritual channels through which God can pour his grace."[12]

How to Overcome Anger with God

When we lay the blame for our tragedies on God, we grieve His heart. For when we believe tragedies are God's will or that God causes illness,

---

[11]Harold S. Kushner, *When Bad Things Happen to Good People*, (New York: Schocken Books, 1981), p. 109. Used by permission.

[12]Warren W. Wiersbe, *Why Us? When Bad Things Happen to God's People* (Old Tappan, N.J.: Fleming H. Revell Co., 1984), p. 96. Used by permission.

accidents, birth defects, or premature deaths, we are accusing God unjustly. We are taking comfort in a lie!

If loved ones or friends are in the throes of grief and angry with God, we can encourage them to be honest with Him and to acknowledge this anger. We can tell them to love God enough to confide in Him everything that is in their hearts. When they cannot pray as they should, we can advise them to pray as they can. Then we need to encourage them to believe that God hears and understands their feelings and that these angry feelings are part of the grief reaction and partly a result of their feeling out of control. God answers prayers by putting new thoughts in our minds and new feelings in our hearts.

It may help them to tell God they are sorry. This is a very simple thing to do, but it helps clear the air and return to a loving relationship. We know this experience works in human relationships; it also works in our relationship with God.

Kushner eloquently summarizes:

> God does not cause our misfortunes. Some are caused by bad luck, some are caused by bad people and some are simply an inevitable consequence of our being human and being mortal, living in a world of inflexible natural laws. The painful things that happen to us are not punishments for our misbehavior, nor are they in any way part of some grand design on God's part. Because the tragedy is not God's will, we need not feel hurt or betrayed by God when tragedy strikes. We can turn to Him for help in overcoming it precisely because we can tell ourselves that God is as outraged by it as we are. In the final analysis, the question of why bad things happen to good people translates into some very different questions, no longer asking *why* something happened, but asking how we will respond, what we intend to do now that it has happened.[13]

How We Respond Is Up to Us

Someone has said, "Loss is inevitable; growth is optional."

During our thirty years in the ministry, my husband and I have seen people respond in varying ways. A man paralyzed in an industrial accident became embittered and drove away his children and anyone else who dared to come near him. Only his wife stayed with him, and everyone wondered how she stood his abusive behavior.

I have seen others stay angry with God for years, blaming Him for their losses. I have seen persons languish in self-pity and despair and merely go through the motions of living.

But I have also seen suffering persons reach out to others who hurt. I have seen persons defy the odds and overcome enormous obstacles.

---

[13]Kushner, op. cit., p. 109.

For some, tragedy prepared them for a special ministry, using the lessons learned in the School of Human Suffering. I have seen persons of faith achieve remarkable feats through persistence and dedication to a cause. And I have read of those who survive tragedy triumphantly.

Iona Henry is one such person. Her teenage daughter died of a brain tumor. Less than a month later, she and her husband and son were in a car-train accident that killed her family and left her badly injured. Losing her entire family left her groping for answers and struggling to survive emotionally. In her grief, she thought through all the simple answers others gave her: (1) It was a planned pattern: "There is a purpose in all of this." This answer has its roots in the doctrines of predestination, a traditional Protestant idea. (2) "God loves you, so He makes you suffer"—emerging from the doctrine that teaches, "Those who suffer greatly earn great 'merit.' " (3) Others said it was "fate." "When your time comes, you just have to accept it." All those answers left her dissatisfied.

What ultimately made sense to her were the words of her father-in-law, a minister: "Some things happen in this world because we human beings act like human beings, not because God makes them happen. It is *human* planning and decision that bring a car and a locomotive to a certain spot at a certain time," he told her.

The answer that came to her was this: "Whatever is, is; you cannot change it. Whatever *has* happened, has happened, and you cannot go back and change any of it, however or 'whyever' it happened. The question is not 'Why did it happen?' but 'What do I do *now*?' " And then she said it came to her, "Stop fighting, Iona Henry! Stop questioning everything. Some questions have no answers; you should know that by now. You should know that only fools persist in seeking the answers to "Why?"[14]

The Open View of God

Dr. Richard Rice's book *God's Foreknowledge and Man's Free Will* explores in depth an alternative to the traditional Christian understanding of God's relationship to the world. He calls it the "Open View of God." Its central thesis is that reality itself—and consequently, God's experience of reality—are essentially *open* rather than closed. This means that God experiences the events of the world He has created—especially the events of human history—*as they happen* rather than all at once in some timeless, eternal perception. This also means that not even God knows the future in all its details. Some parts remain indefinite until they actually occur, and so they can't be known in advance.[15] The actual course of

---

[14]Iona Henry, with Frank S. Mead, *Triumph Over Tragedy* (Westwood, N.J.: Fleming H. Revell Company, 1957), pp. 114, 115.

[15]Rice, op. cit., p. 10.

events is not completely perceptible to God in advance. Rather, it [events] becomes apparent to Him as the participants contribute their individual decisions and actions.[16]

God's relation to the creaturely world is thus subtle and complex. Instead of merely acting upon the world, God also reacts to developments within the world. The influence between God and the world flows both ways. God not only affects the world, but the world also affects him.[17]

When God gave man moral freedom, Rice says, He was leaving undecided whether or not man would obey. He left open man's response to God's expectations of Him.[18] God is *open* to the world of creaturely experience. He is truly affected by our decisions, achievements, and disappointments.[19]

> The open view of God also supports a sense of personal significance by emphasizing God's sensitivity to our experience. God takes an interest in every aspect of our lives. Nothing is too small or insignificant for Him to notice. He concerns Himself with everything that interests, concerns, and worries us. Moreover, God's experiences reflect the actual course of our lives. What matters to us here and now makes a difference to God at this very moment. God feels not only *what* we feel, but also *as* we feel. He is intimately involved in the day-to-day course of our lives. Consequently, our different experiences have different effects upon God. He is pained with our suffering. He is exhilarated by our accomplishments. And He is pleased when we return His affection for us.[20]

This philosophy is contrary to Calvin's view that "not only does God know everything that will ever happen, but everything happens the way it does because He wills it to be so." Dr. Rice's open view of God does not attribute every experience to God's specific intention:

> . . . God did not intend many of the things which happen to us. But once they occur, God nevertheless responds to them in a way that somehow benefits us. Thus, if one is open to divine leading, something as tragic as death of a parent in one's childhood, though not intended by God, can nevertheless result in certain benefits not otherwise likely to occur. In other words, something that happens in spite of God's will can make a positive contribution to one's life, because God can bring beneficial results out of it. This means that anything—no matter how negative in itself—can become the occasion for good as a result of God's infinite resourcefulness. With this in mind, an individual can look back on his life, take it all into account—the bad and the good

---

[16]Ibid., p. 63.
[17]Ibid., p. 39.
[18]Ibid., p. 38.
[19]Ibid., p. 42.
[20]Ibid., p. 100.

alike—and tell himself that nothing is totally wasted. God can incorporate everything into His ultimate design.[21]

. . . God is not responsible for suffering. Suffering owes its existence to factors that oppose His will. But its occurrence does not leave Him helpless. He can act for good in the face of it. And He can accomplish certain things that would not have otherwise been possible.[22]

The open view of God affirms our sense of outrage of what has happened. Some things are simply wrong. They are not what God plans for us. Neither are they in our best interest. At times, people simply fall victim to unfortunate circumstances.

The open view of God affirms that our experiences matter to God here and now. He appreciates to the fullest our loss, our grief, and our pain at the very time we suffer it. His own sense of pain and loss far surpasses ours. . . . nothing lies beyond God's capacity to work for good. In response to any situation, however disastrous, God can work to our benefit.[23]

God Promised His Presence

If our belief structure is based on the knowledge that *God has not promised us anything but to be with us and love us*,[24] then, like Job, our faith will neither be dependent upon rewards nor destroyed when a blessing turns into a loss. For then, God can interact with us through the gift of the Holy Spirit to bring healing to our wounded spirits.

To the faithful, God has promised, "I will never, *never* fail you nor forsake you" (Heb. 13:5, TLB). Jesus called this Presence of God the Holy Spirit, the *Comforter*.

> Though we pray for healing and it doesn't happen,
>   God has promised to be with us.
> Though our disabled or aging body may entrap the spirit,
>   God has promised to be with us.
> Though we may endure unbearable sorrow and loss.
>   God has promised to be with us.
>
> The light of God surrounds us,
> The love of God enfolds us,
> The power of God protects us,
> The presence of God is with us,
> Wherever we are,
> Wherever our loved one is,
> God is.[25]

---

[21]Ibid., p. 69.

[22]Ibid., p. 103.

[23]Ibid., p. 104.

[24]Donald Cole, *Abraham, God's Man of Faith* (Chicago: The Moody Bible Institute, 1977), p. 110.

[25]Adaptation of poem by James Dillet Freeman. Used by permission.

Does God Heal?

Tragic loss can often become the occasion for spiritual growth and change. God can and does heal the spirit through the power of prayer and by allowing the natural grief process to run its course. Grief has a beginning, a middle, and an end. All health and wholeness are from God, and God longs to mend shattered lives. "All healing is a miracle and miracles are signs pointing to the presence of a divine power in nature and history."[26]

Through the centuries since the miracles and ministry of Christ, there are documented cases of persons who have experienced divine intervention and healing for otherwise fatal illnesses. Therefore, believers and unbelievers alike call upon God for a "miracle" cure when faced with a terminal illness. And miracles still happen today, many of which are accomplished with the aid of modern medicine. "Faith and medicine share an intimate connection and the common source in Christ's restoring activity."[27]

Father Francis MacNutt, active in the Catholic healing ministries, says that "*usually* people are not completely healed by prayer, but they are *improved*." Nevertheless, he urges us to ask God for healing, for sickness opposes the will of God. He reminds us that Jesus clearly encourages us to be persistent in our prayers.[28]

But not all who pray for healing are healed. And they ask, like Judy Rodts in Chapter 8, "Why wasn't Justin healed?"

The answer to this question remains a mystery. Even the late Kathryn Kuhlman, one of the most renowned faith healers of our day, was puzzled by it. "No, I don't understand why everyone is not healed physically,"[29] she openly admitted.

Yet that which is essential to our faith remains: Though God does not always heal the body, He can and will heal the soul, the inner heart, of those who believe and trust in His sustaining presence through the work of the Holy Spirit.

Death is not the end of life, merely the passage whereby the soul enters a more glorious life in heaven. Our ultimate hope and healing and wholeness is in heaven.

---

[26]*Rejoicing in Hope—A Promise of Healing and Wholeness* (Minneapolis: Sacred Design, 1971), p. 3.

[27]Ibid., p. 3.

[28]Francis MacNutt, O.P., *The Power to Heal* (Notre Dame, Ind.: Ave Maria Press, 1977), p. 27.

[29]Kathryn Kuhlman. *A Glimpse into Glory* (Plainfield, N.J.: Logos International, 1979), p. 37.

Additional Reading

Dodd, Robert V. *Out of the Depths.* Nashville: Abingdon Press, 1986. (Booklet)

Henry, Iona, with Frank S. Mead. *Triumph Over Tragedy.* Westwood, N.J.: Fleming H. Revell Co., 1957.

McCloskey, Pat. *When You Are Angry with God.* Mahay, N.Y.: Paulist Press, 1987.

Neal, Emily Gardiner. *In the Midst of Life.* New York: Hawthorn Books, Inc., 1963.

Phipps, William E. *Death—Confronting the Reality.* Atlanta: John Knox Press, 1987.

Rice, Richard. *God's Foreknowledge And Man's Free Will.* Minneapolis: Bethany House Publishers, 1985.

Weatherhead, Leslie D. *The Will of God.* Nashville: Abingdon Press, 1944, 1972.

Wiersbe, Warren W. *Why Us? When Bad Things Happen to God's People.* Old Tappan, N.J.: Fleming H. Revell Co., 1984.

Wolff, Pierre. *May I Hate God?* New York: Paulist Press, 1979.

Yancey, Philip. *Where Is God When It Hurts?* Grand Rapids: Zondervan Publishing House, 1977.

◊ **3** ◊

WHEN HELLO MEANS HEARTACHE

The Birth of an Impaired
or Handicapped Baby

With her husband, Gary, by her side, Rhonda Krahl gave birth to her second son on June 3, 1976. The baby was born with a large purple spot on the end of his spine. Rhonda refused to believe the condition was anything serious.

The pediatrician diagnosed the problem as "myelomeningocele with hydrocephalus," more commonly known as spina bifida or open spine. The prognosis? Paralysis of the legs, no bladder or bowel control, enlargement of the head and possible death. Gary and Rhonda couldn't fathom the seriousness of their baby's problem, but their pastor, recognizing the gravity of the matter, encouraged both Gary and Rhonda to hold their newborn. They complied.

The baby was transported immediately to the pediatric intensive care nursery at University Hospital, Iowa City, where a crucial decision about the baby's treatment faced the family. Should the baby be treated, or should nature be allowed to take its course? Rhonda and Gary had always functioned as a team, but Gary, who had followed the baby to Iowa City, was now forced to make this decision alone.

"Treat him," he said without hesitation.

More Problems

Baby Tom was six days old before Rhonda saw him again. When two weeks old, he developed meningitis and was so far gone that Rhonda could arouse no reflex action even when rapping on his incubator. The buildup of pressure in his head caused vocal cord paralysis. A shunt had to be implanted to drain the excess fluid in his brain.

As her baby neared eight weeks, having survived the meningitis, Rhonda was given special training by the staff so she could assume his care at home. His breathing was labored; he made harsh, high-pitched sounds, and his chest contracted as he fought for each breath. This condition had developed before the shunt was implanted, but the shunt had not relieved the condition. Soon after leaving the hospital, the breathing worsened. She rushed him to a small neighboring hospital. His care was so specialized, there was little the hospital staff could do for him except revive him if his breathing stopped. He was again taken to University Hospital. Doctors there inserted a permanent tracheostomy in his throat so he could breathe. He was now ten weeks old.

"His whole life was in my hands," says Rhonda. "I was twenty-one years old and faced with having total care of a critically-ill newborn who didn't make any sound when he cried, had to lie on his stomach at all times, even when taking a bottle, and had to be suctioned every two hours around the clock." As time wore on, Rhonda developed severe tension headaches, so severe she had to ask family members to care for eighteen-month-old Tim, their first child, while she rested, getting up only long enough to care for Tom. Gary also had to learn to suction him so she could get some uninterrupted sleep. Physically, she was totally exhausted.

Passing the Test

"Clinic visits were hard," Rhonda admitted. "The speech, physical, and occupational therapists, social worker, and nurse practitioner went over every aspect of Tom's care. I felt as if I was being judged as a parent. I was a success if he did well; a failure if his condition changed. I had a list on my cabinet of twenty things to do each day for Tom. It was hard to keep track of everything. Tim was still a baby, too."

At sixteen months, the tracheostomy was removed, far sooner than planned.

"Seeing other normal healthy babies sometimes hurt. I remember crying for hours after a family get-together when Tom was three. I watched him clapping and celebrating along with everyone else as his one-year-old cousin took her first steps. Tom should have been running and jumping and playing with other children. It broke my heart to see him so incapacitated, yet he was so happy for her," said Rhonda.

At age three, Tom began special education classes. That same year, he had orthopedic surgery to release the tendons in his hips so he would have more mobility. A large cast framed his small body. At age six, he again had surgery to release the heel cords. This operation was followed by intense pain. "Ossification," or bone buildup, in the muscles occurred. He required painful leg exercises ten to twelve times a day. One day, while exercising his leg, Rhonda felt it give way—she had broken the fragile leg bone. Rhonda felt intense guilt. Tom, now old enough to have feelings of his own, was upset because she blamed herself. But the cast came as a blessing in disguise. It relieved Tom of the tortuous exercises, and he was content to enjoy his sixth birthday party in a cast and wheelchair. Good fusion occurred in the broken leg despite the break.

Doctors call Tom their "miracle" baby.

Sometimes Acceptance Never Comes

"I still mourn at times, especially since the bone hardened in his hip. That lessened his chances for mobility. We had hoped he would become increasingly mobile. Now, that will never be possible," said Rhonda. "It may be necessary in the future for us to decide whether he will be fused into a permanent sitting or standing position. You never totally accept the disability. You always wish it could be different.

"Sometimes I'm angry that we can't do things other families do such as take vacations. We never will."

The Krahl home is especially designed, built with extra wide hallways and doors. Tom has a ramp up to his captain's bed, which has low drawers for his clothes. Today, Tom ambulates with a parapodium and crutches and a wheelchair on occasion. When younger, he used a toy called a "wiz wheel," which he manipulated with his arms.

"A disabled child in a family affects every aspect of life: how you spend your time, where you go, the house you live in—everything! There are daily reminders," adds Rhonda.

"Gary and I have never regretted the decision to do everything possible to sustain Tom's life. I don't think I could have forgiven Gary had he allowed him to die. Conception is an act of God. Tom is God's child. I only regret we could not have had more children—we run the risk of having another child with the same problem."

How Others Responded

"When Tom was born, a relative told me 'You don't deserve this.' Someone else sent a sympathy card, which I didn't appreciate—Tom was alive, not dead. My sisters-in-law gave me a frilly nightie, which thrilled me immensely; I needed the lift. Cards meant a great deal.

"Even in the hospital," Rhonda continued, "I found myself assuming the role of comforting others. I saw a friend, after viewing Tom in the nursery, hurry down the hall in tears. I went after her to comfort her. His condition made people sad.

"But there was no one to comfort me. Over the years, I became bitter, and that developed into a hardness. I decided I wasn't going to expose my hurt, because if others didn't accept my pain, I could be hurt more. As I look back, I believe I should have been more open to accept help from others," Rhonda admitted. Rhonda was fortunate to have help from grandparents and other relatives who lived close by. "Kindnesses such as a casserole from a member of our church or a friend still mean so much. Little things mean a lot. One afternoon, a friend appeared at our door with a game under her arm. 'I've come to play with Tom for a little while,' she said as she greeted me with a big smile. It was one of the nicest things anyone ever did for us.''

Sarah Miller's* birth defects were not as apparent at birth as Tom Krahl's.

"Sarah" arrived a month premature. A few days before she was born, her mother, Janet, had a dream warning her something would be wrong, but in its wrongness, it would be all right. The day her baby was born, Janet read Rom. 8:28, "And we know that in all things God works for the good of those who love him" (NIV). Little did she know that her infant daughter's physical defects would test her faith to the limit.

Her baby girl had a rare defect called "kyphoscoliosis," or forward curvature of the spine, along with three other lateral curves. All ribs on her right side were fused together under the right armpit. Her liver ballooned out like a frog's throat when it croaks.

The best answer doctors could give Janet was that "bone buds 'misfired' on the spine during the first trimester." It looked like a congenital birth defect, but this was not confirmed in genetic studies.**

"When Sarah was born, I had to be the one to take charge in our marriage. I had to call the family and the doctors, or things didn't get done. All of this had a negative effect on our marriage," says Janet. "Ultimately, we divorced.

"At that time, my husband was head of Christian education and evangelism in our church, so we were part of a church staff. We had started a couples' club and teams for youth ministries, so it was hard for me to understand why people didn't call or come around.

"Our first year I was isolated. Sarah was very susceptible to illness. She would go down for a nap and wake up sick. Our pediatrician warned, 'Someday you'll go get her from her nap and she'll be dead.' We couldn't take her out except to relatives—she was too sensitive to change.

"I learned to rely on television ministries for Sunday worship. An older pastor of visitation from our church called on me from time to time. He was accepting, and he had a calming effect on me."

Lessons to Learn

"I didn't ask God *why?* as much as *What lessons do you want me to learn?* or *What decisions do you want me to make?*" Janet commented.

---

*Names have been changed.
**See Appendix A for Known Causes of Birth Defects.

"He put me in charge, so I needed to be clear. I was always worried I would not see something I was supposed to see. I didn't want to make a mistake. With Sarah's condition so critical, it wasn't something I could go back and change.

"God's guidance for me took the form of impressions. Often, my observations told me something was wrong before it showed up on X-rays. Frequently, God prompted me to take immediate action. Had I not followed those promptings, she probably wouldn't be alive today."

So Young and So Much Pain

Sarah Miller has had three major spinal operations. At age five, eight vertebrae in the thoracic region were fused. At age eight, the cervical curve gave way, and five more vertebrae were fused.

Her most serious surgery came at age eleven. The specialist in scoliosis and thoracic orthopedics went to Europe to study the case before performing the operation—there are only five other case studies in the world similar to Sarah's.

The surgery to implant steel rods along her spine lasted nine grueling hours. Janet described her daughter following surgery:

"She was disfigured and bloated almost beyond recognition. Clumps of her hair were missing. Morphine every three hours had no effect on the pain. She became addicted and had to go off cold turkey, and she then had problems with withdrawal.

"I prayed that God would help her in the pain. If it had to be there, I asked God to help us bear it.

"Sometimes I would ask Him to send a person to help me realize what really was happening. One day, when our pastor came, Sarah cried; it was one of the few times that anyone else saw her cry. Few people saw how bad it really was.

"A few days after surgery, one of Sarah's friends came and sat with her. It meant a lot to Sarah that one of *her* friends would bear the pain and the boring idleness with her."

The cost of Sarah's hospitalization and operations have totaled nearly a half million dollars. As a single parent, Janet holds a full-time job and several part-time jobs as a psychometrist to pay off her debts. Most of the surgeries have been paid for by insurance, but there are many things insurance does not pay for—medications, special orthopedic shoes, body braces, appliances, special clothing, transportation to and from clinic visits, and overnight lodging and meals. Illinois Crippled Children assisted with expenses until her divorce. Then, because each parent had separate insurance, their aid was discontinued. Because Sarah's malady is so rare, she doesn't qualify for assistance from other national organizations or funding agencies.

Today, though her growth is stunted because of the steel rods implanted along her spine, Sarah is active in tennis, softball, swimming, bicycling, and basketball. She refers to her surgeries as "time outs" and she ignores her limitations as much as possible. Her hazel eyes sparkle and her soft blond hair frames a face that radiates when she smiles. She has a contagious, indomitable spirit.

Sarah has her own faith, and she is very honest with God. That honesty includes anger at times. "The first thing I'm going to ask Jesus is why we're doing this. Couldn't we have learned these lessons a different way?"

Sarah doesn't accept the prejudices of those who call her "hunchback" or "leaning tower." She is fiesty, and has even been known to clobber those who give her a hard time! She is disturbed when she sees people stare at a disabled person. "Don't they know that that person can't help it?" she asks her mother.

"She always thinks someone has it worse than she has," Janet says.

"She definitely has not limited her own future by limited thinking. And I'm glad I never told her she would never sit up or walk," Janet reflects. "Doctors aren't always right."

"Two friends have helped me over the years, one whose child is handicapped. When she says, 'I know what you are going through,' I know she knows. My other friend has kept pulling me toward normalcy. I needed them both to keep me balanced. It meant a lot when she spearheaded a fund drive in her church so that I could have money to stay with Sarah during her last operation.

"Other friends welcomed and fed my son during my absences. I couldn't have made it without my faith or my friends."

Advice to Offer Parents of Handicapped Children

1. *Realize that you will mourn the loss of your child's potential, depending on the severity and nature of the baby's handicap.* Your projections of your baby's future will be tinged with sadness.
2. *Be aware that you and your spouse will mourn separately and differently.* Each person's grief is unique.
3. *Avoid assigning the blame for the defect on your spouse or yourself.* Self-blame is futile. Seek genetic counseling if the condition is one which your doctor feels may reoccur in subsequent children.
4. *Be honest. Tell others how you feel and what you fear.* Don't mask your feelings and pretend "everything's fine" when it isn't. Let others share your pain with you. Say, "I'm really worried about . . . or I'm feeling . . ." Don't shut yourself off from others, for they will have no way of knowing your needs or what is happening. Be open, not for the purpose of looking for sympathy, but to accept emotional support from others.

5. *Don't confine yourself to the home.* Stay in touch with friends. Occasional outings, church fellowship activities, and worship are essential to good mental health and spiritual renewal. In some communities, there are excellent respite care facilities. Some allow the child to be dropped off for a brief period of time, while others offer a care provider who will come to the home on a daily, weekly, or for a weekend or longer if necessary.

6. *Don't allow limited thinking or labels to impose limits on your child's potential.* Remember that your baby is a child of God and needs your love.

7. *Read and learn* as much as possible about the nature of your child's problem, the agencies or professional help available, and the schooling options. Early intervention is essential if your child is to reach his or her potential. Most states mandate programming from birth for children with disabilities.

8. *Join a Parent-to-Parent support group if one is available in your community.* If none exists, start one.

9. *Remember that God has promised to be with you in the days, months, and years ahead.* Your faith can be a vital source of spiritual strength.

10. *Suggested devotional reading:* Isa. 41:10; Ps. 55:22; 121; 1 Pet. 5:7.

Each year in the United States, 250,000 babies are born with serious birth defects or various types of disabilities. But the families of children with handicaps have special and continuous needs that can often best be met by caring friends and supportive families.

Advice to Caregivers

1. *Acknowledge the baby's birth with a card or gift the same as you would any baby. Do not send a sympathy card.* Phone them or write on the card that you are remembering them and their baby in your prayers.

2. *Don't say, "Isn't this wonderful! God has chosen you as a special parent."* Parents do, however, appreciate being told what a good job they are doing caring for their child.

3. *Offer practical assistance.* Many times surgery or other medical problems necessitate a parent being away from the home with the child. Offer to help by doing small jobs—for example, caring for siblings, taking children to and from school, bringing in food. Remember pride is important to human beings. The parents may dislike having to ask for help again and again. But they may need gas money, a rider to accompany them on clinic visits or therapy sessions, a place to stay while out of town during hospitalizations, or a caring church in a strange city.

4. *Ask the usual questions about a newborn.* For example, "Does the

baby sleep well? Is the feeding going okay? How are you feeling? Are you able to get enough rest?"

5. *Don't ask questions that will induce more guilt.* Don't ask the mother her age. Since the risk of birth defects is greater for certain ages, a mother may hear your question as an accusation.

6. *Don't make projections about the child's potential.* Refrain from making comments like, "Some of these kids end up very bright."

7. *Avoid comparisons.* Each child and each child's problem is unique. Refrain from giving the parents dismal forecasts based on the experiences of other babies with similar problems.

8. *Don't expect the parents to plan the whole life of the baby.* We don't do that for normal children.

9. *Don't always try to be cheery with your friends. Cry with them if need be. In like manner, rejoice with them during their high moments.* Just as the valleys are very low, the highs are very high, and they want to share those as well.

10. *Don't avoid them.* Visit, make a brief phone call, and be there if they need you. Don't be afraid to discuss their baby's condition with them if they want to talk about it. Be supportive without intruding upon the parents' way of dealing with their feelings. The most important thing is to show you care.

11. *Look at and hold the baby.* If the baby's physical condition allows, your holding the baby says, "This handicap is not a barrier. I accept this child."

12. *Don't tell the parents that everybody will accept their child.* The sad truth is, many people have difficulty accepting those with disabilities.

13. *Don't tell the parents what they are feeling or doing is wrong.* Until you understand the reasons behind their feelings and actions, don't criticize.

14. *Avoid second-guessing God's will for their baby.* Who can say with any certainty what the will of God is for another human being? Also avoid interpreting what happened to their baby as punishment.

15. *As the baby develops, rejoice with the parents over even small improvements in their baby's condition.* Don't be afraid to share your child's accomplishments as well. Parents usually don't want to be cut off in any way from the lives of their friends.

16. *As their baby grows, treat the child with respect and love.* Do not convey remorse or pity for the child because of his or her disability.

17. *Offer to care for the child so the parent(s) can have some time away for themselves.*

18. *Remember that disabled children have much to teach us about caring and coping and faith.*

I am indebted to Carol Van Klompenburg for permission to quote some suggestions from her article, "Helping Parents of Impaired Children," *Re-*

newal, February 17, 1982. Special thanks also to Pat Parkhurst for her input.

Additional Reading

Dmitriev, Valentine. *Time to Begin*, 1982. For parents of a child with Down's syndrome. Available by writing: Caring, P.O. Box 400, Milton, Wash. 98354.

Dougan, Terrell, Lyn Isbell, and Patricia Vyas. *We Have Been There*. Nashville, Tenn.: Abingdon Press, 1984.

Ikeler, Bernard. *Parenting Your Disabled Child*. Philadelphia: Westminster Press, 1986.

Johnson, Joy and Mark. *Why Mine?* Can be ordered from Centering Corporation, P.O. Box 3367, Omaha, Neb. 68103. Price: $2.45. (Helpful at time of birth)

Kushner, Harold S. *When Bad Things Happen to Good People*. New York: Schocken Books, 1981.

Melton, David. *Promises to Keep: A Handbook for Parents of Learning Disabled, Handicapped, and Brain-Injured Children*. Franklin Watts, Inc., 1962.

Miezie, Peggy Muller. *Parenting Children with Disabilities*. New York: Marcel Dekker, Inc., 1983.

Noyer, Joan, and Norma MacNeil. *Your Child Can Win*. New York: William Morrow & Co., Inc., 1983.

Perske, Robert. *Show Me No Mercy*. Nashville, Tenn.: Abingdon Press, 1984. (About a Down's syndrome child)

Rabe, Berniece. *The Balancing Girl*. New York: E.P. Dutton, 1981.

Russell, Philippa. *The Wheelchair Child: How Handicapped Children Can Enjoy Life to Its Fullest*. Englewood Cliffs, N.J.: Prentice Hall, 1984.

Shennan, Victoria. *Improving the Personal Health and Daily Life of the Mentally Handicapped*. A Caregiver's Handbook. Englewood Cliffs, N.J.: Prentice Hall, 1984.

Wheeler, Bonnie. *Challenged Parenting*. Ventura, Calif.: Regal Books, 1983.

For a complete listing and the mailing address of the more than 25 national organizations for the intellectually and physically handicapped, consult the *Encyclopedia of Associations* found in your local library.

Instructor/Audio & Video Educational Materials

Ken Moses, Ph.D., is a psychologist who specializes in the effect of trauma, crisis, and grievous loss of human growth and development. He is a dynamic teacher whose presentations have won him acclaim throughout the United States and Canada. His workshop topics include: "On Lost

Dreams and Growth: Dynamics of Grieving and Coping with Disability in Children." His presentations are aimed for parents and professionals who care about disabled children. Write: Resource Networks, Inc., 930 Maple Ave., Evanston, Ill. 60202, or call (312) 864–4522 for more information and additional resource materials.

WHEN HELLO MEANS GOODBYE

Loss of a Baby through Miscarriage, Stillbirth, or Early Infant Death

Tricia Horst waited anxiously for her baby to cry. She heard nothing except the shuffle, shuffle, shuffle of the doctor and nurse working methodically. Moments earlier, her obstetrician had announced, "We have a problem down here." Her husband, Jamie, stood anxiously by her side in the delivery room. The nurse hurriedly left the room pushing the baby in an isolette. Still no sound.

"We have to take your baby to the nursery right away," the doctor explained.

There must be something wrong with my baby, Tricia thought to herself, yet dismissing the possibility of its being anything serious.

"What's the matter?"

"We'll talk about it after I finish the episiotomy*," he replied.

Jamie was alarmed. Tricia was not.

Shortly, the doctor motioned to Jamie.

"Come here; I want to talk to you," he said as he removed his surgical gloves and walked toward the door. Jamie followed reluctantly.

Once outside, he began, "Your baby is anencephalic. That basically means 'the absence of a brain.' The baby is alive but will probably live for only about an hour. It is in the nursery on support systems. You can go back in now and tell your wife." The doctor turned and started to leave.

Jamie was overwhelmed, devastated. His next thoughts were of Tricia. "Wait!" he protested. "She may have questions and I won't have the answers. You'd better come with me."

Slowly, the doctor pushed open the door and went in. Jamie resumed his place by her side. "You'd better tell her," he prompted.

"Your baby is severely deformed, Tricia," the doctor began. "It is anencephalic. The baby will live for about an hour . . ." His voice trailed off.

---

*A surgical incision made to allow passage of the baby and to prevent tearing.

Tricia was stunned, her senses and mind numb. She didn't understand what "anencephalic" meant.

"Was it a boy or a girl?" she asked, her voice flat.

"I'll go find out. I didn't notice," he said as he turned and left the room.

"Well, that's life," she said to Jamie dully. She felt detached and emotionless.

The delivery room nurse came back and reported it was a boy. The baby's birthweight was slightly over four pounds. Though full size, absence of the brain lessened his weight, and he was considered premature.

Tricia was wheeled back to the labor room where an hour earlier she had eagerly anticipated the birth of their first child. She had had a normal pregnancy, and though the baby was three weeks early, there had been no reason to worry, the doctor said.

Jamie was taking it hard. His body shook with sobbing.

Soon after, a nurse came to their room and asked if they would consent to an autopsy. She and Jamie passed knowing glances. Yes, they agreed.

Tricia had told the labor room nurse the names they had selected for the baby before delivery.

"Do you still want to name your baby Benjamin? Since this baby is going to die, maybe you want to save that name for a 'good' baby."

"No . . . no, this is Benjamin. He's been Benjamin since conception. That was the name we picked for him," Tricia said emphatically.

"Well, it just seems like such a nice name," she responded, her voice reflecting her disappointment that they were not following her advice.

Within the hour, they were told the baby had died.

Tricia was puzzled by her own lack of feeling. Jamie was crushed. *Don't I care?* she thought to herself. If someone had said to her beforehand that she was going to have a baby, and the baby would die, she would have anticipated being a basket case. Not only was she not falling apart, she felt as if it didn't matter that much, that she didn't care. She didn't understand her own behavior.

Finally, she admitted to the nurse taking her blood pressure, "I don't understand why I don't care or why it doesn't hurt."

"Well, I don't understand either," the nurse said bluntly. "Do you want to see your baby?"

Having to deal with the reality of seeing her baby frightened Tricia. "It's a pretty good idea to see the baby," the nurse encouraged.

Jamie spoke up, "Yes, I want to see him."

A nurse came in shortly carrying their baby snugly wrapped in blankets. She gently, lovingly rocked the dead baby in her arms.

If I hold him, I may never let him go, Tricia thought. Again, she was afraid and instinctively protected herself from the harsh reality that her baby had died. *No, if I don't hold him, I won't have felt him in my arms.* Tricia's first real emotion was fear. She was determined not to let it hurt.

Jamie reached out and took the baby, then gently cradled him in his arms, swaying gently to and fro. The baby's face and forehead appeared normal. His skull was caved in and deformed.

Tricia was transferred from the labor room to a private room on post-partum with other new mothers. As the numbness and denial waned, she desperately wanted to see and hold her baby. She wanted to touch him, to gently caress him and express her love to him. For months she had eagerly anticipated his birth. Hurriedly, she called the nursery from her room.

"May I see my baby now?" she asked. "I want to hold him."

"I'm sorry, Mrs. Horst, your baby has already been sent down to Pathology."

It was too late. At that, Tricia began to cry, and cried all night and for many months to come.

A graveside funeral for Benjamin was held the next day. The doctor refused her permission to go. "It will be too much for her," he told Jamie. Tricia was angry at Jamie for not responding to her needs.

"There is no way you're going to keep me away," she warned him. Jamie arranged for a friend to come and stay with her in her hospital room during the baby's funeral.

Tricia—like many mothers—was protected against her will, and not included in the funeral planning. Thus, she was not permitted to deal with the finality of death in the formal sociological way our society deals with death—the funeral. Being denied this experience, she lives with the feeling of unfinished business and never having said goodbye to Benjamin.

Grandparents Grieve, Too

Grandparents grieve, not only for the dead grandchild, but for their child as well. Parents hate to see their child suffer such a heartbreaking loss. They can respond in ways to protect themselves and their child in the case of a serious birth defect, such as Tricia and Jamie's baby. Mrs. Horst reacted as most grandparents do by being extraordinarily concerned over her son's feeling that he was to blame for the genetic defect.

Tricia's mother responded with delayed and misplaced anger. This new grief triggered an unresolved grief from her own past. She had never reconciled herself to the fact that Tricia, a Catholic, had married outside her faith.

"You're not really married . . . all your children will be illegitimate," she had warned.

After the baby died, her grief reaction was to lash out. She told Tricia that God had gotten even with her and justice had been served. Unable to deal with any more hurt, Tricia withdrew from her mother. Years later, her mother admitted she was sorry for the things she had said.

The relatives and loved ones closest to the parents may not realize the extent of the grief that occurs in the loss of a "wished-for" child. They were not involved with the dreams, wishes, and love that develops during the prenatal months. The loss of a child is a bereavement of dreams, fantasies, and projections of the future.

These months are unique to the parents alone, the natural bonding that takes place to create a family.

When the process of dreams, hope, and love come to a devastating halt, one cannot hope to understand the bereaved parents unless they have felt the loss themselves.

The Avon Lady

A few months before Tricia's baby was born, the Avon lady made regular stops at her home.

"When's your baby due?" she'd ask, or "You're getting big!" or "The baby's almost here," she'd comment.

Two weeks after the baby died, the Avon lady appeared one day at her door. She asked about the baby and wanted to see him.

"My baby died . . ." Tricia replied.

The woman set down her bag and walked toward Tricia.

"I am *so sorry*," she said as she put her arms around her, giving her a big warm hug.

Tricia burst into tears. Both women sat down on the couch and wept, entwined in each other's arms.

"I am so sorry. I don't know you very well, but my heart goes out to you. I'm going to remember you in my prayers every time I talk to God. I feel so bad."

By her spontaneous kindness, honesty, and sincerity, the Avon lady comforted her more than any other person up to this point. She allowed herself the freedom to cry, allowed Tricia to weep openly, and most important of all, she didn't run away.

Friends often avoided Tricia.

"People were afraid of me, so they avoided me," she said. "It almost seemed like punishment. 'You lost your baby, so I'm not talking to you.' " Nor did friends bring their children to her home, until finally, she begged them, "Please bring your children!"

Tricia one day explained to a close friend. "I know you think by not bringing your children, I'll forget about Benjamin. Yes, your children remind me of my own loss. But I have not forgotten, so there's nothing you can say that's going to remind me or make me forget. I do think of him constantly. I don't want to forget! I want to quit hurting, but I don't want to forget!"

Hurtful Remarks

Hardest to bear were the insensitive remarks about how lucky she had been. "You should be glad he died. Can't you just imagine what he would have looked like had he lived?" one said. She let the comment pass by, but was angered by it. *I just wish I had the chance to see what he looked like*, she thought.

All too common were the reminders, "You can have other babies," as if this baby were replaceable. "Don't get pregnant too soon. You don't want to replace this baby." Then they would add, "But be glad you can have others."

"People say things to console themselves. There is no need to try to say things to make you feel better because *there is not a thing they can say—not a word, not a phrase—that will make you feel better about your loss*," says Tricia.

Fear of Insanity

Sometimes fear of insanity is a normal part of grief. Shortly after coming home from the hospital, Tricia kept hearing a baby cry, and subsequently began to fear she was losing her mind. She was afraid to tell anyone.

"You feel like you're out of control, like you're falling apart. And in a sense, you do fall apart. The jigsaw pieces of your life don't fit together like they used to. It's almost as though you have to fall completely apart before you can put your life back together. It's a healing process. It's a normal part of grieving," says Tricia.

In talking with other mothers who have lost their babies, it is not uncommon to find they, too, have feared losing their mind and have heard "phantom cries." This occurs "most likely after the first week but before the fourth month," says Dr. Glen Davidson. Some hear it for years. He says about the phenomenon, "To see a picture of the baby is the only successful therapy I have yet found to stop the phantom crying."[1]

Questioning God

Tricia questioned God. "Why did you do this to me? What did I ever do to deserve this?" She would think, "God, you think I am strong, but I'm not this strong. I can't take this. This is too much. You've given me a little bit more than I can handle this time."

Added to her own questions were the questions raised by statements others would make about God. One said, "God works in strange ways. He knows what He is doing." Another said, "God has a plan for you. Don't

---

[1]Glen Davidson, M.D., *Understanding Death of a Wished-for-Child*, p. 20.

be in such a hurry to find out, because you won't know until you die." Most hurtful of all was, "God wants babies in heaven." Another told her, "Benjamin is one of God's little angels. You will always have a baby eternally."

Comments like these didn't make her feel any better. Inwardly she rejected and was angered by such statements.

Yet despite her questioning, Tricia found herself clinging to God rather than turning away. She knew she needed Him to get through her loss.

Their minister had been quietly supportive. Having been raised Catholic, she worried about her baby's not having been baptized. Would he go to limbo? The night Benjamin died, their pastor reassuringly told her, "Benjamin is with God and He is taking good care of your baby, Tricia." She was comforted by his assurance that God was caring for her baby.

Decision-Making

"The grieving parent is often disoriented and confused and *vulnerable*," Tricia says. "You want someone to tell you what to do because of your confused state. And there are plenty of people who would like to tell you what to do. They think they'll make it easier for you.

"It's important that parents who have lost a baby make their own decisions. Few, if any, couples go to the hospital prepared to bury their baby, so you have a lot of decisions to make. If somebody makes decisions for you, you're on the other side of that decision, so you haven't really gone through a process vital to working through your grief."

A friend or relative can be most helpful by asking the questions, "What do you think your options are?" and "How do you feel about these options?" and then letting the parents make their own decisions.

"Our psyche has been given a process to go through, and if you're given the support and the environment that gives you permission to grieve, it will be a normal process. You can't push anyone through it by making his decisions for him," says Tricia.

Usually the father goes through a briefer period of numbness, for he is drawn into the demands of home, work, and funeral planning while the mother is hospitalized. This tends to accelerate the grief process. The father may, however, experience a delayed grief reaction. Fathers feel the loss profoundly, nonetheless, and need as much compassion and understanding as the mother.

Mourning Together

As cards and letters from friends arrived for weeks after their baby died, Tricia would save them until her husband came home from work. Together they read them and talked about how they were feeling. "It didn't matter so much what the card said; it just mattered that friends cared enough to send one." This daily sharing helped create for Tricia and Jamie an atmosphere and climate in which to grieve. Grief is a highly fluid process; talking daily helped keep them in touch with each other's feelings, as well as their own. No two persons grieve the same way. Keeping the lines of communication open is vital to the relationship.

"Some couples are brought closer together by this tragedy; others are driven apart. Spouses often look to each other for support, but when both are upset or when one wants to talk and the other wants to forget it, relationships can become strained."[2]

Loss by Miscarriage and Stillbirth

Anita's Story

Anita Purcell's first pregnancy miscarried* at two months. She then had three sons. Her full-term pregnancies were not without complications; she had spotting and had to stay in bed for months before her second baby was born.

In 1981, she was again pregnant, and this time hoped for a girl. Early one August morning, she felt the first pangs of labor. The baby was moving and all seemed to be going well. About 11:30 a.m. she arrived at the hospital. Upon admission, the nurse checked the baby's heartbeat. She tried several times. Soon the doctor arrived and he tried.

"I can't get any fetal heart tones, Anita," he announced. No brain waves registered on further testing.

Anita's heart sank. *He's got to be wrong! Please, God, let them be wrong.*

"It will be easier for you to go through a normal delivery, Anita. A Caeserean section would be unnecessary surgery for you," he explained.

It was hard for her to think of going through labor to give birth to a dead baby. "I don't want to be awake when the baby's born," she told her doctor. "I can't stand the thought of not hearing the baby cry." Deep down, she desperately wanted the doctor to be wrong and for her baby to be alive.

She awakened soon after the baby was born.

The silence in the delivery room was deafening.

"You had a baby girl, Anita," the doctor announced, breaking the silence.

She could see her baby's small, limp body lying in the bassinet. "Can I hold my baby?" she asked. Anita was devastated. She handed the baby

---

[2]Robert B. McCall, Ph.D., "When an Infant Dies," *Parents* (February 1981), p. 82.
*See Appendix B for Facts About Miscarriage.

to her husband, Barnie, who stood by her side. They named the baby Julie.

Anita was wheeled back to the recovery room. "I want to see my doctor," she told the nurse taking her blood pressure.

"He'll be in in a little while," she said as she bent down toward Anita. Softly, she whispered in her ear, "He's crying."

Anita's saddened heart warmed as she thought of her doctor crying alone in the hallway. *He's hurting, too. He really cares!* She would never forget how it felt to know that her doctor was hurting because her baby died. His tears comforted her. His willingness to feel and express emotions was real and appropriate, and in no way jeopardized her faith and trust in him. In fact, it strengthened the doctor-patient relationship between them.

A year later, Anita got pregnant again and all went well for the first few months. The routine five-month checkup revealed this baby, too, had died. It was a boy they named Jeffrey.

But friends discounted her double tragedy. "You *do* have three boys at home," she was reminded. With Julie's death they had said, "It probably wouldn't have been so bad if she had been a boy, since you have three sons."

"God probably took the babies because He knew something was wrong," some interpreted. "God knows best." Anita's reaction to that was, "I wonder how God could take my babies; I am a good mother."

As months passed and Anita needed to talk about her babies, she discovered friends would change the subject when she talked about them. She was disappointed, too, that closer relatives had not gone to the cemetery where Julie and Jeffrey were buried.

Fortunately, she had other friends who would invite her to lunch and openly discuss the babies. The friend who sat with her for hours when Julie was born called on the anniversary of the baby's death and asked if she could go with Anita to the cemetery, a practice she continued for years later.

"She's the only one who remembers Julie's birthday," says Anita. "I can't tell you how good that makes me feel. She's a very *special* friend."

By chance, Anita Purcell and Tricia Horst met. Together, they founded Quad Cities SHARE (A Source of Helping in Airing and Resolving Experiences). They had heard about the SHARE group founded at St. John's Hospital in Springfield, Illinois. SHARE is a self-help group for parents who have lost a baby through miscarriage, stillbirth, or early infant death. It works with parents and hospital OB staff to acquaint them with the normal grief reactions of parents. They show films such as *Memories* and *To Touch Today* and arrange guest speakers. Anyone who has suffered the loss of a wished-for child—parents, relatives and loved ones included—are welcome at their meetings. They present topics of concern:

- The grieving process
- Coping with grief
- Family response to loss
- Impact on marriage
- Working through feelings of anger, jealousy, and guilt
- Unfinished business: the headstone, putting away baby clothes, crib, etc.
- Subsequent pregnancies and children
- Keepsakes of the baby
- Coping with anniversaries and holidays
- Helping the surviving children
- Effect of grief on religious faith

Members of SHARE make themselves available anytime—day or night—to talk or listen with heartfelt understanding to help parents through the initial stages of mourning.

Impact of Health Care Personnel on Long-term Grief

Medical professionals, because of the vital role they play in the baby's delivery, are "first responders" when a baby dies. The doctor's actions, his tone of voice, the nurse's words, an attitude reflected in a raised eyebrow—are etched in the minds of parents for years to come. "Parents' grief response to neonatal death is highly individualized and may depend more on the compassionate concern of care-givers than any other single factor."[3]

"Physicians and nurses," says Elizabeth Kubler-Ross, "may find it extremely difficult to cope with death. They are trained to treat, to cure, to prolong life; yet they must suffer through their own grieving as they face the families of dying patients."[4]

Davidson comments further, "The health care professions, until very recent times, have not been prepared to treat mourning as anything more than pathological reaction."[5]

"It's apparent that 'babies and death' don't go together," says Tricia Horst. "It's uncomfortable for the staff to have a dead baby in the nursery for a long period of time." Through efforts aimed at educating hospital staffs, SHARE has succeeded in winning the cooperation of the hospitals.

---

[3]Drs. Banfield, Leib, and Vollman, "Grief Response of Parents to Neonatal Death and Parent Participation in Deciding Care," *Pediatrics*, Vol. 62, No. 2 (August 1978), p. 176.
[4]Elizabeth Kubler-Ross, *Questions and Answers on Death and Dying* (New York: The Macmillan Publishing Co., 1974), p. 118; Mauksch H.O.: The Organizational context of dying, in E. Kubler-Ross (ed.): Death: *The Final Stage of Growth* (Englewood Cliffs, N.J.: Prentice-Hall, Inc., 1975), pp. 7–24.
[5]Glen Davidson, M.D., *Understanding Death of a Wished-For Child*, p. 16.

The OB departments allow more time for the parents to make their decision to see the baby by holding the body from six to eight hours or longer if necessary.

Tricia and Anita have made an impact on hospital staffs. Karen Sheets, clinical nurse manager of obstetrics at Franciscan Medical Center in Rock Island, Illinois, says about SHARE, "After the SHARE mothers first came to me and presented their program, we [the hospital] decided it was important enough to make it mandatory inservice for all our nursing staff. Talking with SHARE mothers and seeing their teaching films have made my nurses much more aware of the feelings and needs of parents. And they are much more comfortable now dealing professionally with parents who experience the loss of a baby."

Creating Memories

"You go back to memories to work out your grief," says Tricia. "The time is so short. So it's vitally important that hospital personnel are aware of the need to create memories. The more memories you can make in that short period of time, the more you have to cling to in order to work through your grief.

"One mother said the fifteen minutes she was allowed to rock her dead baby were the most memorable moments of her entire life. We have to get over the feeling that 'dead babies are morbid,' " says Tricia.

The wished-for baby is never forgotten. It is not uncommon to discover that women, even in advanced age, when asked how many children they had will nearly always mention the babies that died or the number of miscarriages they had.

SHARE Helps Mothers Like Debbie

Debbie Vretis is a young mother who has found SHARE helpful. Six years ago, she lost her first baby, a son. Debbie remembers her husband and doctor standing over her bed and saying, "Debbie, a terrible thing has happened. Your baby is dead!"

Debbie went into shock. By the time she recovered, the baby had been buried. She neither saw nor held her baby. Her husband and family still find it hard to talk about the baby, and Debbie cries when she is alone. Five years after her baby died, she still was having a difficult time. Now she is "up-dating" her grief, a process that usually happens on the milestones and anniversaries. In SHARE, Debbie has found an environment and friends with whom she can openly mourn the baby she never met.

Several years have passed. Tricia and Jamie now have three daughters; Anita, another daughter; and Debbie, two sons.

All admit they will never forget their wished-for babies and still cry at times when certain reminders touch their emotions. But together, they walk beside others who experience losses such as theirs. They offer this advice to parents:

Advice to Offer Parents

1. *Create memories.* Hold, rock, photograph, take as much time with your baby as you need so that you have a good mental picture of your baby. Allow yourself the opportunity to convey your feelings to the baby. Anything you can do to create memories is important. Grandparents may want to hold the baby also.
2. *Make your own decisions.* It is vital to the grief process.
3. *Include the mother in funeral planning.* Funeral services help to confirm the reality of the baby's death and are a formal way of saying "goodbye." If the mother remains hospitalized, consider having the funeral service in the mother's hospital room.
4. *Allow yourselves permission to grieve separately and together.* No two people are going to grieve the same, so it's important to keep the lines of communication open. Cards, as they arrive, can be shared and create an environment conducive to mutual sharing and mourning.
5. *Don't try to rush yourselves.* Experts say a majority of persons take between eighteen and twenty-four months to work through the mourning process.
6. *If your friends don't call you, call them and let them know you miss them.* By talking openly about it, you will put them at ease.
7. *Avoid assigning blame on yourself or your spouse.* Almost everyone who loses a baby feels guilty. In the case of miscarriage, couples wonder if it was something the mother did—like scrubbing the floors, running, or having intercourse—that caused it. Recognize the fact that guilt, along with sadness, anger, fear, and depression are all part of the normal grieving process and will gradually subside.
8. *Suggested Devotional Reading:* Isa. 41:10, 13; Deut. 33:27; Ps. 22:9, 10; 27:13, 14; 138:8; 2 Cor. 1:3–5.

Advice to Caregivers

1. *Send cards or briefly worded letters,* saying, in essence, "I am so sorry. This must be very painful for you."
2. *Acknowledge the extent of your friends' tragedy and the depth of their grief.* Remember, the depth of their grief has nothing to do with the size or age of the loss.
3. *Tell them you support them and will think of them in your prayers.*

4. *Avoid trying to say something to make them feel better,* especially clichés and statements such as "God knows best," or advice such as, "Don't cry."
5. *Avoid interpreting this as God's punishment, God's plan, or God's will.* Usually, comments such as this are resented, and they are poor theology.
6. *Avoid suggesting they can have other babies as if this baby is replaceable.* By doing so, you *devalue* the baby as if its loss is insignificant.
7. *If you are especially close to the parents, don't be surprised if you experience what is called "third grief,"* a mini-grief period which will last for a brief period of time following the baby's death.
8. *Don't preach, cajole, or scold if you think your friend is wallowing in self-pity.* Give them permission to grieve by listening nonjudgmentally. Allow them to be angry and tearful in your presence.
9. *Don't avoid the grieving parents.* They are still your friends. Call them and let them know you are thinking about them. Ask if they want to talk about their baby. They will usually say yes. Then listen with your heart. They need to talk with friends who care. Grieving is a social process; it requires relationships.

Additional Reading

Church, Martha Jo, Helene Chazin, and Faith Ewald. *When a Baby Dies.* Available from The Compassionate Friends, P.O. Box 3696, Oak Brook, Ill. 60522–3696.

Davidson, Glen W., M.D. *Understanding Death of a Wished-For Child.* OGR Service Corporation, P.O. Box 3586, Springfield, Ill. 62708, 1979. (Booklet)

DeFrain, John D., Leona Martens, Jan and Warren Stork. *Stillborn—The Invisible Death.* D.C. Heath and Company, Lexington Books, 1986.

Friedman, Rochelle, M.D., and Bonnie Gradstein, M.P.H. *Surviving Pregnancy Loss.* Boston: Little Brown & Co., 1982.

Hanes, Mari, with Jack Hayford. *Beyond Heartache.* Wheaton, Ill.: Tyndale House Publishers, 1984.

Ilse, Sherokee. *Empty Arms—Coping After Miscarriage, Stillbirth and Infant Death.* Available from The Compassionate Friends (address above).

Johnson, Joy and Marvin. *Newborn Death.* Centering Corporation, P.O. Box 3367, Omaha, Neb. 68103–0367.

Limbo, Rana K., and Sara Rich Wheeler. *When a Baby Dies: A Handbook for Healing and Helping.* Available from: Resolve Through Sharing, La Crosse Lutheran Hospital, 1910 South Avenue, La Crosse, Wis. 54601, for $8.95 and a $2.00 handling charge.

Mims, Jimenez, and Sherry Lynn. *The Other Side of Pregnancy.* Spectrum/Prentice Hall, 1982.

Miscarriage. Centering Corporation. Available from The Compassionate Friends or the Centering Corporation.

Osgood, Judy. *Meditations for Bereaved Parents.* Available from The Compassionate Friends.

Rando, Therese A. *Parental Loss of a Child.* Champaign, Ill.: Research Press, 1986.

Rank, Maureen. *Free to Grieve.* Minneapolis: Bethany House Publishers, 1985.

Schatz, Bill. *Healing a Father's Grief.* Available from The Compassionate Friends.

Schwiebert, Pat, and Paul Kirk, M.D. *When Hello Means Goodbye.* A guide for Parents Whose Child Dies at Birth or Shortly After, 1981. Available from: University of Oregon Health Services Center, Dept. of Obstetrics & Gynecology, 3181 S.W. Sam Jackson Park Road, Portland, Or. 97201. (Booklet)

Vredevelt, Pam W. *Empty Arms.* Portland, Or.: Multnomah Press, 1984.

Recommended Films/Videos

Memories and *To Touch Today*, video, give insights into the needs of parents, their feelings, and personal experiences; they also assist professionals in gaining a deeper awareness, plus skills in providing comfort and the facilitation of the grief process. Available from: Distribution Department, Health Science Consortium, 103 Laurel Avenue, Carrboro, NC 27510, or St. John's Hospital, c/o Care Video Productions, P.O. Box 45132, Cleveland, Ohio 44145, (216)835–5872.

Death of a Wished-For Child, 28-minute, 16mm color documentary of an actual clinical case. It is restricted to use with the helping professions or organized groups of bereaved parents seeking to provide assistance to parents who have experienced the loss of a baby. It is particularly relevant for obstetrics and pediatric staffs, counselors and social workers. For more information, write OGR Service Corporation, P.O. Box 3586, Springfield, Ill. 62708.

Starting a Self-Help Group

For more information about starting a self-help group in your community, write to the following: *In U.S.:* SHARE St. Elizabeth's Hospital, 211 S. Third Street, Belleville, IL 62222, (618) 234–2415; Unite, c/o Bernadette Foley, Social Services Dept., Jeanes Hospital, 7600 Central Avenue, Philadelphia, Pa. 19111; The Compassionate Friends, National Headquarters, P.O. Box 1347, Oak Brook, Ill.: *In Canada:* Parents Experiencing Perinatal Death Association, c/o Gael Gilbert, 47 Alberta Avenue, Toronto M6H 247, Ontario.

◇ 5 ◇

SIDS—A THIEF IN THE NIGHT

Death of an Infant from
Sudden Infant Death Syndrome*

Kathy Paulson stirred around the kitchen getting breakfast for her family. It was 7 o'clock in the morning but still dark outside in Omaha's bleak January weather.

Kristine's sleeping later than usual, Kathy thought to herself. She called to her husband. "Ken, would you go check on Kristine?"

The Paulsons' two boys, Kurt and Kevin, were still sleeping.

Ken Paulson made his way to the nursery. Suddenly, he screamed, his voice shrill and penetrating, "She's dead!"

Terror raced through Kathy as she dashed to the nursery and switched on the light.

Ken stood frozen, holding up the distorted, discolored body of their three-and-one-half-month-old daughter. Blood-tinged froth had oozed from her mouth staining her pajama top.

As a nurse, Kathy had seen dead bodies before, but seeing her own baby, now stiff and cold, was devastating. Only hours earlier her baby had been warm and sweet, with a smile that crept into Kathy's heart and melted away her cares.

Ken Paulson returned the baby to her crib, then made his way to the phone and dialed the emergency number—911. Kathy followed him, stunned, disbelieving. Soon a voice came on the line. Ken, who was usually never at a loss for words, could not talk. Kathy grabbed the phone from his hand.

"I think our baby is dead! Please send someone." She then gave the operator their address and hung up.

Soon the flashing lights of the rescue unit appeared in their driveway.

---

*Based on an interview with co-founders of Quad Cities SIDS Support Group and co-chairpersons of the International SIDS Guild, and a SIDS mother whose name has been changed.

Paramedics hurriedly made their way to the nursery, following close behind Kathy. They looked at the baby, then turned to leave. There was nothing they could do.

"What is it?" Kathy asked, her voice unsteady.

"I think it's sudden infant death syndrome, or 'crib death' as it is commonly called," one explained. "Apparently she's been dead for a long time."

Excited neighbors began knocking on the Paulsons' door. The flashing red lights had alerted the neighborhood that something was wrong. Kathy decided she had to get the boys out of the house. She called friends and asked them to come for them.

Two policemen arrived, summoned by the emergency operator. Ken explained what he had found. They stood looking down at the lifeless form of the infant hardly recognizable to her parents. Both men, poised with hands on their hips, had tears streaming down their cheeks. Kathy thought it looked strange to see policemen cry. It touched her to see the caring and tender hearts of uniformed men wearing guns and night sticks.

"You'll have to call a funeral home," advised the officer.

"I can't think of anyone," Ken responded, though he bowled every Friday night with a funeral director. Ken's stunned mind now refused to function.

"I'll call one for you," the officer volunteered.

A short time later, a man came to their door.

"I've come to pick up the body," he announced. He was carrying a black case that looked as if it were designed for a tuba or an instrument of some kind.

Ken led him to the baby's room. The man opened the blood-stained case. Ken stood speechless as he watched the man place their baby's body inside, close the lid, and carry her away as if he were carrying a load of bricks.

Kathy watched him pass by her carrying the case. *This is absolutely horrid,* she said to herself. *Carry Kristine in your arms like a baby, wrap her in a warm blanket!* she wanted to scream at him.

The coroner arrived at the same time the funeral director came to pick up the body. He asked a long list of questions. Things went smoothly until he asked, "How many children have you, living or dead?"

"We have two living sons, and a daughter who died in 1970," Ken responded.

The coroner's mood changed from one of empathy to concern. "How did *she* die?" he said in a voice which betrayed his suspicions.

"Our daughter Karen had 'biliary atresia.' She died following a liver transplant. She was three and a half. Operations of that nature were considered experimental when Karen had surgery," Kathy explained.

Tensions eased and the coroner ended his questioning, but not before

Kathy and Ken had felt the poisonous arrows of suspicion and blame.

During the day, relatives were called in Wisconsin and Arizona. Each conversation would begin with a bright cheery greeting on the other end of the line. "Hello, oh, it's so good to hear from you!" and then Kathy would tell them.

"Kristine's dead." And the conversation would quickly degenerate into barely understandable sentences mumbled between sobs and tears.

Before the day was over, the coroner called to give the results of the autopsy.

"I just wanted you to know your baby died of crib death," he began. "There are a lot of old wives' tales going around, but I want you to know it's not your fault and there was nothing you could do to prevent it," he explained.

Kathy called their priest and he arrived shortly after her call. "You don't have to understand this now," he said consoling them. He then went into the kitchen and made coffee.

The Funeral

To be among friends and relatives, the baby's funeral was held in Wisconsin. Kathy and Ken decided that two-year-old Kevin should stay with friends, but five-year-old Kurt would accompany them to the funeral home and the funeral.

The last time Kurt had seen the baby was the night before her death. Ken held Kurt up to the casket so he could see her.

"I want a piece of paper, Mommy. I want to write Kristine a note," he said as he looked at the baby, then his mother.

Kathy shuffled through her purse and came up with paper and pencil. Kurt settled himself at a nearby table and proceeded to write.

"Mommy, how do you spell Kristine?" he asked.

Laboriously he printed, *God loves Kristine*, in a preschooler's shaky, uneven letters. He drew a cross and gravestone marker on the paper.

"I want to put this in with her."

Again, Ken held him up so he could place the note beside his baby sister.

A quick smile formed on Kathy's tear-stained face.

"I want to touch her. Okay?"

"It's okay, go ahead," his parents prompted.

"Kurt, if you have any questions, just come and ask us. If we don't know the answers, we'll find out," Kathy said as he looked from one parent to the other.

Satisfied, he wriggled down out of his father's arms.

Separated by miles, Ken's parents had never seen the baby. They stood weeping in front of the casket of the grandchild they had never met or cuddled lovingly.

Kurt spoke up, "Grandma, you can go ahead and touch her; she's cold and hard and she's going to stay that way."

The funeral director standing nearby overheard Kurt. He bent down and began explaining why the body changes. His gentle explanation on a level Kurt could understand was helpful and relieved the parents of trying to find words appropriate for a five-year-old.

Among those who came for the visitation was a nun. Kathy had assumed she was a friend of Ken's sister, who was also a nun.

"Mrs. Paulson, I'm very sorry. I thought you might find this information helpful." She handed her a brochure about sudden infant death syndrome (SIDS). Kathy learned later the nun had read about their baby's death in the newspaper, and had traveled some distance just to give the Paulsons facts and information vital to understanding what had happened and to reassure them they in no way were to blame for their baby's death. The nun was involved in a SIDS organization in Milwaukee. The Paulsons had never seen her before, nor did they ever see her again.

Kathy and Ken read the brochure over and over.

The Need for Information

Kristine Paulson died January 25, 1974. As they look back, Kathy and Ken are grateful to the paramedics and policemen who responded emotionally and nonjudgmentally. And they are grateful they were given immediate answers by medical personnel and the coroner soon after the autopsy. "If every family were handled as we were, there would be fewer problems," says Kathy.

"In the support group we've formed, I still find parents are not getting the information they need and are not handled well. For instance, I remember seeing headlines in one newspaper, BABY DIES, SIDS? SHERIFF INVESTIGATING. That's accusing parents of murder in the minds of the public.

"You need answers. You need information as soon as possible," says Kathy. "If you don't know what's the matter, you imagine that you, or the babysitter, or the grandparent or the doctor is at fault. The less time that you have to imagine horrible things, the better it is for you, because you don't have to undo negative feelings. You then can handle what's going on right away. The reality of the situation and living with the diagnosis of SIDS is very difficult to handle. Parents need an autopsy report within twenty-four hours after the child's death."

"You can vent your anger on a known cause of death," says Ken. "With SIDS, you don't know the cause, and that compounds your frustration and anger."

Medication?

Kathy strongly advises against taking tranquilizers to get through the funeral or initial grieving.

"The funeral serves a specific purpose: to say 'goodbye' to your baby and to have your family and friends around you to give emotional support in a socially acceptable atmosphere. If the mother has had six doses of Valium just so she won't break down and cry, her mind is in a druglike trance delaying the grief process. A couple of weeks later, when she comes off the drug," says Kathy, "she's going to come out of that state when there are no friends or relatives around to give her support."

Baby's Gone!

"I feel children should be asked if they want to attend the funeral. We knew Kevin at two would not understand, but Kurt wanted to see Kristine. It is very devastating," says Kathy, "to have your children ask questions, but I knew Kurt would always wonder what happened to her and where she was. Children mourn too, but their needs are often overlooked. They need someone to give them answers and help them talk through the grief process.

"I suggest that if parents feel they can't handle their children's questions during the funeral, they should instruct the child to go to an aunt or uncle or grandparent who can talk about death in a positive way and honestly deal with the child's questions.

"In the weeks that followed Kristine's death, Kurt and Kevin asked a lot of questions. They forced me to think about how to answer them. They helped me keep moving in the grief process.

"Two-year-old Kevin would go to the closet where I kept Kristine's car seat and say, 'Baby gone, Baby gone.' It brought home the reality of our baby's death. Though painful, it was helpful."

Facts About SIDS

SIDS is defined as "the sudden and unexpected death of an apparently healthy infant whose death remains unexplained after a thorough post-mortem exam."

SIDS is a definite medical entity. An estimated 6,500 to 8,000 babies die in the United States annually—a rate of 1 to 3 per 1,000 live births. SIDS remains the single largest cause of death among infants between the ages of 2 weeks to 1 year, with the peak incidence between 2 and 4 months of age.[1]

---

[1]Baba, "Possible Role of the Brain Stem in Sudden Infant Death Syndrome," *JAMA*, Vol. 249, No. 20 (May 27, 1983), p. 2789.

SIDS is at least as old as the Old Testament, and seems to have been at least as frequent in the 18th and 19th centuries as it is now.

SIDS cannot be predicted or prevented, even by a physician. It is not caused by suffocation, neglect, aspiration or regurgitation, pneumonia, heart attack, or by changing modes of infant care.

SIDS is not contagious or hereditary. It takes the lives of infants without regard to race or socio-economic status, although Dr. Keith Reisinger, University of Pittsburgh School of Medicine, reports that there is a significant increase in the lower socio-economic class. It does happen more often to males, premature babies, multiple births, and subsequent SIDS siblings.[2]

Medical science has no complete understanding of the cause of sudden infant death. Theories abound; answers do not. Research is being done testing theories of infant botulism, the carotid body (vital respiratory control mechanisms), brain stem structural anomaly, and sleep apnea.[3] The major focus of study has been directed toward respiratory control mechanisms and the problems of periodic sleep apnea and airway obstruction.[4]

Researchers also study "near-miss" SIDS infants—those whose breathing had stopped and were immediately revived by parents or medical personnel. Some "high risk" infants are identified and placed on 24-hour home-monitoring systems. Some medical doctors disagree with home-monitoring. They claim that it creates what some call "a constant state of emotional tension and financial stress, directly attributable to what may be unnecessary monitoring by over-protective parents."[5]

Parents live under the constant threat of fear that they will miss the twenty-second alarm signaling apnea. Prolonged apnea is defined as cessation of breathing for 20 seconds or longer. Some doctors and hospitals are uncertain whether the near-miss apnea contributes to a SIDS death. But most parents prefer taking their chances with monitoring.

Monitoring Subsequent Children

In January 1980, Cindy went to pick up her six-and-a-half-month-old son, Tom, from the babysitter's one morning to find that he had died of SIDS during his morning nap.

---

[2]Gerber Pediatric Basics #27, "Sudden Infant Death Syndrome: Review and Update," Keith S. Reisinger, M.D., M.P.H. Department of Medicine, University of Pittsburgh School of Medicine.

[3]Marie A. Valdes-Dapena, M.D., "Research Developments in the Sudden Infant Death Syndrome," Spring '84 to Spring '85.

[4]Fredric Kleinberg, M.D., "Sudden Infant Death Syndrome," *Mayo Clinical Procedures*, 1984, 59, p. 352.

[5]Betty McEntire, Ph.D., "What Is Crib Death?" *Thanatos*, Vol. 6, No. 1, p. 16.

When each of her two infant daughters were born a couple years later, each baby was monitored for several months. Cindy describes what it was like:

"Some people say that monitoring is a stressful experience. It has its own stresses, but I didn't find monitoring as stressful as the idea that we could lose this child, too. The idea that our baby could stop breathing and we couldn't do anything, and that we could go through the same thing we went through all over again was truly scary."

The Impact of SIDS on the Family

A report published following the National Conference on Mental Health Issues Related to Sudden Infant Death Syndrome in 1977 says: "Because SIDS strikes without warning, these infant deaths are a particularly shattering form of child loss, and the effects on surviving members of the family may last a lifetime, creating serious mental health problems which may erupt years after the death of the child."

Albert C. Cain, Ph.D., professor of psychology at the University of Michigan, has identified the common grief reactions and psychological burdens carried by SIDS parents:

Guilt. Wracking, irrational guilt is one of the most frequently observed psychological burdens of SIDS families and others connected with the child. They are tortured with self-blame and self-hate. Parents question endlessly what their sins of commission or omission were. The older sibling, babysitter, grandparent or other caregiver in whose care the child was at the time of death may face wild, unsupported accusations about his or her role in the baby's death.

Misconceptions about the cause of death. The guilt SIDS families feel becomes even more of a psychological burden if they are uninformed or misinformed about what caused their baby to die.

Anger. Raw, fiercely destructive anger is a frequent reaction to SIDS death. It may be directed toward oneself, family members, friends, doctors, emergency room personnel, God, fate, or anyone who happens to come along. Surviving children can become the brunt of erratic temperamental changes in their parents. Good friends may find themselves and their healthy, living babies objects of resentment.[6]

Sometimes, says Cain, the unacknowledged severity of the SIDS grief reactions precipitates suicide attempts, suicide, and/or admission for mental health therapy. Furthermore, statistics indicate that 6 to 12 months after the traumatic loss of a child, 80 percent of marriages are in trouble. The divorce rate for SIDS parents is high.

---

[6]Albert C. Cain, Ph.D., "The Impact of Sudden Infant Death Syndrome on Families: Some Lessons from Our Recent Past," *Mental Health Issues in Grief Counseling*, DHEW Pub., No. (HSA) 80–5264, pp. 11, 12. Used by permission.

Dr. Cain adds that for every *one* divorce after a SIDS death, he's seen *three* instances of couples who have stayed together, but five and ten years later "holding unforgiving, bone-deep grudges stemming from *emotional* abandonment by a spouse over emotional non-support 'for which nothing he does or says will ever make up,' or for things said 'which can never be unsaid.' "

He reports that in some cases, fathers react by abrupt desertion; unrelenting accusations of his wife's 'having done away with the baby'; turning to the use of alcohol, then drugs; and abrupt, self-destructive behavior at work leading to the virtual ruin of a promising professional career. Dr. Cain suggests that, in general, too little attention has been focused on the impact SIDS death has on fathers.

Ken Paulson agrees. "A father is going to handle the baby's death differently than the mother. Unconsciously men have been conditioned to putting on a front that says, 'You've got to be strong for your wife.' Realistically, men often don't get much emotional support. And men get back into society faster because of their jobs. This adds to the stress, for often the father feels the mother's grief shouldn't be lasting so long. He will often urge her to 'get over it and get on with her life.' "

A Faith Crisis

"Months down the line," said Kathy Paulson, "I believe my faith in God and my Christian friends and all the prayers I knew I was getting really were supportive, but initially—the first couple of days and weeks—I was so angry. On the day Kristine died, if anyone had said my eternity relied on the fact that I accepted God's will right then, I would have punched him in the face right there in the middle of the room.

"If these things happen and there is [God has] no control over them or there is no reason, then what did Kristine die for? I really believe that everything that happens, happens for a reason. If it didn't happen for a purpose—to some effect—then I would be very angry," ends Kathy.

Ken and Kathy have found meaning in helping others. In 1978, they helped found a support group in their community. They have taken a key role in educating professionals and the general public about SIDS and its aftermath. In 1980, they became co-chairpersons for the International SIDS Guild.

Clergy Responses

"Our priest simply said, 'You don't have to understand this now.' On the first anniversary of her death, he called to let us know he was remembering us in his prayers. His phone call a year later really made us feel good," said Kathy.

"Parents in our support group report that pastors often aren't very helpful and will often recite the same platitudes as everyone else—'It's God's will' or 'God knows best.'

"The most helpful, honest statement I heard was made by Earl A. Grollman. He said, 'We don't know why God has babies die. I don't know and I don't know of any clergyperson who can give you an answer unless they've got a special telephone to God and He's telling them, 'I did this for a reason.' I don't know anyone who can give you an answer as to why this happened to you or why your baby died.' "

Vulnerability and Isolation

SIDS parents are especially vulnerable emotionally. Having to explain the sudden death of their baby places them in the position of confronting the question over and over again, "What did the baby die of?" Questions like "Did the baby smother?" "Were you home?" "Did you check the baby?" increase the parents' feelings of guilt and anxiety, and demonstrate the stigma attached to sudden death.

Friends and family are often afraid to talk to parents—because they don't know what to say, they don't say anything. This adds to the SIDS parents' isolation.

Cindy explains, "You feel so isolated within yourself. When people withdraw from you because of their own discomfort, in a way, it's almost like an accusation that you were at fault. You feel you *must* have done something wrong, or this wouldn't be happening to you. On the other hand, you almost feel like they don't want to be around you because they feel it might be catching. I know people don't know what to say. I would rather they'd come and be with me or ask permission, 'Would you like someone to be with you?' rather than feel, 'Well, I don't know what to say so I think I'll stay away.' "

Kathy Paulson adds, "Friends who have well babies often don't know what to do about visiting. Sometimes it is just too painful for the parent to see another baby right at that moment. Some SIDS parents find this painful for as long as a year. I suggest the friend call and simply ask how the parents feel about seeing other babies."

Cindy *wanted* to see other children. "I wanted to see there were children out there who were living and laughing and okay. I needed to see and feel and hope that I could again have that someday. It is always better to ask how the parent feels than to assume they do or do not want to see other babies."

Friends and family need to sit and listen, allowing the parents to express all their intense emotions. Permitting them to talk about many of the same things repeatedly will do much to bring comfort and peace of mind to parents who have lost babies to sudden infant death syndrome.

Advice to Offer SIDS Parents

1. *Call and ask for information about SIDS.* If a support group is not organized in your community and you cannot get literature from your doctor, hospital, or library, call the National SIDS Hotline (1–800–221–SIDS) or write the National Sudden Infant Death Syndrome Foundation, 8240 Professional Place, Suite 205, Landover, MD 20785, and ask for material. Ask for several copies to give relatives and friends.
2. *Remember, no one is to blame.* Nothing you or your spouse or your doctor or other caretakers did or did not do caused your baby's death.
3. *Find a confidant other than your spouse.* You need a friend who can allow you to ventilate and cry and express all your bottled-up emotions without denial and rejection.
4. *Be good to yourself.* Don't expect yourself to function as if nothing has happened. The inability to concentrate, and feeling as though your world has fallen apart are normal grief reactions.
5. *Remember, your children mourn the loss of the baby as well.* Use death language (see Chap. 9). Avoid statements like the baby "was sick," or "is sleeping." The child may then become fearful of being sick or going to sleep. Read books to gain an understanding of how to explain death to your child.
6. *Suggested devotional reading:* Ps. 34:17–19; 46:1–3; 77:1–12.

Advice to Caregivers

1. *If you have access to SIDS literature, give it to the family as soon as possible.*
2. *Avoid asking the parents questions that induce guilt or affix blame.*
3. *Reinforce the belief that the parents are not to blame.* Say, "I know there's nothing you did to cause your baby's death."
4. *Refrain from giving advice or making "be glad" statements.* For example, do not say, "You can have other babies," "Be glad you have other children," "Have another baby, it will help you forget," "At least the baby didn't suffer," "Let's not talk about it, it's too gruesome." And don't urge them to "forget the baby."
5. *Expect to have to tolerate intense emotions and volatile reactions.* Listen, be present physically, as well as emotionally, to render support to the parents. Do not make judgments on their feelings or beliefs.
6. *Reach out to the parents.* Do not let your own sense of helplessness or not knowing what to say keep you from reaching out to the parents, grandparents and siblings. Let your genuine concern and caring show.
7. *Acknowledge the baby's death.* Don't act like nothing has happened. There will be a barrier between you until you do. Say, "I'm sorry your

baby died." Remember a sympathizing tear or a squeeze of the hand also brings comfort and acknowledges the loss.

8. *Do not be afraid to mention the baby's name.* The parents have memories and had hopes and dreams that live on in their memories. Your mention of their baby is usually appreciated. Understand that talking about their loss facilitates healing.

9. *Call and ask before visiting and bringing your children.* Respect the parents' wishes, but *do* call or visit.

10. *Plant seeds of hope that someday the pain will lessen.*

11. *Call parents on the anniversaries.* The baby's birthday, the date of death—especially the "firsts" are always painful. Mother's Day and Father's Day are especially so for SIDS parents, especially if they lost an only child. In their minds, they are still parents. Remembering them with a call means *someone cares.*

Additional Reading

DeFrain, John, Jaque Tayloer, and Linda Ernst. *Coping with Sudden Infant Death.* Lexington, Mass.: Lexington Books, 1982.

Donnelly, Katherine Fair. *Recovering from the Loss of a Child.* New York: The MacMillan Publishing Co., 1982.

Grollman, Earl A. *Living When a Loved One Has Died.* Boston: Beacon Press, 1977.

Johnson, Joy and Marv. *Where's Jess?* Omaha, Neb.: Centering Corporation, Box 3367, Omaha, Neb. 68103. This booklet is intended for surviving brothers and sisters of SIDS victims.

La Tour, Kathy. *For Those Who Live: Helping Children Cope with the Death of a Brother or Sister.* Write to Kathy La Tour, P.O. Box 141182, Dallas, Tex. 75214. $9.95.

Schatz, Bill. *Healing a Father's Grief.* Available from The Compassionate Friends. (See address below.)

Stevenson, Nancy, and Cary Straffon. *When Your Child Dies: Finding the Meaning in Mourning.* Available from The Compassionate Friends.

Filmstrip

Touch the Snow, a filmstrip written by SIDS parents, conveys at a child's level what death is, the expressions of grief, issues of guilt and blame, remembering, and living once again. Purchase price is $125.00; three-day rental fee is $35.00. Available from: The Centering Corporation, P.O. Box 3367, Omaha, Neb. 68103.

National Organizations

The Compassionate Friends
P.O. Box 3696

Oak Brook, IL 60522–3696
(312)990–0010
(Issues a newsletter and has books, video cassettes, and brochures helpful to parents.)

National Sudden Infant Death Syndrome Foundation
8240 Professional Place, Suite 205
Landover, MD 20785.

NATIONAL SIDS HOTLINE: 1–800–221–SIDS

6

SOMEONE MURDERED VICKI

Abduction and Murder of a Child*

It had been a long day, and Dora Larson was exhausted. Her job as a financial advisor and insurance broker was demanding; she had attended an all-day business meeting out of town. She left the house before her children—Shelly, 14, Mark, 12, and Vicki, 10—awakened. Ken and she had made plans to go out with friends later that evening, so when she arrived home she decided to rest a bit while the house was quiet. The family, including Grandmother Larson and Aunt Gail, had gone to watch Mark's Little League game at Andover City Park.

Dora awakened suddenly. It was after 9 o'clock. She had slept far longer than she planned. Hurriedly she dressed, remembering their plans to join friends.

She found Ken, Shelly, and Mark milling about in the kitchen.

"Where's Vicki?" Dora asked.

"Isn't she here with you?" Ken's voice reflected his concern.

"Vicki should be home by now. We'd better look for her." Dora's concern now bordered on panic. She and Ken jumped into their car and made several quick stops at friends. One of those stops was at the home of Scott Darnell, who was visiting his grandparents for the summer. Scott had not returned from the game either. Later, they learned that Vicki was last seen leaving the game with him.

Fifteen-year-old Scott had been a frequent visitor at the Larsons' the past few weeks. Their home had become a hangout for Shelly's teenage friends. Scott was a newcomer to Andover, but he, too, was made welcome. He was tall, slender—big and strong for his age thought Dora—and had curly brown hair. He was polite and frequently quoted Scripture. He seemed attracted to Shelly.

Vicki always frolicked among Shelly's friends, teasing and joking in her usual manner. Her winsome personality had endeared her to not only

---

*Based on an interview with Dora and Ken Larson, whose ten-year-old daughter Vicki was murdered July 12, 1979, in Andover, Ill.

Shelly's friends, but many of Andover's 650 townspeople. She was pretty and petite, with ash blonde hair, a nose spattered with freckles, and an impish smile. She didn't walk, she bounced. Her large blue eyes sparkled with the joy of living, for she lived in a world of love and she radiated that love. She was a straight A student and loved to read and do acrobatics. Vicki trusted Scott the same as everyone else.

At 9:45 p.m., Dora called Henry County Sheriff Gilbert Cady and reported Vicki missing.

"Scott will look after Vicki. He's strong, and I'm sure he'll try to protect her," said Dora. Others agreed. "I'm sure she'll be all right. God will take care of her." One moment Dora felt confident that Vicki would walk in the door, the next moment she was terrified.

By 10:30 p.m. "Gib" Cady had launched an all-out search for Vicki and Scott. Law enforcement agencies from all over the county, assisted by State Police, Civil Defense, and 100 civilian volunteers, marched through fields and woods in the area. A door-to-door search of Andover was initiated with all unlocked doors checked and tagged. Homes of friends where the two might be found were contacted.

By 3:00 a.m., Ken Larson realized his worst fears might become a reality. He began putting up "mental blocks," for he knew he would need to be strong to hold the family together for the ordeal ahead.

Civil Defense volunteers dragged Andover Lake until 5:00 a.m. At dawn an aerial search was begun to scout cornfields surrounding the village.

At 6:00 a.m. Scott Darnell was found walking along a country road. His clothes, hands and fingernails were covered with fresh dirt. He told officials he had been beaten up and knocked unconscious by two men on motorcycles, and that he had last seen Vicki the evening before.

Two hours later, officers found Vicki's body in a shallow grave in a cornfield about 100 yards from the home of Scott's grandparents. The search party was stunned. "How do we tell Dora?" one asked. No words were adequate.

The beautiful, trusting child everyone loved was dead.

By now, nearly a hundred townspeople and friends filled the Larson home and yard awaiting word. Their mere presence during the long wait was comforting to Ken and Dora. It showed people cared. About 10:15 a.m. a patrol car drove up in front of their house. Sheriff Cady, State Trooper Jim Raes, a friend of the family, and Deputy Coroner Lola Odendahl made their way to the Larsons. TV cameras were in the yard and rolling. Promptly friends barred them from entering the house. Dora studied Gib Cady's somber face; his eyes betrayed the bad news he bore.

"She's dead, isn't she?" Dora asked.

The sheriff slowly nodded his head yes.

Dora collapsed.

Coming out of the safe harbor of unconsciousness, she felt herself being lifted up by what seemed like a thousand loving arms. Tearful eyes filled with pain surrounded her everywhere she looked. She leaped to her feet and bounded for the door. Her mind refused to believe the horrible truth—Vicki was dead! She ran and ran until she collapsed again. Ken and Mark found her in some bushes several blocks from their home.

"Ken, what have I ever done to deserve this? Why is God punishing me like this?" she asked, her voice sobbing, her body trembling.

"If God is punishing you, then why do *I* hurt so much?" he responded.

His words helped dispel her belief that God was punishing her personally for Vicki's death.

Later that morning, Scott Darnell confessed. He had lured Vicki away from the game by telling her he had a small horse for her. He raped her, then strangled her from behind with a bandana, and buried her in the grave he had dug several days before. She had been dead about eighteen hours. The coroner believed she died at 9:30 p.m.—the time Dora had awakened suddenly from a sound sleep.

Further investigation revealed the youth was a child molester. He had been in and out of mental Institutions and juvenile correction centers since he was ten years old. He was arrested for an attempted rape of a ten-year-old girl in 1977. No one in the town of Andover knew of his lengthy criminal history until a month after the murder.

Retired Pastor John Stuebe, a friend of the family, was called and asked to come to the Larson home.

"God didn't do this, Dora; sin did!" he forthrightly told her. He moved among friends and relatives, speaking softly, yet convincingly, for wherever he went, his presence conveyed comfort and calm.

Dora had not eaten for hours. Friends brought in enough food to fill two refrigerators, but eating was unimportant to her. Sensing her needs, Pastor Stuebe asked, "What would you like more than anything else to eat right now?"

"A milkshake," she replied. She would long remember the gesture, for it expressed a concern for her body as well as her aching heart and numbed mind.

Departing from tradition, visitation was held in the Larson home rather than the funeral home. Some friends found it hard to face them. Everyone hurt so badly. Dora saw the deep pain in their eyes and felt compelled to comfort them. She couldn't believe that one little girl had touched so many lives.

The ordeal of seeing Vicki's body lay ahead. She was not prepared for what she saw. It didn't look like Vicki. Dora couldn't bring herself to touch or kiss her daughter goodbye, something she would later regret. Oh, how she wished she had said "I love you" one last time! Only the family saw her; the casket was closed during the service.

During the service, Dora's mind wandered—the long wait, her haunting words. . . *She's dead, isn't she?* She felt so guilty. How could this have happened? And then she heard Pastor Stuebe's closing comments.

"Even her name 'Victoria' means victory over death!"

The Trial

Seven months later, Scott Darnell was tried for murder as an adult because of apparent premeditation. His defense attorney entered a plea of insanity, claiming that Scott's "body was the instrument" that caused the violent act. "A person is not responsible if there is mental disease," he claimed. Eminent psychiatrist, Dr. Bruce Danto, testified that the defendant had a psychopathic and sociopathic personality and he was a "homicide waiting to happen."

At a bench trial* in February 1980, Scott Darnell was declared legally sane. Six weeks later, he was sentenced to spend the rest of his natural life in prison with no provision for parole.

"Society must be protected," said the judge.

What Helped, What Hurt

"When I looked up at the funeral and saw the doctor who delivered Vicki, that helped. I can still see him standing there with pain on his face. He didn't get a chance to come over and talk to me but I knew he was there," said Dora. "People think they have to say something—but it's their presence that counts."

Dora said she appreciated the gestures, the silent hugs.

"It was comforting for me when people said, 'God will be with you.' It was raining the morning after Vicki was found. When we awakened, my sister-in-law said, 'I think God is crying, too.' That was comforting."

Living in a small town where everyone knows one another had its rewards. People responded promptly, appropriately, and empathically. "The town surrounded us—you could feel it. They were all so compassionate and good to us," said Dora.

Well-meaning people said things to Dora like, "It's God's will and it was destined," "God won't give you any more than you can handle," "You won't understand this now," or "This is your cross to bear." These phrases didn't offer the Larsons comfort.

Says Dora, "I believe the instant Vicki was killed, God permitted her to enter heaven—that's the kind of thing God does—but he didn't 'take' her back."

Dora, during the initial grieving process, didn't find comfort in church,

---

*A bench trial is one in which the defendant is tried and sentenced by a judge rather than a jury.

although she is a woman of deep faith. She says she didn't feel free to cry there. When she talked to others, people meant to be kind by changing the subject from Vicki, or expressed the opinion that the situation could be worse. After all, they said, she and Ken still had two children.

It was even more painful when mothers inferred, directly or indirectly, that the Larsons' negligence or irresponsibility was the cause of Vicki's death.

"Everyone tells you you're going to get over it. But you never do. The pain lessens, your heart heals, but things come along—such as the first day of school and birthdays—that make you hurt all over again. Weddings I attended were difficult; I would think, 'Vicki will never have a wedding.' "

A week after Vicki's death, the Larson family went to a community mental health center for family therapy.

Notoriety No One Wants

Dora and Ken were upset with television reporters who broadcast that Vicki and Scott had a "summer romance." They begged them to stop, but they had to contact their lawyer, who in turn contacted the station. Finally the reports stopped.

Their lawyer advised them to go out of town during the trial to avoid the press. Time and again, the Larsons were reminded of their pain when stories about the murder would appear in the newspaper.

Spectators drove by the house. "Shortly after Vicki's funeral, I went outside one day to address thank-you notes. Cars were driving by just to see where we lived. I finally went into the house," said Dora. Dora said she learned to tell the difference between those who really cared about them and those who wanted information.

The entire family suffered. On one occasion, fourteen-year-old Shelly was taunted by a carload of teens: "How does it feel to have helped kill your sister?" Twelve-year-old Mark overheard classmates say, "You remember the girl that was killed? That was Mark's sister." The remarks were like twisting the knife of pain still deeper. Says Dora, "Vicki was the victim, but it just goes on and on for the family years later."

Please, Lord, No Nightmares

Like most parents of murdered children, the imaginings of their child's last hour haunted the Larsons. Dora felt that as a mother, she was supposed to protect her child, and she hadn't been there to do that. She prayed to be spared nightmares, and she was. But still, she was haunted by recurring questions: "Did Vicki cry out for me? Was there anything I could have done to prevent this? Did she know how much I loved her?"

Ken Larson, too, had questions. Why did God allow this to happen?

Why doesn't He stop it from happening to others? He coped with his imaginings by erecting mental blocks. "I have tried to deal with it in small portions as time has gone along because I couldn't deal with it all at once. I couldn't handle it and give the support the rest of the family needed."

The "Shoulds" and the "Oughts"

Dora went back to work two weeks after Vicki's death. She was flattered when people would say, "You must be made of rock to smile and come to work and go on," implying how strong she was. She felt she had to show the world what a great, strong Christian she was. She might let God down if she let her weakness show, so she pretended to be fine. She wanted people to see the victory in all this. Dora wouldn't allow herself to be angry with God.

Inside she felt as if she were on trial as a mother and as a Christian. When people asked her, "How do you do it?" she went home and cried because it caused her to question herself. She felt guilty about everything; she even felt guilty if she didn't think about Vicki. Dora was not fine at all. She wanted to tell others how bad she hurt, but she couldn't.

Seven months after Vicki's death, Dora learned she was pregnant. She felt this baby was a gift from God, for she had had surgery and wasn't supposed to get pregnant. Dora had a son born with a serious birth defect, a cleft palate.

But it was a new beginning, and Dora and Ken welcomed him. They named him John, "messenger of God."

But how could God let him be born with a birth defect? Dora questioned, "Why is God piling all this on me?" Her depression grew worse. She wanted to be happy, but the pain persisted.

Dora became suicidal.

Ken Larson was aware of his wife's despondency.

"Her voice was dead," said Ken. "She was emotionless. I knew there was something wrong and I knew she needed professional help. She said she would go to the doctor and we bargained that if she went, she would not have to be hospitalized."

Dora admits, "One day something within me clicked. If I could die, I could stop the pain. I was going to have the doctor give me something to help me sleep. Then I would come home and take the whole bottle of pills."

Dora says she suffered a mental breakdown. Her sister came to be with her and help with the baby. When Dora wasn't sleeping, there was time for Ken and Dora to talk. Dora says she thinks this helped save their marriage.

"Each of you is going off in a different direction trying to heal yourself, and you become angry with your spouse. You actually hate each other at times. Fortunately, we never blamed one another for Vicki's death.

"The guilt is a horrible thing. We had a very difficult time. Both Shelly and Mark were allowed to scream at me. They had to take it out on someone. One day Shelly, who feared for her own safety and felt terrible guilt, shouted, *'What kind of God could do this?'*

"The kind of God who sent Jesus so Vicki could go to heaven," Dora replied.

Must I Forgive?

After her breakdown, Dora went for more therapy. Her psychologist, Paul Skinner, Ph.D., said of Dora, "A year after the child's death, the numbing effect had worn away and the raw horror of losing her child through an excruciating kind of death plagued her. She felt guilty and family members seemed to heap their anger and guilt on her, everyone thinking, 'If only we had. . . .' Dora began isolating herself because she was afraid she would break down and weep in any social situation."

At first, Dora thought she had forgiven Scott. As a Christian, she *ought* to forgive. That's when she had real problems. Finally, she admitted that she literally and totally and utterly hated the boy for what he had done to Vicki.

"But I knew I had to fight this battle," said Dora. "He killed Vicki, but he *will not* kill me or the other children. I'm not going to stay depressed about this. He is not going to win the final battle."

Dora went to Father Gary Dalmasso for help.

"Dora," he began, "knowing you, you will learn to forgive him. You must, because then you will no longer be tied to him."

Now, after eight years, she says she seldom thinks about him.

The Turning Point

"After Vicki was found," Dora said "I was overwhelmed with the darkness—the power of evil." She could feel it in the air, and she felt that God didn't love her.

Dora talked with Father Dalmasso and his wife Judy about her fears. They assured Dora of God's love for her and gave her permission to be angry. Judy reminded Dora of another mother who had watched her son's murder on a cross in an effort to save mankind. It helped Dora put her daughter's death into perspective on a personal level.

That discussion and little unexpected surprises, which she attributed to God, seemed to be the beginning of a turning point for Dora, whose own father had died three months before Vicki. Dora tells about one memorable occasion in the cemetery when she felt Vicki's presence while she was crying at her grave.

"Why are you crying?" Vicki asked her mother.

"Because I hurt!" she replied.

"Well, I don't," she answered.

"But I want you back!" Dora protested.

"Someone has to take care of Grandpa," Vicki ended.*

All of these experiences were very real for her, Dora says. It helped her realize Vicki was in better hands and never had to hurt again.

"I have come to rely on the Holy Spirit and found emotional healing through prayer. Today, I have a deep inner peace with God that not only comforts me, but gives me the strength and courage to go on," she adds.

Turning Anger into Action

Charlotte Hullinger is co-founder of the Parents of Murdered Children (POMC), a self-help organization made up of parents whose sons and daughters have been murdered. "Violent death," she says, "brings anger so intense most people can't handle it." The Hullingers publish a newsletter, *Survivors*, and help found chapters throughout the country.[1]

From the beginning, Dora and Ken worked to change laws and chose to channel their anger into constructive action. With the aid of Jeremy Margolis, Inspector General for the State of Illinois, Dora has initiated Illinois Senate Bill 1853 which, if passed, will establish criteria that the Department of Corrections must utilize prior to discharging a delinquent minor from its custody and control. It provides for a discharge hearing prior to release of the minor with notice given to interested parties, including the State's Attorney, Probation Department, the victim and the committing judge. It also provides that the committing judge shall have continuing jurisdiction to modify or revoke the discharge of the minor from the custody and control of the Department of Corrections.

Dr. Paul Skinner summarized Dora's efforts: "One would have thought that her emotions had been drained away to be replaced with sheer fatigue. But this was a strong woman who had to fight back at something. She chose to fight a giant—the legal system—that had turned its head when the murdering youth had demonstrated earlier that he was sick and dangerous."

In 1986, Dora was appointed by the Governor of Illinois to serve on a statewide panel, The Illinois Campaign to Protect Our Children. She is the only private citizen on the panel. Its purpose is to recommend new pro-

---

*Experiences of this nature are reported occasionally and seem to be somewhat of a common phenomenon in the grief process.
[1]*People Magazine* (March 16, 1981), p. 116.

grams and legislation at the state level and offer suggestions to the National Campaign to Protect Our Children and the President's Child Safety Partnership.

"Dora is an indomitable fighter. She brings to the panel her vast knowledge, experience, and dedication," said Inspector General Margolis.

Protecting Other Children

"Most of the time," says Ken, "a father wants to go out and do something violent. I tell fathers to turn their anger into something positive. If they go out and injure the alleged perpetrator, they could get put into jail themselves. If the child has been molested and is living, that child already has enough guilt. If the father is arrested because of something that has happened to him or her, the child only feels worse. That's not going to help the child or the family."

The Larsons founded Protecting All Children Together (PACT) which serves a two-county area. The group cooperates with I-SEARCH, local police officers, and other organizations interested in child safety. Members participate in lobbying efforts for child protection laws and to inform the public of the danger of crimes against children. A spin-off of PACT is COURT WATCH. Members of COURT WATCH monitor how the child who has been sexually or physically abused is treated in the courtroom. "The laws are very lax with child molesters," says Dora.* "The public must demand better laws to protect children.

"The more people attending the trial wearing a COURT WATCH badge, the stronger the message that someone cares about what happens to the child," she adds. "Court watching for children is telling every judge, attorney, police officer and court official that there are people concerned about the real victim—the abused child."

Delphine Wright, parent supporter of the founding of I-SEARCH, says, "Adding to the frustration and bitterness for many parents of murdered children is our judicial system, which allows for plea bargaining for lesser terms, short-term imprisonment, and parole for the murderer. Tension mounts as parents count the months, then days until the murderer is released, knowing full well he will be free to kill again." She adds, "Parents are left with the feeling that the system doesn't work, and this insecurity invites them to take the law into their own hands."

Reaching Out to Others

Ken and Dora speak to PTA meetings, parents' groups, school programs, and church fellowship groups, warning them of the dangers to

---

*See Appendix C for Facts About Child Molesters.

children. When they talk with other parents of molested or murdered children, they begin by saying, "We know what you're going through. We're here to help you through the pain and grief. We've traveled the same road."

"It would be easy to say, 'Vicki's dead and gone; then let the world go on,'" says Ken. But he is angered by the complacency of society and the criminal justice system. "Most people think it can never happen to them," he adds. "We've paid a price [for our involvement] but it's worth it."

"We won't let her die in vain," says Dora. "I can hear her saying, 'Go get 'em, Mom.'

"I'll never stop wanting her back. But if you dare to love, you risk being hurt. I never would have *not* had her. All of this pain is worth it just to have had her."

The Larsons say they are thankful God allowed them to find her body. "Unlike many parents of missing children, we know where our child is. The thing I resent most," says Dora, "is that she didn't live long enough to leave any legacy. All we have left is a memory of her, and in our memories, she never grows any older. Vicki will always be ten."

Advice to Offer Families of Violent Death Victims

1. *Generally it takes eighteen to twenty-four months just to stabilize after the death of a family member. It can take much longer when the death was a violent one.* Recognize the length of the mourning process. Beware of developing unrealistic expectations of yourself.
2. *Your worst times usually are not at the moment a tragic event takes place.* Then you're in a state of shock or numbness. Often the most difficult time is four to seven months after the death. Strangely, when tempted to despair, this may be the time when most people expect you to be over your loss.
3. *When people ask you how you're doing, don't always say, "Fine."* Let some people know how terrible you feel.
4. *Talk with a true friend or with others who have experienced a similar loss.* These people will speak your language. Other survivors can be very helpful. Only they can really say, "I know; I understand. You are not alone."
5. *Often depression is a cover for anger.* Learn to find appropriate ways to release your bottled-up anger. What you're going through seems so unfair and unjust, and you need to vent these feelings.
6. *Take time to lament, to experience being a victim.* This time is necessary and can be therapeutic.
7. *It's all right to cry, to question, to be weak.* Beware of allowing yourself to be put "on a pedestal." Others may tell you what an inspiration

you are because of your strength and your ability to cope so well. If they only knew!

8. *Don't expect too much of yourself.* This may be the first violent death you've coped with. You need help. A support group can help you cope with your intense grief.[2]

9. *Seek family therapy counseling from a qualified professional counselor with experience in grief counseling.* Women and men handle anger and grief differently. Siblings, too, are angry. These pressures create tremendous strains on relationships.

10. *Refrain from seeking revenge on the perpetrator.* "Remember, Beloved, never avenge yourselves, but leave it to the wrath of God; for it is written, 'Vengeance is mine, I will repay,' says the Lord" (Rom. 12:19, RSV).

11. *Channel your anger into constructive action.* "Be angry but do not sin" (Eph. 4:26, RSV). Call your Congressman. Work toward changing laws to protect children.

12. *Protect your family from the news media whenever possible.* If the news reports are painful, turn them off, but save newspapers; you may need to refer back to them.

13. *Refrain from using alcohol or drugs to ease the pain.* Alcohol is a depressant and will only cause more problems and more depression.

14. *Avoid those persons or things that bring you more pain.* Don't let other people make you feel guilty. As healing occurs, these feelings will lessen. Try to ignore the innocent but hurtful things people say.

15. *Forgive yourself; God does!* There is true guilt and there is false guilt. True guilt comes from actual wrongdoing (sins of commission) or things left undone (sins of omission). False guilt is unwarranted and purely imaginary. It may stem from things other people said that make you feel guilty. Confess all your guilt to God and ask forgiveness, for He alone knows your heart and can forgive you—then *accept* His forgiveness.

16. *Allow yourself to heal before you begin reaching out to other parents of molested or murdered children.* But do reach out and try to help others in some small way at least. This little step forward may help prevent you from dwelling on yourself.

17. *Many times of crisis ultimately become times of opportunity.* Mysteriously, your faith in yourself, in others, in God can be deepened through crisis. Seek out persons who can serve as symbols of hope to you.

18. *Stay in touch with the State's Attorney during the trial.* You may need to be informed of your rights.

19. *Suggested devotional reading:* Ps. 11; 31:14–16; 1 John 4:18, TLB.

---

[2]Nos. 1–8 were written by Father Kenneth Czillinger, Cincinnati, Ohio. Used by permission.

Advice to Caregivers

1. *Reach out to the victim's family.* If you are a total stranger or casual acquaintance, write a note; if you are a close friend, go to them or call. If you are a very close friend, hug them and let them cry—be present for them and let them know you hurt with them. Don't let your pain keep you away.
2. *Assure them this is not God's will.* If God has given the Commandment, "Thou shalt not kill," then how could it be God's will that their loved one is murdered?
3. *Recognize the fact that other people hurt besides the parents.* Siblings, grandparents, aunts, uncles, cousins, the perpetrator's family—all who touched the victim's life may be hurting. Acknowledge their grief and reach out to them as well.
4. *Offer to do menial tasks that will help them during the initial phase.* Bring food or helpful items such as dishtowels; offer to do cleaning or laundry. But ask before you launder the victim's clothing; the mother may have strong feelings about doing these chores herself.
5. *If members of the victim's family tell you how angry they are, tell them they have a right to be angry.* Allow members of the family to talk about the victim; don't change the subject.
6. *Recognize your friend's grief will be of long duration.* Lend emotional support in the months ahead, especially during the trial or news announcements. This is an emotionally trying period for the victim's family. They need your understanding and continuous support.
7. *Don't be critical of the victim's family if there is a distraction and laughter.* Laughter is a form of release from tension, and therapeutic.
8. *Lend your support in passing legislation that strengthens laws to protect children.*

Additional Reading

Lindberg, Anne Morrow, *Hour of Gold, Hour of Lead.* New York: Harcourt Brace Jovanovich, 1973.

Magee, Doug. *What Murder Leaves Behind: The Victim's Family.* New York: Dodd, Mead and Company.

Overly, Fay L. *Missing.* Denver, Colo.: Accent Books, 1985.

Phillips, Steven. *No Heroes, No Villains: The Story of a Murder Trial.* New York: Random House, 1977.

Schiff, Harriet Sarnoff. *The Bereaved Parent.* New York: Penguin Books, 1978.

Wolff, Pierre. *May I Hate God?* New York: Paulist Press, 1979.

Support Group

For more information write:

Parents of Murdered Children (POMC)
% Charlotte Hullinger
1739 Bella Vista
Cincinnati, OH 45237
(513) 721–5683.

John Walsh, founder of the Adam Walsh Child Resource Center, recommends *The Child Awareness Game* and the video, *Too Smart for Strangers* by Walt Disney Productions, for educating your children about strangers.

7

A MISSING CHILD: THE TORMENT THAT NEVER ENDS

Loss of a Child Through Abduction by a Stranger, Fate Unknown*

Papers were late the morning of August 12, 1984. Eugene Martin, 13, left his home at 4:45 a.m. to deliver the Sunday issue of the *Des Moines Register*. He delivered only on Sundays. Most Sundays, his older step-brother, Don, went with him, but he had stayed overnight with a friend. "Gene" sat alone on the corner of S.W. 14th and Highview waiting for the truck that would bring his papers.

"Gene, you better get under the light," another paper boy warned as he rode by him at 5:45 on his bicycle. Several paper boys waited together just two blocks farther down the street.

Gene Martin was last seen at 6:00 a.m. talking to a tall man wearing dark brown slacks and a camel-colored jacket.

At 7:15 a.m. route manager Paul Porter called Gene's father, Donald Martin.

"Don, did Gene get frustrated and come on home? His bag and papers are still at the corner." Paul said he had driven by once, noticed the bag and papers were still there, and thought maybe Gene had left some, since the papers were especially heavy. Paul finished his route, then drove by again. He stopped and counted. All the papers were there. None had been delivered. Paul was worried.

Only two years before on September 5, 1982, paper boy Johnny Gosch had been abducted. National TV crews were in town doing a follow-up on the Gosch case.

Donald Martin hurriedly searched the house and car. Once Gene had locked himself out of the house, curled up in the car, and gone to sleep. Gene was nowhere to be found.

---

*Based on an interview with Donald and Sue Martin of Des Moines, Iowa.

Donald was frightened. Sue, Gene's new stepmother, called the police. Fifteen minutes later, two Des Moines police officers knocked. Sue opened the door. A few minutes later, several FBI men were there, too.

Des Moines law officials responded in force this time. Two years before, even though five witnesses had seen Johnny Gosch being kidnapped, police didn't act. According to law, no crime had been committed. Johnny was kidnapped one block from his home only six minutes after leaving home. Noreen Gosch had predicted it would happen again.

This time it was Gene. Gene was a friendly boy with dark brown hair and eyes and olive complexion. He was small for his age. He enjoyed swimming and roller skating and he had a girlfriend. He attended Salvation Army worship services.

"Gene loved to talk and would help anybody. I think the man lured him by asking directions. Knowing Gene, he would try to help him," said his father.

"A picture. Do you have a recent picture of him?" one man in uniform asked. Donald Martin hurried to his mother's home. She had a recent 8×10 school picture of him. By 12:30 p.m. Gene's picture was broadcast on television.

Police and FBI set up a hot-line number and extra phone lines coming into the Martin home. One line was kept open in case Gene tried to call home. All incoming calls were tape-recorded.

The four persons who were in the neighborhood at the time of the abduction and who might have seen the abductor or his vehicle were flown to Texas to undergo hypnosis so that they might come up with a description. From this, a composite of the man's face was drawn.

The national television crews covering the Gosch case were called. They soon appeared and milled about the front yard of the Martin's modest white frame house on Frazier Street. Donald stood near the street outside his home watching the commotion. A man in a red pickup truck drove by, turned around, then drove by again. The driver stopped near Donald and motioned for him to come over to his truck. He reported seeing a car on S.E. 14th headed east toward Easter Lake. "He had a kid with him. The kid was pretty beat up," he said. The informer drove off before Donald could get his name or a license plate number. The television crew rushed their videotape to a studio to see if they had the license number on film. Unfortunately, the incident was not on film. Police rushed to Easter Lake and found nothing.

A search party was formed; hundreds of volunteers scanned the surrounding wooded areas. Without his parents' knowledge, young Don and some of his close buddies skipped school and joined the search party. It meant a lot to him that his friends wanted to help. He blamed himself for not being with Gene that morning. "If onlys" were going through his mind.

That first week, leads kept coming in. The Martins were afraid *not* to talk to the media. It was important to keep attention focused on Gene in hopes someone would see him. But the Martins were exhausted, surviving on a couple of hours of sleep each night, hurriedly eaten sandwiches, or meals brought in by kind neighbors.

Sue and Donald kept in constant touch with the local police. They suggested the Martins come to the station and listen to the tapes of incoming calls. All kinds of calls were coming in from psychics and possible sightings. One call came from a psychic in Grinnell, Iowa. She described where she envisioned they would find Gene. "Go to Waterworks Park. You will see a red pilon and a piece of white paper lying on the ground and a bridge." Police searched the park and found what she had described, but not Gene.

The search parties continued looking for two weeks.

As days turned into weeks and weeks into months, Gene's father felt completely lost. He kept his feelings all locked inside. He didn't know where or whom to turn to. He didn't know what to do. Donald Martin had been awarded custody of Gene when he and Gene's mother divorced. At first he refused to allow Gene to have a paper route. When he found out Paul Porter would be his manager, he finally relented. Paul had been Don's route manager for two years.

Sue and Donald had been married only since the first of April. Gene had come to live with them when they moved into the house on Frazier Street. Sue and Donald worried whether Gene and her son Don would get along. "From the beginning, they hit it off. Gene and Don went everywhere together," said Donald.

A Community Responds

Donald and Sue were overwhelmed at the community's response to his son's abduction. Grocery stores donated rolls and doughnuts for the search parties. Strangers called and told them they were thinking about them and wanted to help in any way possible. Donations started coming in. Letters crammed their mailbox. Several local churches held prayer vigils. Donald's employer gave him a leave of absence with pay. Fellow workers from years past called Donald to let him know they were remembering him. They had never experienced such an abundance of caring.

One day, there was a knock on their door. A mother with two small children stood outside. "My children had a Kool-aid stand. They wanted to give you this." Sue tearfully accepted the children's donation of $12.63 they proudly handed her. She called Donald in from the backyard so he could meet the young mother and children; they were deeply touched.

Disillusionment Sets In

As time passed, fewer leads came in. Active investigation by the police department slowed to a halt. More than 150 psychic leads had been received, but the police placed little faith in their information.

Both Sue and Donald felt increasingly helpless. They were hurt and disillusioned because the leads that were coming in were not being followed up on.

Sergeant Jim Toma of the Des Moines Police Department, investigator assigned to the Martin case from the beginning, said 47 investigators were initially assigned to the case. The active investigation, which went on for months following the abduction, cost the department well over $200,000. "It's impossible to follow up every time a psychic says, 'Go to where you see a shirt hanging on a fence post.' Do you know how many fence posts there are in Iowa? There comes a point when there's nothing solid left to go on," said Toma.* The leads and tapes were now considered confidential information and they were no longer permitted to review them. "I believe they felt Gene was dead," said Sue.

The *Des Moines Register* hired Harry Braafhart, former bodyguard to Governor Ray, as a security officer and as liaison between the families and the Register.

As in most missing child cases, the parents of the missing child put their faith in, and are dependent upon, law officials to help find their child. As time passes, cooperation and efforts wane because of fewer and fewer leads. Police may believe the child is dead. Often, by necessity, law enforcement agencies must decrease their all-out efforts. When this happens, parents become disillusioned and angry with the police and FBI. *The missing child will always be a top priority for those parents.* Search efforts then become the responsibility of the parents.

Donald and Sue refused to give up. They hired a private investigator at $35 an hour plus expenses to help them find Gene. The investigator helped them get organized. Donald bought a computer to record the names of anyone ever involved in the case. He programmed in a cast of characters and chronology, listing alphabetically the names of contacts, the date of contact, and content of the message given and action taken.

One incident occurred in October but was not reported until December. A teacher in a small neighboring town had seen a man get off a motorcycle, then hurriedly carry the limp body of a young boy beneath a bridge. The boy's eyes were wide open; he was either drugged or dead. The man told his wife what he had seen. "Don't get involved," his wife

---

*Phone interview August 19, 1987.

warned. But the teacher was haunted by what he had seen. Finally, long after the trail had grown cold, he reported it to the Martins. Sue Martin and Harry Braafhart went to the exact location and took pictures of the bridge and river beneath. The river was dragged, but no body was found.

The emotional toll a missing child puts on a family is disabling and devastating. Four months after the abduction, Sue was ready to walk out on her new marriage. "I can't take this; I can't live like this anymore," she told Donald.

Donald had grown up in a family in which he had been conditioned to keeping his feelings to himself. "If I had a problem, my parents didn't want to hear about it," said Donald.

What bothered Sue most was Donald's unwillingness to talk about it. It was all bottled up inside him. Donald was blocking out of his mind the things that could be happening to Gene.

Teenager Don was silent, too. He didn't want to talk about it, even with his friends. Sue and Donald knew he was hurting.

In the short time that her son Don and Gene had lived together as stepbrothers, they had grown close. They knew Don missed Gene and blamed himself for not being there with him at the time of the abduction. Don was angry at the abductor. "I'd like to get the guy who took Gene," says Don.

The Unanswered Question: Dead or Alive?

Much time has passed since Gene's abduction. Some people believe he is dead. "If he is dead, I would like to have his body so we can give him a decent burial. I want to believe he is still alive," says his father. "I can't quit! It's like an emotional roller coaster. Your hopes rise when there's a new lead. One day you're up, the next day you're down."

In 1985, a flier picturing Gene produced by the ADVO System based in Milwaukee under the slogan, "America's Looking for Its Missing Children," produced more than 200 responses from 36 states of possible sightings.

A Nation Rallies

Significant strides have been made in efforts to publicize the pictures and descriptions of missing children. America is waking up and responding to this horrible crime against children.

Barbara Chapman, media director for the National Center for Missing and Exploited Children, in 1985 gave these figures: Children missing through parental abductions are estimated between 25,000 and 500,000 cases annually; children missing due to unknown abductors is estimated at 4,000 to 20,000 annually; and runaways are estimated at one million annually. The Center claims, however, that "estimates from various organizations of the number of children who are the victims of noncustodial parental kidnapping vary from 25,000 up to three quarters of a million cases each year. There are no reliable surveys or estimates of the incidence of parental kidnapping. No one knows the true parameters of this part of the problem of missing children because there currently exists no effective record-keeping system to determine the extent of the problem."[1] The U.S. Justice Department reports that over 2,000 unidentified children's bodies are buried each year.

The Martins have nothing but praise for the National Center for Missing and Exploited Children based in Washington. "Jim Scutt, our technical advisor, has never let us down," said Donald.

Barbara Chapman says, "We just don't give up. The Congressional definition of a missing child is that of an infant through age seventeen; however, if we've been given the child's name before age seventeen, we don't drop them or stop working on their case at eighteen. That's very reassuring to parents.

"At the Center, we have terrible ups and downs. When a child is found, we all celebrate. When a child is found dead, we all can hardly talk to one another. We are so enamored by that child and so determined to help those parents, it's hard to lose one," she adds.

The Dark Side of Child Abduction

Noreen and John Gosch in public lectures give more information. Of those children abducted by strangers, 98 percent are abused sexually. Organized rings of profiteers abduct children between the ages of ten and fourteen. The ten to twelve age group is preferred by molesters/abductors because they prefer to use children on the brink of puberty for their sexual satisfaction. "Organized rings will pay up to a quarter million dollars for a picture-perfect blue-eyed blonde-haired girl, age eleven. They can earn more than a half million dollars in a two-year period in child pornography with that child," says John Gosch.

Pioneering Parents

The pioneering efforts of parents like John and Noreen Gosch are beginning to make an impact. The Gosches have made hundreds of speeches, gained the support of Governor Branstad, and made guest appearances on *Good Morning America, Hour Magazine, The Phil Donahue Show, 20/20, Sunday Morning with Charles Kuralt,* and *The 700 Club.* They

---

[1]Taken from a report "Background Information on Missing Children," May 1985, published by the National Center for Missing and Exploited Children.

have testified before Senate hearing committees and have introduced a bill in Iowa that would stiffen the penalties for child abductors. They actively support those who work against the efforts of the North American Man-Boy Love Association (NAMBLA), an organization of pedophiles* that seeks to lower the age of consent to eight years of age. In other words, if a child of eight "consents" to sexual activity, the offender cannot be prosecuted for sexual offenses committed against that child. NAMBLA's motto is: "Sex by eight is too late."

Since the airing on NBC of "The Adam Walsh Story" in 1984, parents are developing a healthy paranoia and taking steps to protect their children. Adam was the six-year-old child who was abducted from a shopping mall and murdered in Hollywood, Florida, in 1981.

A National Network

The National Center for Missing and Exploited Children, a government-financed organization, was opened May 25, 1984, in Washington, D.C. It serves as a national information center which serves police and parents throughout the nation. The Adam Walsh Child Resource Center, under the leadership of John Walsh, Adam's father, is based in Florida. The National Child Victim Network was organized and put into operation in 1984 by the National Coalition for Children's Justice (NCCJ) headed by Ken Wooden. Ralston Purina was the first corporation in America that had the courage and vision to give financial support to NCCJ's network. Another organization called "Find the Children" is a non-profit foundation whose purpose is to raise funds to be distributed to those regional and national organizations most directly engaged in the search for missing children. CHILD FIND concentrates its efforts on putting out names and pictures of parentally abducted children. I-SEARCH (Illinois State Enforcement Agencies to Recover Children) was created in 1984 and is a division of the Illinois State Police.

Support groups and organizations have sprung up in thirty-two states. A few states like Iowa have set up a computerized clearing house for information about missing children. Police departments and some hospitals provide parents with LOVE PRINTS or fingerprints of their children. Parents are videotaping their children. Microscopic computer chips can now be bonded to a child's tooth for helping police identify abducted children and provide doctors with emergency medical information.

A City Remembers

The people in Des Moines continue to support and aid in the search for both Gene and Johnny. Outraged mothers in Des Moines invaded the

---

*A pedophile is usually a male that prefers to have sex with youngsters.

adult bookstores and tore magazines filled with child pornography from the shelves. Some semi-trucks, as they travel coast to coast, display larger-than-life pictures of Johnny and Gene. The *Des Moines Register* contributed reward money offering $125,000 for any information leading to the recovery of the boys. Additional reward money is offered by businesses, friends and relatives. The *Register* will now, upon request by parents, deliver the newspapers to delivery boys' homes.

The Torment Continues

Donald and Sue Martin still live with the torment that never ends. They still hope and pray Gene is alive—and so do many others. At a recent fundraiser, a large cake bearing a likeness of Gene was sold twelve times to different bidders, raising $1550. No one would take the cake home; it was one time Donald admits being in tears. The Martins now have the cake in their freezer. "We'll have the cake when Gene comes home," he says.

Until then, they wait. "I believe it will be the man on the street that finds him," says Donald. "I'll never give up believing he's alive. I can't. I just can't give up hope!"

How to Prevent Child Abduction

Despite efforts to educate the public and increase public awareness, there is much to be done. The first problem to be overcome is accepting the fact that it can happen to you and your child.

The best defense begins in the home by educating yourself and your child about strangers and keeping current information such as a Child I-Dent Record on file. Ken Wooden, a national investigative reporter for *ABC NEWS* 20/20, prompted Congressional inquiries and legislation dealing with missing children. The information in his booklet, *Child Lures—A Guide to Prevent Abduction*, is based on interviews with convicted child molesters and murderers. At the end of this chapter are additional books you can use to educate your child about child molesters.

Advice to Parents

1. *Educate yourself and your child to the dangers and lures of bad strangers and child molesters.* As earthly protectors of our children, it is our God-given responsibility to arm them with clear, practical steps to ensure their own safety. Knowing what to do does much to dispel the fear such teaching engenders. You and your child need to be careful, but you do NOT need to be afraid.
2. *Keep a complete description of your child.* Take color photographs of

your child every six months. Have your dentist prepare dental charts for your child and be sure that they are updated each time an examination or dental work is performed. Know where your child's medical records are located. Arrange with your local police department to have your child fingerprinted.*

3. *Communicate your love to your child and let him know you would never stop looking for him if he were lost.* Child abductors will often tell the child their parents don't love them or care about them.

4. *If your child is missing and you believe he or she has been abducted, immediately call law enforcement officials.* Stay in close contact with the police and FBI. Also report your child's disappearance to the National Center for Missing and Exploited Children, 1835 K. Street, N.W., Washington, D.C. 20006, *1–800–843–5678*.

5. *Remember, media attention is vital, so cooperate with television and newspaper representatives.* It is important to keep the story alive and in front of the public. You need their services to alert the general public to be on the lookout for your child.

6. *Always be polite to callers and people who offer leads.* There is always the possibility the lead they give you will help you discover your child's whereabouts.

7. *Become organized.* Record the dates of leads, write a summary of phone calls. Establish a card file of names and addresses and phone numbers of contact persons such as police officers, The National Center for Missing Children, your state's clearing house if one is organized—any person whom you may need to get in touch with again. Save all business cards. In some instances, it was discovered that someone involved in the search was also involved in the abduction.

8. *Keep the faith.* If you give up, so will everyone else. Efforts to find your child often depend on your continued efforts and persistence. Be assertive if necessary.

9. *Attend benefits and other fund-raising events held on behalf of your missing child.* Public support is vitally important. Sponsor fund-raising events if necessary.

10. *Help educate the public regarding the dangers our children face today.* Contact your state representative and any other politician in a position to fight for important legislation that will aid missing children. Keep them, and the public, informed of new laws which need public support.

11. *Suggested devotional reading:* Ps. 55:4–8, 22, 23; 57:1–3; 62:1, 2; 71:14; 130:1–6; Rom. 14:8.

---

*These are the five steps that the National Center for Missing and Exploited Children recommends in its brochure "Just in Case . . . Parental Guidelines in Case Your Child Might Someday Be Missing."

Advice to Caregivers

1. *Give the family of a missing child continued moral support.* Call or write and let them know you care. Response from the human family does much to restore their faith in goodness. Remember the person most precious to them—their child—has been taken from them, shattering their belief in humanity.
2. *Volunteer your services.* Search parties are often needed. Food is necessary to keep the family going. Someone to care for other children is essential, especially during the first week or so. Their whole household has been disrupted. Practical assistance is the best kind.
3. *If you have information about their missing child, call the family and police immediately.* Valuable time is lost if you hesitate because you don't want to get involved. Consider how you would want someone to respond if your child was missing.
4. *Give donations to fund-raising events.* Parents often have to be off work and need financial assistance. As police investigation dwindles, the search efforts are often up to the family, and the ongoing search is costly.
5. *Let the family know you are praying for them and their child.* A note or phone call months after the abduction is appreciated. It says their child is not forgotten.
6. *Don't avoid the parents.* If you are a friend of a family with a missing child, don't avoid them because you don't know what to say. Risk bringing up the subject. They usually will appreciate your concern. If they choose not to talk about it, at least you will have let them know you still care and are concerned about them and their child.
7. *Pray daily for the child and members of his or her family.*

Additional Reading

Berenstain, Stan and Jan. *The Berenstain Bears Learn About Strangers*. New York: Random House, 1985.

Kraizer, Sherryll Kerns. *The Safe Child Book.* New York: Dell Publishing Co., 1985.

Newman, Susan. *Never Say Yes to a Stranger.* New York: Perigee Books, 1985.

Wooden, Ken. *Child Lures, a Guide for the Prevention of Molestation and Abduction.*

Prey—Missing and Murdered Children.
Special bulk rates 1–10: $3.00; 1–150: $2.00; 150 and more: $1.50.

Request from:
The National Coalition for Children's Justice

Child Lure
3345 Shelburne Road
Shelburne, VT 95482.

Other brochures and literature can be obtained by writing:
Find the Children,
11811 W. Olympic Blvd.
Los Angeles, CA 90064 or P.O. Box 463, Pound Ridge, NY 19576.

The National Center for Missing and Exploited Children will send one free
copy of each of the following:

Directory of Support Services and Resources for Missing and Exploited Children—a descriptive listing of nonprofit or public support groups throughout the country dedicated to assisting missing and exploited children and their parents.
Parental Kidnapping Handbook—a handbook to assist the parent of a child who has been taken by a noncustodial spouse.
Summary of Selected State Legislation—a guide to the most effective state child-protection laws in the country.
Child Protection Guidelines—safety and precaution tips for preventing child abductions and exploitation.
Informational brochures:
Child Protection—Safety and Precaution Tips
Just in Case . . . Your Child Is Missing—Preparation and Action for Parents
Just in Case . . . Your Child Is Sexually Abused or Exploited—Guidelines for Parents

Request by writing to:
The National Center for Missing and Exploited Children
1835 K. Street N.W., Suite 700
Washington, D.C. 20006.
1–800–843–5678

Child Information Packets can be ordered from:
Help Find Johnny Gosch Foundation, Inc.
Box 65332
West Des Moines, IA 50267.

Films for Parents and Children

Better Safe Than Sorry. Can be obtained by writing Film Fair Communications, 10900 Ventura Blvd., Studio City, CA 91604. This film comes

in a series of three for varying age groups:
Better Safe Than Sorry—Primary/Elementary/Junior High
Better Safe Than Sorry II—Kindergarten/Primary
Better Safe Than Sorry III—Junior/Senior High School.

◇ **8** ◇

SUFFER THE LITTLE CHILDREN

Children with Cancer*

Death by Cancer

Justin's Long Battle

In August 1979, four-year-old Justin Rodts was pale and listless. Rather than play, he lay on the floor. By late afternoon, his temperature rose over 100 degrees. His mother Judy was worried. She had discovered enlarged nodes in his neck, so she took him to the doctor. As weeks passed, Justin complained that his foot hurt. On the fourth visit to the doctor's office in a month, cancer cells appeared in the microscopic studies of his blood. Justin was diagnosed as having acute lymphoblastic leukemia, a cancer of the bone marrow tissues in which blood is formed.

"His odds are a fifty-fifty chance for survival; ninety percent chance for remission," the oncologists at the University of Iowa Hospitals and Clinics told Frank and Judy Rodts.

Through treatment, his cancer did go into remission, but in the fall of 1981, two years later, Justin suffered a relapse. The cancer mustered its forces for a battle that would last a year and a half.

"I felt such hurt and such exhaustion," said Judy. "The physical drain is terrible when you know your child is dying. It's a very scary, helpless feeling. It was so hard to keep a smile while inside I was falling apart. I was constantly fighting back tears till I thought I was going to explode. But for him, I wanted to stay happy. From the time he relapsed until the time he died (two and a half years), the stress was constant. Even when he was seemingly doing well, and he looked strong and beautiful and happy, we were always worried. The fear was always there."

"The pressures were tremendous, too, trying to make a living when

---

*Based on interviews with members of Candlelighters, a self-help organization for parents whose children have cancer or who have died from cancer.

92

things were bad," Frank added. "So that Justin could remain home, we arranged for chemotherapy to be given at a local hospital as an outpatient. But because of that, insurance wouldn't pay the $720 per treatment which he had every other day for seven weeks."

An Outpouring of Love

Almost every single day through Justin's entire illness, a secret pal remembered Justin.

"Someone would anonymously send Justin an envelope containing a stick of gum, a balloon, a dime, something to color or a joke or riddle—and always a Bible verse," Judy recalled.

On other occasions, he would receive big manila envelopes filled with cards made by school classes; a radio station had made an appeal for cards, some had a dollar tucked inside. "He would save the dollar bills and play with them, then finally spend them on something he wanted. He looked forward to the mail so much," said Judy.

Friends loaned Justin a small, gas-powered race car to ride. "He felt free in that car. His hair blew back, and he had a big smile—he was happy. It was a wonderful gift," said Judy.

During his final hours, Judy and Frank Rodts lay beside their dying son in front of the fireplace in their family room, Justin's favorite place.

"We kept telling him how much we loved him," recalls Judy. "Finally, Justin could no longer speak to us."

Judy told Justin, "I know you want to tell us how much you love us. You just squeeze our hands and we'll know you're telling us you love us," she remembers. "With his last breaths, Justin squeezed our hands."

Justin Rodts died in the arms of his parents on May 19, 1983. During those final moments, they spoke of heaven with their son.

"God was with us all through Justin's illness," said Frank. "And He has definitely guided us through many tough times. When Justin died, we felt Jesus' presence. It was a peaceful warmth—free of worries—at the time of his death. His dying took the fear out of death for Judy and me."

"I don't feel it was God's will Justin died, because I believe God is good. But I have to admit, *I'm confused.* God does heal, and *I don't understand why Justin wasn't healed*," said Judy.

Heather's Story

On March 12, 1983, Heather DeKeyrel had the flu—at least her doctor thought so. "Give her aspirin," he advised. She was nauseous and had a low-grade fever. Her father Frank was alarmed when, a short time later, she could barely walk, for his blonde, brown-eyed middle daughter had been exceptionally strong.

Late that afternoon, the doctor saw Heather in the emergency department at a local hospital. Blood work confirmed that something was terribly wrong, possibly leukemia. Nurses talked among themselves, tears filling their eyes. Heather was rushed to a university medical center some sixty miles away. On March 15, a diagnosis of acute lymphoblastic leukemia was confirmed.

Chemotherapy would begin immediately, but she should be home in four days, they said. She had an 85 percent chance of complete recovery; girls' chances were better than boys'.

But by the end of the week, it was apparent complications were developing. Her mother Pat never left her side; Heather wanted to be held and wanted to go home. Frank felt helpless.

"She's not doing too good today," the cleaning lady told Frank as he entered the unit. She was a simple woman, yet always honest and caring. Frank liked her.

One day she motioned for him to follow her. "Come, I want you to see this picture," she said. It was a picture of Jesus' footsteps in the sand, the text closing with, "During your times of trial and suffering, when you see only one set of footprints, it is then that He carries you."

"Jesus will carry you," she told Frank.

Heather DeKeyrel's condition grew progressively worse. Finally, her lungs filled and she died on March 25—her elder sister Melanie's birthday—only twelve days after she became ill.

"The loss was too much for some to bear," Frank said. "As Pat and I and the teary-eyed doctors and nurses stood in her room just after she died, a priest said, 'Sometimes I really wonder if there is a God.' We were all too embarrassed and speechless to reply. There was silence in the room. My faith sank."

But others brought hope and comfort. The minister who helped them most during Heather's hospitalization was Reverend Peterson who came frequently and merely listened.

A parent whose child enters the hospital, who is told the chances for survival are good, and then watches the child die of complications, is often left in a state of utter disbelief, groping for answers.

"Afterward, what hurt me so bad was that Heather trusted us. We would tell her, 'This might hurt but this is going to make you better.' She trusted and never cried," Frank said.

"I know God gave her to us," Pat added, "but if He wanted her back, why did He let her go through all that pain?"

"I always feared someone would take Heather, but I never thought it would be God," said Frank.

"People would tell us it was God's will. Another said, 'I want you to know God didn't do this.' Neither of those statements said what we needed to hear. What you really want and need to hear is that God is there with you through it all," Frank emphasized.

God's perspective came through a Jesuit priest who counseled, "Frank, you were victims of a severe injustice. But stop and think of the most severe injustice that ever happened on the face of the earth. This man Jesus came—the very man that created you, the world, the earth*—His own people turned against Him. Can you imagine that man hanging on a log . . . nails driven through his hands and feet. . . .'

"As many times as I have seen the Crucifix," said Frank, "nothing touched me as much as that did. I could feel the pain.

"When there's hope, faith is easy. But when all hope is gone, faith really is tested."

But some of the worst counsel came from well-intentioned acquaintances.

"Someone told me," Pat said, "It is probably a good thing she did die, so she wouldn't suffer.' It tore me up for someone to say it was a good thing for a child to die. They haven't been there themselves."

Another said, "Maybe it's a good thing Heather died, because when she got older, she might have gotten into all kinds of trouble."

Statements of this nature merely added to her pain.

Living with Cancer

Karina's Story

Fifteen-month-old Karina Carson had an extremely rare tumor called "juvenile fibromatosis" extending into her spinal column and depressing the spinal cord.

During surgery, root-like projections of the tumor were removed from the toddler's spinal cord. Five days later, a biopsy revealed the remaining mass was inoperable because of massive involvement with the brachial plexus and the nerves leading to the right arm. Amputation of the arm and shoulder was ruled out because of the tumor's involvement with the major vessels leading to the brain. At that time, Bob and Nancy Carson, Karina's parents, were told it was a benign growing tumor. Only ten days after the biopsy, however, Nancy discovered the lump was growing rapidly. Further tests revealed it was malignant. Oncologists advised chemotherapy to stop tumor growth.

Hoping she might be helped by radiation therapy, in July 1985, the Carsons went to the University of Arizona Medical Center. The specialist counseled against radiation, for such massive doses of radiation would cause significant growth arrest and deformity in years to come. After hear-

---

*John 1:3.

ing the radiologist's report, Nancy and Bob drove for hours, crying. Their hopes were dashed.

The following October, because doctors were divided in opinion, Nancy and Bob decided to discontinue therapy. While off chemotherapy, Karina's hair grew back and she seemed healthy. But tests the following spring revealed some tumor growth, so chemotherapy was started again. The Carsons await the effects of this round of treatments.

Staying Up

Karina, now four years old, became self-conscious of her resulting hair loss, so Nancy has bought hats, frilly dresses, and pink outfits for Karina so people would know she is a girl rather than a boy. Her brothers, Matt and Tony, warn their friends not to laugh at her baldness and inform them that the medicine their sister is taking causes her to lose her hair.

"We try very hard to keep things as normal as we can," Nancy says, "and to have an 'up' attitude. I try not to show depression about going to the clinic. I always try to think of something good for her to do there, like seeing her favorite nurses."

Nancy believes one secret is trying to keep life normal.

"Bob and I go out one night a week by ourselves because we have to maintain a strong relationship," said Nancy. "People ask, 'How can you go out when your child is so sick?' They don't realize you have to keep your sanity, and life and other relationships go on."

Though the Carsons were informed about Candlelighters, a support group for parents of chronic or terminally ill children, it took a long time before they were ready to try it. "I pictured a room full of very depressed people, and I didn't want to go," said Bob.

Bob feels differently now. "Your friends mean well, but they don't understand. In Candlelighters, everybody in that room knows how you feel and that is a good feeling. They can give you a lot of tips. They are part of our extended family."

You Must Be Special

A common remark made to parents of children with cancer is, "You must be a special person, and God must really love you to give you a child like this."

But Nancy says, "I'm not special; I don't want to do this, either. In essence they're saying, 'God would never pick me for such things because I'm not strong.' "

Some people say to her, "Well you *have* to be strong. You don't have any choice." "I *do* have a choice. I could choose to crack up; some people do," Nancy admits. "What I want them to say to me is, 'You're doing a good job caring for Karina and you're coping well.' "

"A lot of people give unsolicited advice about chemotherapy," Bob says. "They'll say, 'I wouldn't give her that stuff; people die from that.' You work so hard to make decisions—that responsibility is awesome—and people who don't know anything about it question you. Rather than saying, 'Why did you do that?' they should say, 'What made you come to that decision?' or 'That must have been a hard decision to make.' "

Nor do parents want to hear stories about cancer. "It seems like people think cancer is my hobby now and they're going to tell me about the same hobby," said Nancy, "so they keep me updated on everyone they know who has cancer."

If I Couldn't Believe in Heaven . . .

Though Nancy and Bob concentrate on "now," at times they think about losing Karina.

According to Nancy, "One of the hardest things for me to deal with—one of my biggest nightmares—is, if she dies, how we can put her in a box in the ground. You have to believe in heaven, because if you don't, what do you have? What do you have to live for?"

At times, Nancy questions God's existence. "Sometimes I think if there was a God, He would not take little children or let them suffer and have pain." Other times, she can say, "She is God's child, and we've been able to have her for a while; if God chooses to take her, then she's going to a better place. There's a reason; we just don't know what it is."

Surviving Cancer

Andy, the Miracle Child

Darlene Katherman has posted on their refrigerator door this statement: *Through the healing activity of the Holy Spirit, I am totally well and strong.*

It serves as a constant reminder to the Kathermans—John and Darlene—to keep a positive, faith-filled attitude, for their six-year-old son, Andy, is truly a living miracle.

Andy's story began in January 1981, when he was twelve months old. He and his identical twin, Jeff, were both sick with the flu. Both babies were whiny, lethargic, and feverish.

"Jeff has an ear infection," said her pediatrician, "but Andy has something far more serious. He has a large mass in the abdomen. I have called Iowa City and they are expecting you." By evening they began what both John and Darlene describe as a "painful ordeal." More tests at the University Medical Center confirmed the malignant tumor was concentrated on the right lobe of the liver. The diagnosis was hepatoblastoma. Surgery soon followed, during which over 85 percent of Andy's liver was removed.

A friend's mother, Berniece Lynch, opened her home in Iowa City to Darlene, John, and his mother for as long as they needed. It was her way of repaying the many kindnesses given her when her husband died the year before. Darlene was extremely grateful, for she had been living in a dormitory near the hospital.

Despite chemotherapy, in the months that followed, X-rays revealed that the malignancy had metastasized to the lungs. The doctor had exhausted his knowledge of things to do. Aggressive surgery to remove the cancerous growths was considered, but it had never been done before on a child with this type cancer. While the doctor was at a convention in Baltimore, however, the question was raised, "Why *not* try?" A thoracic surgeon performed surgery the end of June and chemotherapy followed to arrest further growth. The following September, more spots were found and more surgery was done.

John and Darlene put Andy in God's hands. And then they waited.

A Real Thanksgiving

A CT scan the week before Thanksgiving showed Andy's lungs free of cancer.

One day, the phone rang and John answered. A friendly voice said, "I'm Reverend Steve Richard from Spokane, Washington. Several months ago, a member told us about your little boy. How is he doing? We've been praying for your little boy for quite some time now."

Darlene was overwhelmed. "I ran into Andy's room and he was sleeping. The tears were falling and I said, 'Andy, people all over the country are praying for you and you don't even know them.' "

John and Darlene have learned that Andy is the only survivor among children for whom the cancer had involved the lungs. "Andy is in a league all by himself," said their specialist. His form of cancer in children is rare: two out of one million. Every night, John and Darlene kneel and thank God for Andy, their miracle child.

A Nurse Who Knows What to Say

Pediatric oncology nurse Carole Six and her husband regularly attend Candlelighters.

"I went so I could learn how to help parents of ill or dying children. I learned that most parents found nurses to be supportive and loving, but the real problem for parents is dealing with doctors. Most of us are used to dealing with one doctor. In a teaching hospital, the patients see as many as twenty-five doctors. There are a lot of differences between a private hospital and a statewide institution.

"I learned parents want to be leveled with, no matter what the outcome.

"I always tell children the truth. One of the mothers had to literally carry her screaming child into the hospital for treatments. I asked her to bring him in to talk with me.

" 'I'm never ever going to lie to you,' " I told him. " 'If it is going to hurt, I will tell you. I'll be here with you; I'll be crying with you. But we'll get through it together.' " The mother had no more problems bringing him for treatments.

"Kids are made of extra durable stuff. In my twenty-four years of nursing, I've never seen a child give up. Adults give up, but kids fight with everything they've got. And they always have a big smile and a hug for you.

"You've got to give parents hope. You can't take away hope. No one— only God—knows when and if a child is going to die. I don't believe in telling someone how much time they have, for no one really knows.

"One of the worst things anyone can say to a parent of a sick or dying child is, 'I know how you feel.' You have to have suffered the loss of a child to know how it feels."

Advice to Offer Parents

1. *Educate yourself about your child's disease.* If no information is available locally, call the CANCER HOTLINE 1-800-422-6237, or write the National Cancer Institute, Room 10A18, Bldg. 31, Bethesda, MD 20205.
2. *Keep a journal.* Record the dates of all diagnostic procedures and results, treatments, medications and their dosages, reactions, if any, and blood test results. Include the names of physicians and their phone numbers. If your child is taken to another doctor or a hospital emergency room, your records will be an aid to medical personnel. Compile a brief synopsis of your child's case listing the date of diagnosis, diagnostic tests and results, surgeries, and so on, to present to each new doctor. It will save you from answering the same questions again and again.
3. *Join a support group as soon as possible.* You will be among persons who truly understand what you are going through.* Other parents can be reliable sources of information for you.
4. *Try to maintain a positive attitude.* Your attitude will do much to sustain the quality of life for you, your child, and your family. Avoid

---

*Information about Candlelighters and The Compassionate Friends is given at the end of this chapter.

persons with a negative attitude, if necessary. Keep your daily routine as normal as possible.

5. *Tell your child if a procedure will be painful.* Don't tell your child a procedure won't hurt when you know it will. Establishing an honest relationship with your child and medical personnel will do much to allay the child's fears. Answer your child's questions honestly.

6. *Be assertive with medical personnel if necessary.* You have certain rights as the parent of a patient. One of these is the right to know. If you don't understand what your doctor is telling you, push for clarity.

7. *Don't be afraid to say no.* If a finger puncture will suffice for a blood test in lieu of a venipuncture, then be assertive.

8. *Show your appreciation to medical personnel.* They're human, too, and need affirmation. Express your gratitude for caring treatments and unexpected kindnesses.

9. *Fathers, participate in your child's treatments as often as possible.* Decision-making about your child's treatment and care is best done as a couple.

10. *Don't take what one doctor tells you as absolute truth.* Seek other opinions if necessary.

11. *If your child must be protected from infection, don't be afraid to refuse visitors or family members who have had a recent infection or contagious disease.*

12. *Create loving memories with your child.* The memories you create are like an internal emotional scrapbook for you to cherish in years to come. Live so you will have no regrets.

13. *You may want to take pictures of happy times and tape record your child's voice.* These keepsakes will be treasured later. Though painful, they may help you work through your grief if your child dies.

15. *Cling to hope.* Each child is a unique individual; no one can predict how long your child will live, and when or if your child will die.

15. *Rely on your child to carry you through.* Often your child is sensitive to your needs and will say and do the right thing to help you over the most difficult times. Listen and take your cues from the child.

16. *Parents, take time out for yourselves.* Communicate feelings, remembering that each person responds differently to stress. What is good for you as a couple is also good for your child and family. The overflow of your love has a profound influence on your children, so your relationship is of primary importance.

17. *Each parent may need to find a friend, other than the spouse, in whom they can confide and verbalize pent-up emotions.*

18. *Remember, the grandparents, aunts, uncles, and your friends are hurting, too.* Share your feelings and help them cope.

19. *Trust God to be faithful to His promise to be with you always.* For He has said, "I will never fail you nor forsake you." Hence we can con-

fidently say, "The Lord is my helper, I will not be afraid" (Heb. 13:5,
6, RSV).
20. *Suggested scriptures for reflection: Deut. 33:27; Ps. 34:18; 46:1; 2 Cor.
1:3, 4; 5:1; Rev. 21:4.*

Advice to Caregivers

1. *Listen with your heart.* Parents need to verbalize their fears and frustrations.
2. *Be supportive of the difficult decisions parents must make concerning their child's treatments.*
3. *Make specific offers of assistance.* For example, encourage the parent(s) to go out, or offer to stay with the child while they go out. Ask if you can bring them anything from the store. Offer to care for other children so the father can participate in treatment. Parents feel awkward asking, so general offers of help are seldom accepted.
4. *Bring the child a new game, a library book, or other diversion to keep the child entertained if confined to the home.* If the child is in protective isolation, mail cards or small gifts, a Bible verse.
5. *Refrain from entering the home of a child with cancer if you have had a recent infection.* Their bodies cannot fight infection.
6. *Avoid telling parents other depressing cancer stories.* They need to hear encouraging, upbeat stories.
7. *Pray for the child and parents.* Say, "I'm thinking of you in my prayers." Your prayers are interpreted as caring.
8. *Doctors, nurses, ministers, grandparents: affirm the parents.* Parents need to hear that they are doing a good job caring for their child.
9. *Medical personnel: if you have done a procedure on the child that brought unnecessary pain, apologize.* It's doubly painful for the parents if none is made.

If the Child Has Died:

10. *Avoid using statements prefaced by: "Be glad," or "It's a good thing," or "He or she is better off."* Nor should you say, "I know how you feel." Simply say, "I am so sorry."
11. *Feel free to cry with parents.* They seldom forget those with whom they've shed tears.
12. *Allow the parents to talk about their child.* Don't change the subject if they bring up his or her name.
13. *Remember, the child's birthday, Mother's and Father's Day, and Christmas are extremely painful times for parents who've lost children.* Take time to call them and let them know you are thinking about them.
14. *Refrain from telling parents they should be glad they have other chil-*

dren. This kind of statement discounts the lost child.
15. *Refrain from removing the child's clothing or possessions to spare parents pain.* There are no set rules on when this should be done. The parents know when the time is right for them.

Additional Reading

Baker, Lynn S. *You and Leukemia: A Day at a Time.* Write to Mayo Comprehensive Cancer Center, Rochester, Minn. 55901. Written for children, informative for whole family.

Bayly, Joseph. *The Last Thing We Talk About.* Elgin, Ill.: David C. Cook Publishing Co., 1973.

Bluebond-Langer, Myra. *The Private Worlds of Dying Children.* Princeton, N.J.: Princeton University Press, 1978.

Buckingham, Robert W. *A Special Kind of Love—Care of the Dying Child.* New York: The Continuum Publishing Co., 1983.

Hickman, Martha Whitmore. *I Will Not Leave You Desolate.* Nashville, Tenn. The Upper Room, 1982.

Jackson, Edgar N. *Telling a Child About Death.* New York: Channel Press, 1965.

Jensen, Amy Hillyard. *Healing Grief.* Issaquah, Wash.: Medic Publishing Co., 1980. 22-page booklet. To order, write the publisher at P.O. Box 89, Redmond, Wash. 98073-0089.

Knapp, Ronald J. *Beyond Endurance: When a Child Dies,* New York: Schocken Books, 1986.

Lancaster, Matthew. *Hang Tough!.* New York: Paulist Press, 1985. (Written by an 8-year-old cancer victim.)

Martinson, Ida Marie, Ph.D., R.N. *Home Care for the Dying Child—Professional and Family Perspectives.* New York: Appleton-Century Crofts, 1976.

Miles, Margaret Shandor. *The Grief of Parents ... When a Child Dies.* Oak Brook, Ill.: The Compassionate Friends, 1978.

Moster, Mary Beth. *Living with Cancer.* Wheaton, Ill.: Tyndale House Publishers, 1979.

Rosen, Helen. *Unspoken Grief—Coping with Childhood Sibling Loss.* Rutgers, N.J.: Lexington Books, 1986. (Rutgers State University)

Schatz, William H. *Healing a Father's Grief.* 22-page booklet can be ordered from Medic Publishing Co., P.O. Box 89, Redmond, Wash. 98073–0089.

Stevenson, Nancy C., and Cary H. Straffon. *When Your Child Dies: Finding the Meaning in Mourning.* Lakewood, Ohio: Theo Publishing Co., 1981. For copies write: Philomel Press, c/o St. Paul's Episcopal Church, 2747 Fairmont Blvd., Cleveland Heights, Ohio 44106.

Young People With Cancer—A Handbook for Parents. U.S. Dept. of Health and Human Services, Public Health Service National Institutes of Health, NIH Publication No. 82–2378, April 1982.

Support Groups

The Candlelighters Childhood Cancer Foundation
2025 Eye Street
N.W., Suite 1011, Washington, D.C. 20006
Candlelighters publishes a quarterly newsletter.

The Compassionate Friends
P.O. Box 3696
Oak Brook, IL 60522-3696
Compassionate Friends has a brochure, "Suggestions for Doctors and Nurses," available for 15 cents each or 100 for $10.

Various other pediatric oncology support groups exist. To find out if there is a group in your area, call the CANCER HOTLINE, 1–800–422–6237.

Films

When a Child Dies is available on a free loan basis through local funeral directors who are members of the National Funeral Directors Association through their state association (although some states may not have it). It is recommended for use by churches, schools, libraries, hospitals and other health care services, as well as family-oriented organizations and individuals.

9

HOW TO TALK WITH CHILDREN ABOUT DEATH

Some Do's and Don'ts

Health professionals agree that the effects of loss on children are severe, lasting into adulthood if not resolved.[1] It is impossible to estimate the anguish and sadness children have suffered by thoughtless comments parents or other adults have made to children. Thus, how we communicate with children about death is vitally important. Author Duane Mehl tells his story. "After my brother died, a close relative said to me, 'God took your little brother because he had a tendency to lie. If he had grown up, he might have gone to hell.' Looking back on this remark, I am surprised that I didn't feel shocked by it at the time. Instead, I became worried that God would also take me—and for the same reason."[2]

Fewer and fewer children today are exposed to the realities of farm life. As a young girl living on a farm, witnessing the death of animals was a common occurrence for me.

My father's faithful companion and watchdog, Shep, was run over by a car, and our family mourned his death as though we had lost a trusted, faithful friend. The calf I was raising ate weeds sprayed with weed killer and was poisoned. A baby bunny was hit with a mower while Dad cut hay. A sow lay on one or more of her piglets, killing them. Baby chicks sickened and died if not kept warm. Our work horse, Dick, died of old age. Chickens, pigs, and steers were butchered for meat. In my mind death became a part of the plan for all life.

Because we are no longer an agrarian society, Elisabeth Kubler-Ross claims children are seldom exposed to the natural life cycle of plants and animals. And people seldom die in the home as they once did. Therefore,

---

[1]Claudie L. Jewett, *Helping Children Cope with Separation and Loss* (Harvard, Mass.: The Harvard Common Press, 1982), p. x.

[2]Duane Mehl, *At Peace with Failure* (Minneapolis: Augsburg Publishing House, 1984), p. 13. Used by permission of the publisher.

"death is a subject that is evaded, ignored, and denied by our youth-worshiping, progress-oriented society."[3]

Most parents want to shelter their child from death. I once read about a mother who hurried out to the nearest pet shop to buy a new parakeet so her daughter would not have to face the fact that her bird had died. She believed her daughter would never know the difference, and she wanted to shield her from the experience of loss.

This mother, like many parents, made two wrong assumptions: (1) that the death was abhorrent to her, therefore it would be equally as abhorrent to her daughter, so she felt she must protect her child; and (2) that her daughter would never learn the truth.[4]

Such overprotection tends, however, to rob a child of the opportunity to develop coping skills for handling loss of those objects or persons dear to them. This kind of behavior perpetuates the cycle of death denial so typical in our society today.

"Children are not as fragile as we tend to think," says Jerome Frank, a psychologist at Johns Hopkins University. "It's only in this century that children have been so shielded from death."[5]

Usually, adults are reluctant to talk with children about death. A prime factor may be the parents' inability to face their own mortality. Because children ask questions which probe the mystery of death and the afterlife, some adults may lack a mature understanding of their own faith, and find it difficult to talk about a subject they know so little about. Some may believe that children simply cannot understand and therefore offer nothing more than empty euphemisms.

Social scientists have studied children at various ages and stages of development concerning their understanding of death. For infants and toddlers, their greatest fears center around separation. Before children are old enough to be familiar with the term or have any concept of death (at about the age of two), they already have some notion of *here* and *not here*, of having and losing, holding and dropping, appearing and disappearing [peek-a-boo]. This is the beginning of the child's experience with change of condition, experience of parting with objects, or with persons.[6]

Preschoolers ages three to five view death as sleep or a temporary state and as reversible: "Bang, Bang! you're dead. Now get up!" At this stage in their development, their minds are filled with magical thinking and fantasy. Often a child is overwhelmed if he or she thinks that bad

---

[3]Elisabeth Kubler-Ross, *Death: The Final Stage of Growth* (Englewood Cliffs, N.J.: Prentice-Hall, Inc., 1975), p. 10.

[4]Marguerita Rudolph, *Should the Children Know?* (New York: Schocken Books, 1978), pp. 34–35. Used by permission.

[5]*New York Times* (March 29, 1986), p. 6.

[6]Dixie R. Case and Darrell Chase, "Helping Children Understand Death." *Young Children* (November 1976).

thoughts or something they said or did caused the death of a loved one. "Children worry over the power of bad thoughts,"[7] says Rudolph. Again, their greatest fear is that of separation.

From ages five to nine, children gradually realize that death is final, universal, and personal.[8] They personify death as a person or a ghost figure who catches and carries off its victims.

Swiss psychologist Jean P0iagèt claims children go through stages of distinguishing what's alive from what's dead.[9] By age nine or ten, the child understands that death is inevitable and irreversible and that they, too, will die someday.

How to Help Your Child Understand Death

1. *Teach with animals and plants.* When a pet dies, a child mourns. By doing so, the child is developing the ability to work through grief. This experience will give your child the opportunity to gain a gradual understanding of human death. Don't replace the animal right away. You can also use the life cycle of plants to teach about death. The same language is used for plants (plants live, plants grow, plants die) as for all living things.
2. *Be open to a child's questioning about death.* Don't avoid or change the subject. Children need to know it is not a closed subject. If you don't know the answer, say, "I don't know." Talk about death without fear or denial. You also communicate nonverbally and children are perceptive to body language. The unknown is what children fear most, for it stirs anxiety and fantasy. It is wise to talk naturally about death with a child before it impacts them personally. Read books about death with them. Arm your child with knowledge before he or she is faced with a crisis. If possible, take them to the funeral of a casual acquaintance like a neighbor or friend of the family so they witness the rituals involved with funerals *before* they lose someone close to them.
3. *Give accurate information promptly.* There is usually a precise reason for death. "Grandpa's heart stopped beating." ". . . children *want to know* everything. For this, they are endowed with curiosity, equipped with powers of observation, and they possess an unmeasurable capacity for discerning details."[10] If we remain open and respond hon-

[7]Marguerita Rudolph, *Should the Children Know?* (New York: Schocken Books, 1978), p. 51. Used by permission.

[8]Linda Jane Vogel, *Helping a Child Understand Death* (Philadelphia: Fortress Press, 1975), p. 18. Used by permission of the publisher.

[9]Sylvia Anthony, *The Discovery of Death in Childhood and After* (Middlesex, Eng.: Penguin Books, 1973), p. 51.

[10]Rudolph, op. cit., p. 58.

estly each time the topic of death comes up, the child's concept of death will grow.[11]

4. *Be honest.* "It is important to be truthful to children, even pre-schoolers," Vogel says, "about the facts of death as they come up, and about the feelings of sorrow from loss that need to be expressed. This builds a healthy, trusting relationship between children and adults, gives personal knowledge of significant events in the children's lives, and corrects harmful misconceptions."[12] Avoid cover-up stories. Secrets and mysteries tell the young child that there are areas he cannot share with his parents.[13]

5. *Ask what truth the child is seeking.* We may assume they want a lot of information when a simple fact will do. Don't assume; answer questions with questions until you are able to find out what it is they are really asking. Begin with where the child is. Answer only what they ask.

6. *Avoid judgmental statements and don't moralize.* Don't say, "You mustn't say that," or "Don't feel that way." Don't tell the child how he or she should feel.

7. *Use "death" language; avoid euphemisms.* Say, "He died," rather than "he passed away" or "we lost him." Euphemisms are vague and create confusion in understanding. "Lost" means he was lost, not dead. Don't give the impression the deceased is coming back such as from "a journey." By misunderstanding common adult expressions, children frequently arrive at serious misconceptions.

8. *Don't equate death with sleep or sickness.* The child may confuse sleep with death because he or she recognizes both states as being still. He needs reassurance that death is not a long sleep. The sleep he takes each night is rest.

9. *Differentiate between minor illness and fatal illness.* Children learn that other children die, but you need to reassure them that it is only when a child is very sick or has an accident that they die. Most children grow up and live to be old.

10. *Explain the terminal illness.* If there is advance warning of the death of a loved one, tell how the disease will be treated and of the chances for recovery.[14] Point out the advances being made so the child can maintain hope. Share the fact that many diseases have been wiped out and doctors and scientists are trying to find more cures. Let them know that everything possible is being done to help their loved one

[11]Ibid., p. 61.
[12]Vogel, op. cit., p. 21.
[13]Hardgrove and Warrick, "How Shall We Tell the Children?" *American Journal of Nursing* (March 1974), p. 448.
[14]Kathryn Allen, M.S.N., Hospice Coordinator, Lutheran Hospital, Moline, Ill., *Daily Dispatch* (April 1983).

be more comfortable. Clarify the requirements necessary for the body to function, and point out how the disease prevented the body from functioning properly.[15]

11. *Do expose the child to the dying person.* Sometimes it can be helpful for a youngster to share in the process of watching a person die. However, this experience must be supported and guided by parents or other caring adults, so that a child can talk about his fears and express himself.[16] The dying person can minister to loved ones, as is often done in the hospice setting. "Death itself is not so bad as their fears and is more easily integrated when it has been seen and known and the farewells said."[17]

12. *Reassure the child that he or she will be cared for and not abandoned if the dying person is a parent.* If you are the surviving parent, reassure your child that you are taking care of yourself and probably won't die until you are old. It is important, however, that children know that everybody will die someday. It is vitally important for parents to have a will and guardianship assigned for their children in the event of simultaneous death of both parents. It is wise to discuss this with your children; tell them who would care for them in the event of your death.

13. *Give the child the option of attending the funeral and other religious rituals.* Never force, but do encourage. Davidson believes children of all ages should be included in the family's rituals of leave-taking.[18] Vogel feels that children by age five should participate in services for the dead.[19] When parents deny them participation in funeral procedures, the children feel isolated and burdened by confusion and by unexpressed grief. "Communicating the truth to children, fact and feeling, when death in the family occurs, encouraging their expressions of grief, and bringing children in on whatever religious, spiritual, or ethnic forms of funeral are important in developing family feeling and respect for traditions."[20] By viewing the body and seeing the casket left at the cemetery answers some questions the child has about where the body has gone.

14. *Understand that humor may serve as a release of tension.* "Children under the age of twelve have a short span of enduring grief (compared

---

[15]Chaplain Ron Hasley, Director of Pastoral Services, Moline Lutheran Hospital, *Daily Dispatch* (April 1983).

[16]Kathryn Allen, M.S.N.

[17]Beverly Raphael, *The Anatomy of Bereavement* (New York: Basic Books, Inc., 1983), p. 356.

[18]Glen W. Davidson, *Death . . . What Do You Say to a Child?* (Springfield, Ill.: OGR Service Corporation, 1979), p. 13.

[19]Vogel, op. cit., p. 46.

[20]Rudolph, op. cit., p. 69.

to adults), and they need and usually seek distraction (they even joke about the event) and they resort to various defenses against grief.[21]

15. *Don't say, "God needed her," or "God took her," or "God punished her," or that "It is God's will."* It is unwise to tell a child that God wanted their loved one. God may want him next. When the child feels this threat, God, in his eyes, may become a hated Being of little comfort.[22] Assure your child God is very sorry when tragedies happen and that He understands our pain and will help us through it.

16. *Don't try to stop the grieving process.* Be accepting. Give the child permission to grieve. To help prevent future emotional difficulties, encourage the child to talk about feelings of grief such as fear, anger, guilt, and loneliness. Explain that these feelings are appropriate and normal, and so is crying. Allowing the child to grieve, openly and freely, will allow him to move from hurt to health.

17. *Be aware of irrational guilt feelings.* Reassure the child that he or she did not cause the death and could not have stopped its happening. Children need to be told that their bad thoughts toward a loved one did not cause death.

18. *Give the child affection.* Be nonverbal and open to physically comforting your child.

19. *Don't fragment the family or initiate more change than necessary.* Try to maintain the family routine as much as possible to reinforce feelings of security.

20. *Be open about your tears and feelings.* Say, "I feel very sad because Grandpa died." Let the child know that you will not always feel this way. Don't pretend as though nothing has happened.

21. *Don't use the child as a "parent replacement" for a lost spouse.* Nor should the parent assign to the child the absent parent's role. Don't say, "Now you are the 'man' or 'woman' of the house." This is an unfair burden and robs the child of his or her childhood. It is assigning the child an impossible task.

22. *Encourage reminiscing about the deceased.* Remembering good times and wonderful things about the person who has died creates memories that help the child accept the death.

23. *Encourage the child to write a letter or draw pictures.* Experts say the very act of writing letters to the survivor, to God, or to the deceased is a way for children to heal emotional hurts.

24. *Speak of heaven in terms of relationship with God rather than a place.* Tell them, "Heaven is where God is. 'God is love' and the life of heaven is a life of love. Children will understand this; they know that nothing is more important than love."[23]

---

[21]Ibid., p. 77.

[22]Hardgrove & Warrick, op. cit., p. 450.

[23]Elizabeth L. Reed, *Helping Children with the Mystery of Death* (Nashville: Abingdon Press, 1970), p. 30. Used by permission of the publisher.

25. *Pray for wisdom.* Ask God to direct you in knowing how to respond to your child's questions about death.

Linda Vogel in her book, *Helping a Child Understand Death*, tells us how to explain death in a simple way.

"We can say to our children, 'We miss Grandpa but we can be glad Grandpa doesn't hurt or feel sad anymore. His body is in the ground, but all that loved and was loved by Grandpa is with God and we believe God will love him and care for him in a way more beautiful and more wonderful than we can imagine. When people say Grandpa is in heaven this is what they mean."[24]

In summary, young children believe in parent-power. The parent who listens, who answers questions simply but adequately, who leaves space for the child to voice any and all concerns and who does not moralize is building a bridge to last a lifetime. This pattern of honesty and openness can ease the pain by strengthening the bonds with others.[25]

As a parent, your attitude in times of grief, as at all times, is the most important influence on your child. Your feelings, both conscious and unconscious, are quickly sensed and assimilated by your child. For the Christian, the attitude of prayer, praise, and thanksgiving has healing power in the mind and heart. Only the Christian, who understands that God gives life and warmly receives back those who love Him, can affirm the goodness of God when all others despair.

Knowing what death is, and learning to face it, is one of the most important things we must learn and teach to our children. The Christian who understands that it is the gateway to eternal life walks through this life with assurance—and courage. If we know that death is walking into the arms of God, nothing will make us cower from it![26]

Additional Reading

For Parents:

Davidson, Glen W. *Death . . . What Do You Say to a Child?* A Short Guide for Adults. Can be obtained from OGR Service Corporation, P.O. Box 3586, Springfield, Ill. 62708.

Dodd, Robert V. *Helping Children Cope with Death.* Scottdale, Pa.: Herald Press, 1984.

---

[24]Vogel, op. cit., pp. 63, 64.
[25]Hardgrove & Warrick, *AJON*, p. 450.
[26]Daily Family Devotions, P.O. Box 1246, Pacific Palisades, Calif.

Grollman, Earl A. *Talking About Death—A Dialogue Between Parent and Child.* Boston: Beacon Press, 1970, 1976.

Jewett, Claudia L. *Helping Children Cope with Separation and Loss.* Harvard, Mass.: Harvard Common Press, Inc., 1982.

Reed, Elizabeth L. *Helping Children with the Mystery of Death.* Nashville: Abingdon Press, 1970.

Rogers, Fred. *Talking with Young Children About Death.* Available from: NFDA Library of Publications, 11121 W. Oklahoma Ave., Milwaukee, Wis. 53227. (Mr. Rogers' Neighborhood)

Rudolph, Marguerita. *Should the Children Know?* New York: Schocken Books, Inc., 1978.

Schaefer, Dan, and Christine Lyons. *How Do We Tell the Children: A Parents' Guide to Helping Children Understand and Cope When Someone Dies.* New York: Newmarket Press, 1986.

Vogel, Linda Jane. *Helping a Child Understand Death.* Philadelphia: Fortress Press, 1975. (Christian viewpoint of death)

Ward, Elaine. *Helping Children Understand Death.* Educational Ministries, Inc., 765 Penarth Ave., Walnut, Calif. 91789.

For Children Ages 3–7:

Alex, Marlee and Ben. *Grandpa & Me—We Learn About Death.* Minneapolis: Bethany House Publishers, 1982.

Alexander, Sue. *Nadia the Willful.* New York: Pantheon Books, 1983. (For grades K–3)

Barker, Peggy. *What Happened When Grandma Died?* St. Louis: Concordia Publishing House, 1984.

Buscaglia, Leo. *Freddie the Leaf.* New York: Holt, Rinehart, and Winston, 1982.

Cera, Mary Jane. *Living with Death.* For ages 4–10. Storybook/Workbook. Both books can be ordered from Kino Publications, 6625 N. 1st Ave. Tucson, Az. 85718.

Graeber, Charlotte. *Mustard.* New York: The Macmillan Publishing Co., 1982.

Hazen, Barbara Shook. *Why Did Grandpa Die?* New York: Golden Books, 1985.

Hickman, Martha Whitmore. *Last Week My Brother Anthony Died.* Nashville: Abingdon Press, 1984.

Lee, Virginia. *The Magic Moth.* Boston: Houghton Mifflin, 1972.

Kopp, Ruth. *Where Has Grandpa Gone?*—Helping Children Cope with Grief and Loss. Grand Rapids: Zondervan Publishing House, 1983.

Mellonie, Bryan and Robert Ingpen. *Lifetimes—A Beautiful Way to Explain Death to Children.* New York: Bantam Books, 1983.

Mumford, Amy Ross and Karen E. Danhauer. *Love My Hurt Away.* Denver: Accent Publications, Inc., 1983.

Sanford, Doris. *It Must Hurt a Lot.* Portland Ore.: Multnomah Press, 1985.

Stein, Sara Bonnet. *About Dying*—An Open Family Book for Parents and Children Together. New York: Walker and Company, 1974.

Stickney, Doris. *Water Bugs and Dragonflies.* New York: The Pilgrim Press, 1982.

For Children Ages 8–14:

Beckmann, Beverly Ann. *From.* St. Louis: Concordia Publishing House, 1980.

Bisignano, Judith, O.P., Ed.D. *Living with Death.* (For ages 11—adult) Home and Classroom, Journal/Resource Guide. Kansas City, Mo., 1985.

Blume, Judy. *Tiger Eyes.* New York: Dell Publishing Co., 1981.

Fassier, Joan. *My Grandpa Died Today.* New York: Behavorial Publications, Inc., 1971.

Forral, Marie and Anders. *Rebecca, a Look at Death.* Minneapolis: Lerner Publications Company, 1978.

Mann, Peggy. *There Are Two Kinds of Terrible.* New York: Doubleday & Company, Inc., 1977.

Norris, Louanne. *An Oak Tree Dies and a Journey Begins.* New York: Crown Publishers, Inc., 1979.

Orgel, Doris. *The Mulberry Music.* New York: Harper & Row Publishers, 1971.

Olsen, Violet. *Never Brought to Mind.* New York: Atheneum Publishers, 1985.

Sims, Alicia. *Am I Still a Sister?* Available from The Compassionate Friends, P.O. Box 3696, Oak Brook, Ill. 60522–3696. (For ages 7–10)

Smith, Doris B. *A Taste of Blackberries.* New York: Thomas Y. Crowell, 1973.

Vogel, Lise-Margaret. *My Twin Sister Erika.* New York: Harper & Row Publishers, 1976.

White, E.B. *Charlotte's Web.* New York: Harper & Row Publishers, 1952.

Zim, Herbert. *Life and Death.* New York: William Morrow & Co., 1970.

10

I GAVE MY CHILD AWAY

Releasing a Child for Adoption*

Karen was fifteen, a sophomore in high school, popular, attractive and a leader. She had been class president her freshman year. And now she was pregnant. She was embarrassed and couldn't face her classmates, so arrangements were made to have a tutor. The question uppermost in everyone's mind was: "Who's the father?" But Karen wouldn't tell.

"Don't tell Dad . . ." Karen begged her mother, Lynda. But neither of them could keep this a secret—not for long anyway.

"We've got to talk," Lynda blurted as her ex-husband walked in the door. "Karen is pregnant!"

Karen saw the pain in their faces, and it magnified her own: her mother was bewildered; her father, devastated.

Earlier that day she had gone to their family doctor.

"What are you going to do with the baby?" the nurse asked as Karen was leaving the treatment room.

The thought startled Karen. *What would she do with the baby?*

"I don't know," she answered, her voice breaking.

"Have you ever thought about putting your baby up for adoption?" the nurse suggested, handing Karen a slip of paper with the name of an agency and a telephone number to call.

That evening, the phone rang. It was the baby's father. "Well, are you pregnant?" he asked, his voice registering panic. He had urged her to get an abortion without telling her parents. But abortion was unconscionable to Karen. She had to tell her parents. "Yes," she said hanging up the phone.

A few days later she called the agency.

The first four months, she wanted and needed her family near her. She stayed at home alone, with nothing but her thoughts, and the isolation was getting to her. Then she heard about the Florence Crittendon Maternity

---

*Based on an interview with a twenty-year-old woman who gave up her son for adoption when she was sixteen. Names have been changed.

Home ninety miles away. Arrangements were made. The baby's father was willing to help pay the expenses involved. Karen decided to go to the home, have her baby, and place the child with an agency for adoption.

At the maternity home, Karen found she was surrounded with mothers-to-be from ages fourteen to thirty, who could give her the companionship and understanding she had been lacking. Her family could not give her the same support that being around other pregnant girls gave. Most of them had decided to keep their babies, but in the back of Karen's mind she kept wondering: What do they have to offer a baby? Somehow it seemed selfish to keep a baby just to avoid the pain involved with giving it up.

Karen gave birth to her baby in early May.

"In the delivery room, I wanted to know what it was—a boy or a girl. Somehow I knew it was a boy. I told them I didn't want to see him, so they put a washcloth over my face. By 7 o'clock that evening, I changed my mind and I asked them to bring him to me," said Karen.

"The nurses didn't know what to say. They didn't know if they should bring me a birth certificate. Of course, the baby had to have a birth certificate! It seemed the nurses left me alone a lot; they were hesitant to talk with me. For them, giving up a baby seemed unnatural," said Karen.

"The birthing process was a miracle to me. I was on a natural high for several days. I couldn't believe I had given birth to something . . . someone . . . so perfect. It was hard to believe he was real."

Up until the time of birth, she and members of her family had thought of the baby as an "unwanted pregnancy." Karen's mother admitted that she, too, had given little thought to the baby's birth. "It wasn't until I saw him in the nursery that I realized this was Karen's child—my grandchild! I had thought of all the reasons why she couldn't keep the baby; once I saw him, I desperately wanted her to bring him home."

Giving him up was not going to be easy. Karen's decision to place the baby for adoption was now under attack. Phone calls from her sister, her grandmother, and other members of the family started the first day. "Bring him home," they pleaded. Her own heart was pleading, too, but she knew she must think about what was best for her baby. Later that day, she refused all outside calls. There was only one person to whom she could turn: Mrs. Smiley, the cook at the maternity home. All the girls called on her when they needed help. Soon after she was called, Mrs. Smiley appeared and sat by her bedside.

"Karen, what have you planned this whole time?" she began. "You're not going to have *this* baby with you right now, and you might never see him again. But that's a small price to pay considering you can spend eternity with him. Whether it's eighteen or eighty years until you see him, don't jeopardize him . . . don't hurt him, and don't hurt yourself. Just think about when you get to heaven and he's there and you'll be together for eternity. That's a long time compared to your short life. You know what your feelings are, and you know what you can't do for this baby. These people who are advising you to keep your baby aren't thinking of all these things," she advised Karen.

Her words reaffirmed Karen's decision to go through with the adoption. She knew what she wanted her baby to have: *two* parents, a home, brothers or sisters, financial security. Karen couldn't provide any of these for her baby.

Karen's observations of other young mothers at the home had convinced her what she was doing for the baby was right. "All I could see were women with no futures," said Karen. "They didn't have a dime, and they were going to keep their babies. I asked them, 'How are you going to get the formula?' 'What about the clothes?' 'What about the diapers?' 'What about the rent?' "

Several days later, her family apologized for making it so difficult by bombarding her with their wishes. "We had given her *no* encouragement or support until then to keep the baby," said her mother. "I can remember asking Karen, 'How are you going to pay for insurance for the baby?' It seemed like such a trivial thing to worry about after he was here. It was unfair of us to question her decision, because she was thinking about what was best for her baby."

Loving and Letting Go

The baby stayed in the hospital two days; Karen, three days. She had gone to the nursery and viewed her baby with her parents on the second day. He was crying, and she remembers feeling so helpless.

She was permitted to hold her baby one last time before he left the hospital. The agency's social worker, tears streaming down her face, brought him in to her. Karen lovingly caressed her baby, knowing full well it would be the last time she would ever see him. Her heart told her to run after him, to bring him back. Her reason told her that if she loved him, she must let him go.

Later, the social worker told Karen's mother, "Karen's got so much love—unselfish love—in her to give her baby up, to make sure he has everything he needs or eventually desires."

The baby's father had signed the adoption papers and given a medical history, and vital information for future reference in the event there were genetic or transmittable diseases.

The hospital had agreed to take pictures of the baby, but failed to do so. Karen felt angry and betrayed, for this was part of the agreement.

Karen returned to the maternity home for a few days after leaving the hospital. She was treated like a queen by the other girls. She had made close friendships while there, and hated to leave. But things were different now—she was no longer pregnant. She had looked forward to going home. Now she hated to leave her "safe" environment—surrounded by girls who understood what she had gone through. But it was time to face the real world and begin again. She cried all the way home. There was an emptiness inside her that defied description.

Trying to Forget

That summer, Karen spent a lot of time with her old friends at the beach. They had a lot of questions. They asked her about birth control, abortion, and pregnancy—questions usually reserved for adults. Karen answered them candidly. Her pregnancy had brought her prematurely into womanhood; at the age of sixteen, she was handling grown-up problems.

Karen had learned that experimenting with sex was dangerous and morally wrong. She accompanied a friend to an abortion clinic and was sick for days afterward. She was thankful she had not gone that route. Karen at least had the satisfaction of knowing that her baby was alive and well—somewhere.

Six months after giving birth, the realization of what she had done hit her. Parties led to excessive drinking and smoking dope—anything to forget.

Now she hated the social worker, who she had always felt was sensitive and caring. It was unnatural. How could she take a woman's baby from her? It should be illegal. Karen vented her anger by writing a vindictive letter, which was never mailed.

Karen was in with the wrong crowd and headed on a path of self-destruction, lashing out at everyone around her. During her senior year, she and others at a drinking party were caught and suspended from high school for three days.

As a result, she was forced to seek counseling. "Drinking is not your real problem—there's something else, Karen," the counselor told her. She began crying, then told him about giving up her baby and how sad she felt.

"Getting caught is probably the best thing that ever happened," said Karen. "It made me realize drinking was a way to escape. I gave up drinking when I knew what I was running from."

The Need for Replacement

When Karen was nineteen, relatives in another state thought of her when their friends Marilyn and George separated. Their baby, Amy, was only weeks old. Would Karen come and take care of Amy? Marilyn had left both her husband and the baby.

Karen felt compelled to go. She couldn't hold her own baby, but here was a baby that needed her. George saw Karen as a means to an end—a way of getting custody of his baby. Months later, he married Karen, thinking she would join in the fight for custody. But George was wrong. Karen loved the baby, but she was not willing to take another woman's baby from her. George lost the custody battle; the marriage lasted only five months. "It hurt because he never really loved me. He just wanted me to help get Amy," said Karen. "All my friends—and George—knew how desperate I was for a 'replacement baby.' "

Five Years Later

The adoption agency had agreed to act as an intermediary for Karen to receive developmental information and pictures of her baby at ages three, six, nine months, and at a year. She has channeled letters and gifts to her son on his birthday.

"Each year on his birthday, I write a letter begging to have another picture of Jerry. I'd be lost without those pictures," said Karen. She knows that her son has two brothers, who are also adopted, lives on a farm, and that he talks about his "birth mother." "I am no threat to the adoptive parents. I would never do anything to hurt him or his future. I do want to be told, however, if something happens to him or his family.

"There isn't a day that goes by that I don't think about him. I try to imagine what he is like. Sometimes when I lie in bed at night thinking about him, my arms *literally* hurt. I ache from the top of my head to the tip of my toes—I would give anything just to see and to hold him. But I know adoption was the best choice because all benefited—the baby, the adoptive parents, and me."

Asked when she began the grief process, Karen answered without hesitation. "I began grieving immediately when I learned I was pregnant. I cried every day for nine months, and for days after coming home. It has affected and hurt my whole family—and the lives of many other people as well. My grandparents mourned the loss of their only great-grandson; we're a family of girls."

Karen speaks to high school students and warns, "Don't make the same mistake I did and get pregnant. Learn from my mistakes." She also speaks to adoptive parents, and persons interested in adopting a baby. Her message to other pregnant girls is pragmatic, "Do you want to wait tables and earn a minimum wage the rest of your life? That's what will happen if you keep your baby."

Karen is now twenty-one, has a good job, and is attending a community college evenings.

How Others Responded

Rumors ran rampant. After giving up her baby for adoption, the question uppermost in people's minds was "How could she do it?" Rather self-righteously, most conversations would usually end with something like, "I could never give *my* child away." Others said, "She just gave her baby away so she could go out and have a good time." But Karen wasn't having a good time: her heart was breaking.

"I used to ask myself that same question: 'How could I do it? How could I give my baby to a total stranger?' " said Karen. "At first I didn't know how I was going to do that. Then I realized that I had to give my baby to the Lord. I had to entrust Him with his care. I felt like the Lord was leading me through all of this, so the only thing I could do was give him over to the Lord. Any parent only has temporary custody of a child."

Karen says her strengths came from her support system and religious beliefs. Though saddened by her pregnancy at such a young age, her parents stood by her. The social worker assigned to her was caring and sensitive. The girls at the home were supportive. The counselor at the alcoholic treatment center was perceptive and saw behind her facade of bad behavior to the real pain that drove her to escape through drink and drugs.

Karen is perceptive of her own inner thoughts and feelings, articulate, and able to reach out to others who need help

Changing Attitudes and Adoption Practices

In the past, "sealed record" adoptions were vital to protect children from the age-old stigma attached to being a child born out of wedlock. The word "illegitimate" could mean a lifetime of scorn and ridicule for the child. The birth mother lived in fear of discovery, which could heap public disgrace upon her and her family. She bore the brunt of shame; the father's identity was seldom disclosed.

Suzanne Arms, in her book, *To Love and Let Go*, writes:

> The standards of adoption we now take for granted arose from within a society different from today's. Adoption, in a world where unmarried women who became pregnant were considered immoral and dangerous to society, and where the children of such unions were branded illegitimate, *had* to reflect those uncompassionate attitudes. It is no wonder that early maternity hospitals and homes for unwed mothers went to great lengths to keep the identities of the women hidden or that names were changed on birth certificates and files kept under lock and key. Women and children deserved to be protected from stigma. They had no economic or political power, and it was nearly impossible for children born out of wedlock or their mothers to move freely in the world if their background was made known. The stigma still exists but is no longer so great; yet the secrecy of this tradition continues to be the rule.[1]

---

[1]Suzanne Arms, *To Love and Let Go* (New York: Alfred A. Knopf, 1983), p. 223. Used by permission of the publisher.

On January 1, 1976, California adopted a law called the Uniform Parentage Act which says that *every* child is to be considered as legitimate. Three categories are used to designate paternal parentage. The father is named as: (1) the mother's husband; (2) the "alleged" father; or (3) he is the "unidentified" father. Similar laws are being adopted in other states across the country.

Several factors have greatly influenced the supply of and demand for adoptable babies. Improved methods and availability of contraception and legalization of abortion in 1973 caused a sharp decline in the numbers of babies available. In addition, girls and women who carry their babies to full term are more likely to keep their babies. As recently as fifteen years ago, about 85 percent of all pregnant teenagers who gave birth released their babies for adoption. The latest data indicates that about 93 percent of all teenagers now keep their babies. Some experts claim only 3 percent of pregnant minors who give birth without being married currently choose adoption. Yet more people are seeking adoptions because women delay having children in lieu of a career. Infertility therapy groups estimate that one in six couples of reproductive age has difficulty conceiving.

Changing mores and social awareness, plus the assertiveness of women pioneering new, more humane ways of "letting go" of their babies, have brought about change in attitudes and adoption practices. In addition to agency adoptions, some states now permit what is called *direct independent adoptions*, which avoid foster homes, unlike agency adoptions, and allow the baby to be given directly to new parents upon discharge from the hospital. The birth parent may select the adoptive parents for her child, based on biographical information about them. Therefore, she may know their identity, and may have been in contact with them—either by telephone or in person.

Now some agencies, like Catholic Social Services, in some states agree to facilitate a reunion between the child and his or her birth parent(s). For example, at the age of eighteen, with the permission of the adoptive parents, the adoptee can initiate a request for a reunion. At the age of twenty-one, either the adoptee or the birth parent can request to be reunited *without* the adoptive parents' permission. And some states have a state registry where either the birth parents or adoptee may register his or her name in the event the parent/child wishes to initiate a search and reunion.

Because of the lengthy waiting periods of agency adoptions (the waiting period can be four to seven years), some adoptive parents choose the *legal private adoption* handled through intermediaries—lawyers, physicians, the clergy—who help facilitate the placement, rather than an adoption agency.

These methods are controversial because of the lack of regulations surrounding such adoptions, and the fact that, for the most part, lawyers have not been trained to find homes for children. Opponents say that confidentiality of adoptive parents is not protected; that custody fights have resulted when biological parents have later sought, and successfully won, the return of a child; that adoptive couples are not adequately screened; and that biological parents do not receive enough counseling about their options, such as temporarily placing a child with foster parents.[2]

The Pain That Never Goes Away

In the mid-seventies, Arthur Sorosky, Annette Baran, and Reuben Pannor did research into the lives of what they called the adoption triangle—birth parents, adoptive parents, and adoptees. Letters from birth parents verified the hurt and pain they have carried for years. The authors found:

> Fifty percent of the birth parents interviewed said that they continued to have feelings of loss, pain, and mourning over the child they relinquished. Examples of such expressions were: "I never got over the feeling of loss"; "I still have feelings of guilt and pain when I think about it"; "Whenever I see a child, I wonder if it's her"; "Giving up the child was the saddest day in my life"; and "I pray that the child will not blame me or reject me. I think about him always."[3]

They found two factors especially caused unwed birth mothers continued pain: (1) the concern that the child would not understand the reason for the relinquishment and grow up feeling rejected and abandoned; and (2) a worry that the child would think poorly of them and never know what they [the birth parents] had done with the rest of their lives.[4]

Advice for Women Considering Adoption

1. *Thoroughly investigate the adoption options available to you.* There are public or private agencies, Christian or church-related agencies, or legal private adoptions. Beware of those who would buy and sell your baby! Study the risks involved with each before making your decision.
2. *Decide what you want.* Do you want to hold the baby? Do you want to select the adoptive parents for your child? Do you want to meet

---

[2]William G. Greer, "Private Adoptions Are Legal but Still Controversial," *New York Times* News Service, *The ARGUS* (November 23, 1986), B3.

[3]Arthur Sorosky, M.D., Annette Baran, M.S.W., and Reuben Pannor, M.S.W., *The Adoption Triangle* (Garden City, N.Y.: Anchor Press/Doubleday, 1978), p. 52. Used by permission of the publisher.

[4]Ibid., p. 72.

them? Do you want to hand the baby to them? Do you want to have them pick up the baby from the hospital? Do you want developmental information and pictures? Remember, in years to come, you will never stop wondering about your child and the adult he/she becomes.

3. *Decide how much information you will want to have in the future.* Although you give up all rights to the child, there can be *sharing of pictures and information*, or the *semi-open option* which allows you to meet the adoptive parents and exchange information pertaining to the *parents only.* The *open option* allows you to meet with the parents and exchange background information about the parents and child. These options must be negotiated at the time of the adoption; you will not be given the opportunity to participate in later years if you fail to include it in the initial agreements. Those parents who cooperate in the sharing option usually do so for two, five, or eighteen years. These options vary from state to state and agency to agency.

4. *Know your own strengths.* It will help you decide how much you want to be with your baby when he arrives, the persons to whom you will or will not listen when they give advice, or whether you can parent the baby.

5. *Decide what you want for your baby.* Write everything down. Evaluate whether you can now, or in the near future, provide your child with these basic needs.

6. *Think of your own future.* Weigh and evaluate your support systems. Will you have to count on your parents to take over for you? Are *you* ready to become a good parent *on your own*? Evaluate your chances for finishing school, or starting a career if you keep the baby. Now do the same by projecting what your future would be like if you place the baby for adoption.

7. *See and hold your baby so that you know he/she is real.* Create memories with your child during the brief moments he/she is yours. Hold, rock, take pictures of your baby, say goodbye to your baby. These things will help you as you work through the grief process.

8. *Don't let others talk you out of your decisions.* Remember all the rationale you used to decide what was best for you, your baby, and your family.

9. *Accept the fact that you are going to grieve.* Giving up a baby is like a "psychological amputation." You will feel a great sense of loss.

10. *Don't stifle your feelings.* Talk about your pain with empathic friends or relatives.

11. *Think about a brighter tomorrow.* Trust God to direct your life by relying on His guidance through the Word and the Holy Spirit. "I will instruct you . . . and guide you along the best pathway for your life. I will advise you and watch your progress" (Ps. 32:8, TLB).

11. *Entrust your life, and the life of your baby, to God's loving care.* Pray daily for your child.

12. *Suggested devotional reading:* Ex. 1:15—2:10; Ps. 73:21–26; 121:1; Jer. 29:11, 12; Phil. 3:13–14.

Advice to Caregivers

For Parents:

1. *Don't force your decisions on your daughter, disregarding her feelings about whether to keep or release her baby.* Regardless of her age, it is a decision she will live with for a lifetime. Making the decision for her can result in great bitterness toward you if she is told what to do and not allowed to participate in the decision-making about her baby.
2. *Explore the options fully and carefully with your daughter.* You may be approached by friends or relatives who want to adopt the baby. Evaluate the risks involved with each method of adoption. Secure literature from various agencies and make comparisons. Explore the support systems available to your daughter if she keeps the baby.
3. *Give emotional and spiritual support to your daughter.* She needs your love and concern regardless of the circumstances. Resolve to stand by her.
4. *Don't isolate your daughter.* She needs to be surrounded with caring, supportive persons who will give her encouragement to make difficult decisions.
5. *Keep the lines of communication open.* Discuss feelings—hers and your own. Don't deny her the right to express her feelings of love and maternal concern for the baby. Be nonjudgmental and compassionate.
6. *Understand that feelings of guilt and failure as a parent will influence your thinking.* Most teenagers say parents could not have prevented the pregnancy.
7. *Know that this baby is a human life—your grandchild—not just an unwanted pregnancy.* This baby deserves your love.
8. *Support your daughter's decision once it is made.* Don't withhold love if her decision goes against your wishes.

For Relatives and Friends:

1. *Don't pry or ask embarrassing questions.* If the woman wants you to know, she will tell you.
2. *Short-circuit rumors.* Let them stop with you. Words and thoughtless comments do hurt.
3. *Never refer to the child as "illegitimate."* The stigma associated with the word is damaging. All children are precious in the sight of God and don't deserve a label that denigrates them—or the family—an entire lifetime.

4. *Offer encouragement to the pregnant woman and her family.* Show sincere concern and love for them.
5. *Don't question the woman's love for her baby if she gives him up for adoption.* A woman usually releases her baby because she can't provide for the child's physical needs, not because she doesn't love him.
6. *Understand the woman's need to talk about her baby.* She is filled with remorse and grieves the loss. Her pain is real and long-lasting.

Additional Reading

Arms, Suzanne. *To Love and Let Go.* New York: Alfred A. Knopf, Inc., 1983. (About open adoption)

Heckert, Connie. *To Keera With Love.* Kansas City, Mo.: Sheed & Ward, 1987.

Lindsey, Jeanne. *Pregnant Too Soon.* Buena Park, Calif.: Morning Glory Press, 1980.

Sorosky, Arthur D., M.D., Annette Baran, M.S.W., and Reuben Pannor, M.S.W. *The Adoption Triangle.* Garden City, N.Y.: Anchor Press/Doubleday, 1978.

Strom, Kay Marshall. *Helping Women in Crisis.* Grand Rapids: Zondervan Publishing House, 1986. (For Christian leaders)

Witt, Reni L., and Jeannine Masterson, M.S.W., C.S.W. *Mom, I'm Pregnant.* (A Personal Guide for Teenagers.) New York: Stein & Day, 1982.

Zimmerman, Martha. *Should I Keep My Baby?* Minneapolis: Bethany House Publishers, 1983.

HOTLINES
Bethany Christian Services: 1–800–238–4269
National Adoption Hotline: 1–202–463–7563
National Pregnancy Hotline: 1–800–233–6058

Films

Adoption—Another Choice
Available from:
Archdiocese of Hartford
Office of Radio & Television
785 Asylum Ave.
Hartford, CT 06105

We Were Just Too Young
Available from:
MTI Teleprograms
7825 North Scott Street
Schiller Park, IL 60176

◇ **11** ◇

I KILLED MY BABY!

*The Emotional Aftermath of an Abortion**

Jan was pregnant—and scared! How would she tell her children? Would they think less of her? She was divorced with three children; the baby's father was divorced and had children, too.

Both Jan and Todd loved kids—that was no problem. He was unemployed and had been for some time, but that was not the problem, either.

Todd was a silent and loving gentle giant of a man—a free spirit— and she cared for him deeply. But he would go off for weeks, sometimes months, without saying why. Jan understood, but she needed someone who would be there day in, day out. She knew she could never marry Todd. He needed time and space; she wanted more in her life. But warnings that sexual relationships belong in the confines of marriage had gone unheeded, and now she was pregnant.

Todd was upset when she told him. His reactions were similar to her own: *It can't be! There's a mistake. This can't be happening.* At first he said, "It can't be *my* baby."

"It's not going to go away," she told him. "We have to make some decisions."

Jan felt alone. She wanted the baby, but Todd's life and her childrens' lives were a consideration, too. One day, mustering enough courage, she asked her three children, "How would you feel if I ever had another baby?"

"It might be fun," answered the seven-year-old. But as the conversation evolved, her teenagers worried about things they couldn't do or places they couldn't go *if* she had a baby. A baby would change everything. *They don't want anything to change, nor do they want to share their mom,* thought Jan.

Since her divorce, she had tried to better their lives in every way she could. Knowing her children as well as she did, she knew they would adjust if she went through with having the baby. But did she want to do

---

*Based on an interview done ten months after a woman in her thirties had an abortion. Names have been changed.

that to them? She wasn't worried about their thinking less of her because she had become pregnant, but she didn't want them to think less of her because of the choice she now had to make.

The timing was all wrong for her to have a baby. Todd felt like a failure, and he didn't need one more thing to make him feel even worse. In Jan's eyes, Todd was not a failure; he had a college degree and was extremely intelligent. But there were no jobs to be had, and there was no way he would be able to support the baby. All Jan would have expected of him was to stay with her through the baby's birth.

But time was a factor. She knew it had to be done soon—during the first trimester. The nearest abortion clinics were nearly a hundred miles away, and each had waiting lists, she was told. One was more clinical, less supportive; the other offered an advocate who would go through the whole painful procedure with her. She was hoping it would be the latter. Jan called and found that there was a cancellation. She could go within the next few days. *I can always cancel the appointment,* she told herself. She didn't know how Todd would feel about an abortion.

Painful Alternatives

Jan had never been faced with such a painful decision. *How do I choose that this child should die?* she asked herself, agonizing over her belief that each child is a gift of God.

Deep down, she knew Todd *knew* it was his baby—he was going through the process of denial, as she had done. She waited a few days after telling him. Then one day she talked to him. "We've got to talk," she began.

"Yes, I know," he answered.

"How do you feel, Todd?"

"I'm scared," he admitted. "I don't know what to do."

She knew Todd loved children. Watching him with kids—both hers and his—was beautiful. If she kept this baby, she would always have a part of Todd with her. But somehow, she felt that was being very selfish.

Jan didn't know what she wanted. It was just so much easier to see what Todd needed and what he could handle. She sought help from a counselor at a local maternal health center. After a long discussion, the counselor said to her, "I don't think you want to do this. I think your decision has already been made. You're not going through with it."

"I don't know what I'm going to do," Jan replied. "But once I make the decision, it's a decision I have to live with the rest of my life, no matter which way it goes. If I decide to keep this baby, after so many months, I can't change my mind. And yet the abortion will be just as final.

"I could never give my baby up for adoption. I could not stand knowing my baby was living with somebody else."

Jan agonized alone over the decision she had to make. Her heart said, *No, keep the baby!* But how would she work things out? Finally, fighting against everything she believed in, she decided she must have the abortion.

She told Todd.

She would have to come up with the money; Todd couldn't help her, and that, too, was hard for him. He agreed to take her to the clinic.

At the Clinic

Before going in for her lab work, Jan handed Todd an envelope. Unlike others, this clinic would allow him to stay with her during the entire procedure, but Jan chose not to put him through it. Todd was given literature to read explaining the procedure.

He read her letter while waiting.

In her letter to Todd, Jan told him it was going to be a boy. Somehow, she said, she knew this baby was a boy, and she had named him Jake.

When she rejoined Todd after completing her lab work, he asked, "How did you know?"

"Know what?"

"Jake—it was my father's name."

Jan and Todd were startled by the coincidence.

With this realization, Jan broke into tears. Tears welled in Todd's eyes as well.

"Are you sure we're doing the right thing?" Jan asked, regaining her composure.

"I don't know . . . I just don't know," he said.

Todd grasped her hand; she felt he wanted to leave—to go home—and not go through with it. His touch was firm, but questioning.

And then they looked at each other, and they both knew. She knew Todd was where she had been weeks before in her thinking. Just a couple of weeks earlier, she would have kept her baby regardless of what anyone thought and whether she had his support or not. *But it's not fair to the children we have now, and it's not fair to the baby's father,* she had rationalized. She remembered a billboard's message, "A baby is forever." She was prepared to make a commitment to the baby, but she just didn't want to put everybody else through hell because of it.

She felt she had to have the abortion.

Jan describes what it was like.

"It was like being in the twilight zone. It was the most awful experience I've ever been through. They assign you a support person who's been through an abortion, and that person goes with you every step of the way.

"It was hard hearing life being sucked* out of me. Once it was started,

---

*Aspiration method of abortion.

there was no turning back," Jan sobbed quietly.

"So many pro-abortion people refer to the 'fetus.' They say there's no feeling . . . that it isn't a baby . . . that it doesn't have a soul. I don't believe any of it. I never did.

"It was like lining up four children—all of my babies—and saying, 'Choose. You can have only three.' And I had to play God. I had to decide whether this baby lived or died . . . in my heart I killed my baby."

I Need to Hold a Baby

Jan wept as she poured out her feelings.

"I miss my baby . . . I mourn for my baby. I want to feel him . . . and I just haven't done that. There's just an emptiness and nothing takes its place . . ."

She paused, her eyes red from weeping and her voice broken. Slowly, she began talking again.

"I hate to hear a baby cry. I need to hold a baby until I'm ready to let go, but I don't know anybody who has an infant, and I wouldn't know how to explain to them why I have this need. I need to rock a baby. I wore out rocking chairs with my other three babies. I want him back so much. If only I could have him for just *one* day. I don't even have a grave to go to.

"It is a death to me. In time, it will get easier, but it will never get better, nor will it ever be right. A woman whose baby has died is free to mourn; it is socially acceptable. She can talk to anyone about her baby's death, but I can't talk about my baby. It's not socially acceptable.

"I keep waiting for someone to fix it, and no one can fix it. I want it to be final. I don't want to hurt because of it anymore, but I know I always will."

The Fear of Being Judged

"It's comforting to know that my baby is with God, and on a one-to-one basis I talk to God a lot about my baby. I haven't confessed what I've done. I haven't been to church since I did it. The hypocrisy on my part keeps me away—and on the church's part, too, because of the judgment. There are so many people who are so opinionated one way or the other about abortion. They make strong statements, and they don't stop to think about who's around, or what the person who has had an abortion may have been through, or the emotional pain. A few remarks bring back all the pain. I wish the church were as forgiving as God.

"It's very hard to make the decision to abort your baby. Sometimes the choices seem like all the right answers, and they're all the wrong answers. A person who isn't living it can't understand."

A Lasting Memory

"I know I have to face that baby someday, and I don't know what to say. I don't think I'll go to hell because of it; I think I'm in hell now. It will take a lifetime to get over," said Jan.

"There's a part of me that stopped growing because of this experience. I'll never be the same. I don't care if I live to be a hundred years old, I know there will still be that memory. I *would not* do it again."

It was important for Jan to finalize the relationship with her unborn baby, so she asked that I end her story with this message to her baby:

"I love him. His mommy and daddy love him, but we chose to spend our lifetime with the babies that we have." But Jan's sense of guilt remains.

"We plan to spend eternity making it up to him," Jan ends.

One Among Millions

During the years 1973 to 1981, 11,194,601 abortions were reported. In 1982 alone, there were 1.57 million legal abortions in the U.S. As in previous years, the majority of women obtaining abortions were young, white, and unmarried. Approximately 63 percent were under 25 years of age, 70 percent were white, 78 percent were unmarried, and 58 percent had had no live births.[1]

Unlike Other Losses

Each woman's story is unique; no one story gives the whole picture. Yet consistencies occur. One thing is certain: Jan is one among millions of women who bear their pain and guilt in silence.

The problems related to a woman's mourning the loss of an aborted baby are unique:

1. There is no external evidence that a baby ever existed—no validation or proof—of the fact that once there was a tiny life growing inside her. No baby to hold or say goodbye to. Her unborn baby lives only in her mind and heart—and it haunts her.

2. There is no formal leave-taking or ritual, such as a funeral, for the mother of an aborted baby to attend where others publicly acknowledge her loss and share her grief.

3. Often only a few friends, perhaps a family member or two, are told about the abortion, so there is virtually no support system. Twenty percent of the women who abort their babies never tell their male partner.[2]

4. Aborting a baby, though permitted by law, is still socially unac-

---

[1]Centers for Disease Control Abortion Surveillance, U.S. Department of Health & Human Services, Annual Summary 1981 issued November, 1985, p. 1.
[2]Arthur Shostak, *Oprah Winfrey Show*, September 16, 1986.

ceptable (even among people unopposed to abortion), so no one gives her permission to grieve openly. No one acknowledges her grief, so her suffering is done in secret and in silence.

5. Unlike other deaths, the woman bears the burden of guilt for having ended her baby's life. She is the one who endures the procedure, and she lives with the guilt of that action. Many find it difficult to forgive themselves. She may have succumbed to societal pressures to have the abortion—either from a boyfriend or parents or friends—but this does not lessen her feeling of guilt. It intensifies her pain and feeling of isolation. Often she becomes angry at those who encouraged her to undergo an abortion, especially if deep down she wanted her baby and felt it was wrong to end its life.

6. She may experience rejection, disapproval, anger, humiliation, and harsh judgment from the people she loves the most once she reveals the truth. This, added to her own feelings of guilt and loss, can be devastating.

7. Too few clergy, psychologists, psychiatrists and social workers have been trained to take these women through the steps necessary for healing and reconciliation with God. Currently fewer than twenty post-abortion healing outreach programs are organized in the United States. Some have tried support groups, but Kathy Deema, organizer of WEBA (Women Exploited by Abortion) in Illinois, and Vicky Thorn, Director of *Project Rachel* in Milwaukee, report one-on-one counseling has proven to be the most effective.

8. Abortion advocates provide no classes, no role models, no movies, no education to prepare the woman (or man) for the tremendous sense of loss they will feel after abortion.

9. The grief cycle for abortion is different than for other types of losses. At first, some women feel relieved and happy it's over. Usually, grief over a loss is most intense in the initial stages. The woman who has aborted may repress her feelings for many of the reasons stated earlier. "She may remain in a state of denial for a prolonged period of time. This unresolved, complicated grief may not surface for from six to ten years,"* says Vicky Thorn.

According to Arthur Shostak, author of *Men and Abortion: Lessons, Losses and Love*, "bottling up emotion" is typical for men as well. Shostak states that 75 percent of the men he interviewed in an abortion clinic had talked to no one except their sex partner about the abortion. Men, too, feel tremendous loss.

"Because these feelings are often buried and never processed, they often come up later on," says psychologist David McEchron, of Davenport, Iowa. "You can't ignore the concepts that go with abortion. You have to

---

*Coordinator of Project Rachel and co-director of the Respect Life Offices, Archdiocese of Milwaukee, Wis. Interview October 23, 1986.

have the thought, 'Is this murder?' Abortion forces you to deal with the issues of life and death. This awareness has been heightened within us culturally. So when this grief and guilt is not processed, it comes up later and the person feels, 'This is my unpardonable sin and now I'm being punished.' "*

Healing Ministries

The first conference held in this country dealing with post-abortion counseling and healing was convened in August 1986, at Notre Dame University. It was called "Healing Visions," co-sponsored by the university and the National Youth Pro-Life Coalition (NYPOC). The earliest organized attempts to counsel post-abortion women through healing ministries were started in 1979 by Jan Krocheski in St. Paul, Minnesota. *Project Rachel* was organized in 1984 in the Archdiocese of Milwaukee, a ministry operated by priests and professional counselors that provides professionals to help women deal with abortion. *Project Rachel* serves as a model for organizations springing up in this country and abroad. Father Michael T. Mannion's book *Abortion & Healing: A Cry to Be Whole* is among the first books on the market to help women and professionals understand the unique phenomenon of post-abortion grieving and steps toward reconciliation with God.

The Need for Forgiveness

Vicky Thorn of *Project Rachel* reports that women generally have not been helped by easy dismissal of guilt. "When women are told, 'Don't worry about it. You did the best you could under the circumstances. Get on with your life,' it hasn't proven helpful for them. They inwardly feel the abortion was wrong, and they want and need someone to be honest with them and say, 'Yes, it is wrong to take a baby's life.' They can then accept that fact and get on with mourning."[3]

Father Michael Mannion says, "I see guilt as healthy and productive when it leads the woman to come to grips with the reality of what she has done. It can be a part of the way back to wholeness and inner peace through a personal relationship with a loving and forgiving God, and a commitment to embark upon the journey of that relationship. Once the 'commitment to healing' process is set in motion, there is no value in

---

*W. David McEchron, Ph.D., P.C., is a psychologist in private practice in Davenport, Iowa, Private interview October 8, 1986.
[3]Vicky Thorn.

guilt whatsoever."[4] The healing process takes place in its rhythm between God and the soul of the woman.[5]

Of itself, psychology can only help a woman understand the past and cope with it, but that is not enough. Knowing the whys and the hows of the past do not liberate a person from the shackles of repetition and the reliving of the continuous pain of the past. Forgiveness does. That is not an invention of humankind, but a gift of God. Spiritual healing is God's seal on the human heart that the past may not just be coped with, but healed.[6]

Advice for Women Who Are Mourning the Loss of an Aborted Baby

1. *Allow yourself to feel the pain, to grieve.* Avoid suppressing the pain, for it will merely lie buried until it is worked through. Pain must be faced before it can be healed. This process is called "grief work."
2. *Allow yourself time to grieve.* Give into grief when you feel the need to, but then proceed to other more pleasurable activities. Gradually lessen those grieving periods.
3. *Share your feelings with an empathic friend, partner, relative, or counselor.* You cannot grieve alone; it is done in the context of relationships. Give names to your feelings of anger, fear, and so on. Expressing and naming them helps dissipate their intensity.
4. *Select a professional counselor carefully.* You may decide to talk with your minister, rabbi, or priest. Mental health centers also have trained counselors who can be helpful. But depending on their attitude, they may either increase or decrease your guilt feelings. At this moment, strong pro-life advocates *may* prove devastating for you.
5. *Name your baby.* Naming and visualizing what your baby may have looked like will make your baby real. How can you grieve over someone if you haven't given him or her personhood?
6. *Envision your baby in the loving arms of Jesus.* In heaven there is no pain, no bitterness, so your baby is in a state of perfect peace with God and has already forgiven you.
7. *Ask God to forgive you.* There is nothing you have done that could make God stop loving you. God's love is not limited in understanding or compassion as is human love. Rely on the truth: "If our heart condemns us, God is greater than our heart" (1 John 3:20, KJV). Accept God's forgiveness.

---

[4]Michael T. Mannion, *Abortion & Healing: A Cry to Be Whole*, (Kansas City, Mo.: Sheed and Ward, 1986), p. 73. Used by permission of Sheed & Ward, 115 E. Armout Blvd., Kansas City, Mo.
[5]Ibid., p. 47.
[6]Ibid., p. 21.

8. *Forgive yourself.* This is often the hardest part. Trust in the promises that God can cleanse you thoroughly: "Though your sins be as scarlet they shall be white as snow" (Isa. 1:18, KJV). God forgets our past deeds. "For I will be merciful to them in their wrongdoings, and I will remember their sins no more" (Heb. 8:12, KJV). You have no right to continue to condemn yourself if God has forgiven you. God wants you to be whole again.

9. *Forgive those with whom you are angry or blame for your having had the abortion—the male partner, parents, friends, medical professionals who performed the abortion.* You cannot be healed if you harbor bitterness in your heart. You may also feel as though you have been deceived by the language describing a baby as a "blob of tissue" and the pro-abortion slogans.

10. *Ask God to heal your memories.* Envision Jesus standing beside you during those painful moments in the past. If you commit them to God, through the work of the Holy Spirit, you will gradually be healed.

11. *Avoid getting pregnant again to "atone" for the abortion.* This is a common reaction, an attempt to replace the baby. It is important to understand that there is no replacing the aborted baby.

12. *Avoid being around destructive, critical persons* who feel they want to punish you for your misdeeds or make you feel guilty. Remember, no one has the right to judge you. Avoid those who are only interested in exploiting your story, but don't seem concerned about you as an individual, or the pain you are presently suffering. Unfortunately, these people can sometimes pop-up in the best pro-life groups. Remember, however, that pro-life organizations are often full of people who are willing to help.

13. *Reach out and help other women.* As you heal, reaching out to others, little by little, can be therapeutic.

14. *Recognize irrational fears* such as the fear of losing future babies because God may punish you or take them from you. Some also fear losing the children they presently have.[7]

15. *Suggested devotional reading:* Isa. 1:18; Micah 6:8; Mark 10:16; 2 Cor. 7:1–10; Heb. 8:12; 1 John 3:20.

Advice to Caregivers

1. *Love and support your daughter, friend, or loved one.* If you are a parent, remember it was extremely difficult for her to tell you. No doubt, many a fearful teenager has opted for abortion rather than deal

---

[7]I am indebted to Father Mannion, Vicky Thorn and Judy Gillespie of *Project Rachel*; Mary Ann Hughes of NYOPC; and Kathy Demma, organizer of Illinois WEBA, for the above recommendations.

with the imagined or real parental consequences. Though you may feel intense anger, rejection, shame, humiliation, or betrayal, remember your reactions may leave a lasting impression on her that affect your relationship in years to come. Never underestimate the effect your words and actions will have on her. She needs your unconditional love now more than ever before and she needs your compassion, not condemnation.

2. *Listen with your heart.* Never underestimate the pain she is now experiencing. She needs nonjudgmental understanding, acceptance and caring. Cry with her. Embrace her lovingly.
3. *Fathers of aborted babies need the same loving understanding.*
4. *Be accepting of her feelings.* Your openness will allow her to vent and articulate those feelings.
5. *Give her permission to grieve.* Don't encourage her to get over it, forget it, or act like it never happened. Grieving for an aborted baby takes time, the same as any other loss.
6. *Keep confidences; never violate confidentiality.* When confidences are broken, trust is destroyed. Her support system may consist only of a select few.
7. *Be sensitive to those around you.* Before you judge others harshly, remember they may be in great pain. It is not your right or duty to judge them. Our Lord Jesus had great compassion for those who were in spiritual pain, and spoke words of compassion to them, but He spoke words of condemnation toward those who were insensitive and unforgiving.
8. *Anniversaries will be painful for her*—the date her baby would have been born, the first year anniversary of the abortion. Remember her with a phone call that says you care about her.

Additional Reading

Demma, Kathy. *Reaching Out.* Can be ordered by writing author at P.O. Box 314, Dolton, IL 60410. Enclose $1.00 and self-addressed stamped envelope.

Garton, Jean Staker. *Who Broke the Baby?* Minneapolis: Bethany House Publishers, 1979.

Hanes, Mari, with Jack Hayford. *Beyond Heartache.* Wheaton, Ill.: Tyndale House Publishers, Inc. , 1984.

Koerbel, Pam. *Abortion's Second Victim.* Wheaton: Victor Books, 1986.

Linn, Dennis & Matthew, S.J. , and Shelia Fabricant. *At Peace with the Unborn: A Book for Healing.* Mahwah, N.J.: Paulist Press, 1985.

Mannion, Michael T. *Abortion and Healing: A Cry to Be Whole.* Kansas City, Mo.: Sheed & Ward, 1986. May be ordered by calling a toll free number: 1–800–821–7926. Total cost: $6.95.

Michels, Nancy. *Helping Women Recover from Abortion.* Minneapolis: Bethany House Publishers, 1988.

Shostak, Arthur. *Men and Abortion—Lessons, Losses, & Love.* New York: Praeger, 1984.

A complete packet of information containing articles, lists of additional books, and a list of healing outreach programs can be obtained by writing The National Youth Pro-Life Coalition, Jackson Ave., Hastings-On-Hudson, New York, NY 10706. Enclose $7.50 plus $2.40 for postage and handling.

Videocassettes

Presentations on the subject of post-abortion counseling and healing ministry are available from Sheed and Ward, P.O. Box 419281, Kansas City, MO 64141–0281. Write for more information or call 1–800–821–7926.

The Psychological, Emotional and Spiritual Impact of Abortion: A Profile of Women, Men and Families in Need, featuring Vincent Rue, Ph.D.

The Healing Process: Models for Evaluation and Response, featuring E. Joanne Angelo, M.D.

Post-Abortion Counseling Techniques, featuring Terry L. Selby, M.S.W., A.C.S.W.

Post-Abortion Reconciliation: Integrating One's Faith into the Healing Process, featuring Rev. Michael T. Mannion, S.T.L., M.A.

Healing Outreach: Congregation and Community Programs That Work. A panel discussion featuring Vicky Thorn (coordinator of *Project Rachel*, Archdiocese of Milwaukee), Pat Morris (Director of WEBA Illinois), Cecile Hecker (Member of Board of Directors for LifeLine), and Bill Thorn (Professor of Communications at Marquette University). Each of the above are available in VHS or Beta from Sheed & Ward. Cost: $69.95.

Post-Abortion Healing Outreach Programs

After Abortion Helpline, Providence, RI – (401) 941–3050
American Victims of Abortion, Washington, D.C. – (202) 626–8832
C.A.R.E., Pittsburgh, PA – (412) 572–5099
Conquerors, Minneapolis, MN – (612) 920–8117.
Counseling Associates of Bemidji, Bemidji, MN – (218) 751–9510
Open Arms, Federal Way, WA – (206) 839–8919
PACE, P.O. Box 35032, Tucson, AZ 85740
Project Rachel, Milwaukee, WI – (414) 769–3391
Puzzle Project, Rev. Gary Bagley; 795 Main St.; Diocese of Buffalo, NY 14203

RETURN, Diocese of Joliet; St. Charles Center; Route 53 & Airport Rd; Romeoville, IL 60441

Save-a-Life, Birmingham, AL – (205) 933–9393

WEBA, Antioch, IL – (312) 549–8197

WEBA/Illinois, 8 South Michigan Avenue, Suite 1100, Chicago, IL 60603 – (312) 263–1175

◇ **12** ◇

VIOLATED!

*The Emotional Aftermath of Rape**

Jennifer knew Sid from high school days. He was popular, and she hadn't believed all the rumors she'd heard about him. He seemed like a nice guy. When she came home from college for the Thanksgiving holidays, he asked her out and she accepted. She would be nineteen in a month; Sid was twenty-one.

But Jennifer discovered that the rumors about Sid's reputation were true. On the date, he tore her clothes, physically abused her, and raped her. Fearful her parents would discover what had happened, she waited until it was very late before sneaking into the house and her bedroom. She hid her clothes in a shoe box; she would take them back to college with her and dispose of them there. She couldn't believe what had happened. For the next few days, she wore a long-sleeved sweater to cover her bruises so her parents wouldn't know. She feared her mother and father might blame her, or her father might go after Sid. She wasn't sure how they would react, and she wasn't willing to find out.

She confided in Pam, her hometown college classmate. "He's a popular guy," Pam told Jennifer, somewhat envious it hadn't happened to her. Pam was no help at all; she had no idea how horrible the experience had been. Jennifer felt dirty, worthless, cheap, and used. She was filled with self-loathing and feared pregnancy.

It was a month before Jennifer could sleep without having nightmares. By this time, she had convinced herself it was her own fault. She was edgy and cried for no reason. Then she began to get angry, and that anger permeated every aspect of her life. She was inexperienced when it came to men—if only she had been more knowledgeable. Now Jennifer feared all men. Fortunately, her parents moved from the small town where they were living, so she was not faced with seeing Sid. Jennifer felt relieved—she never wanted to see him again.

---

*Based on an interview with a woman in her late thirties. The names have been changed.

Still, Jennifer told no one.

Years later, she married, but was unable to tell her husband about the experience for fear he might think less of her.

Not until Jennifer was thirty-three did she seek psychological counseling, some fourteen years after the traumatic assault.

Jennifer describes the process: "I had neatly 'packed away' those feelings and they were eating me up inside. The psychologist made me go back and remember the details of the rape, forcing me to take a look at it again. When you work that hard to bury something, it's scary to bring back all the ugly pieces so you can make sense of something that happened years ago."

Jennifer required only a few therapy sessions. She describes them as necessary for "cleaning out the wound." The skilled counselor also helped Jennifer sort out the issues of culpability: She was not to blame, for she had been the victim of a violent crime.

"I don't think my fear of men has ever completely gone away. Nor has the feeling of rage. This has never tempered," she admits.

The FBI reports in the *Uniform Crime Report* that each year in the United States, a reported rape occurs every six minutes. One in three women will be a victim of sexual assault at some time in her life. The number of unreported rapes is unknown, of course, but some experts believe that only one in ten victims alert authorities.

Berlinda Tyler-Jamison, former director of the Quad Cities Rape/Sexual Assault Counseling Center and member of the Illinois Coalition of Sexual assault, says that rape victims go through three phases of what is called "Rape Trauma Syndrome."*

Phase One, the acute phase, is *shock*. The victim feels she has lost control. She has a sense of crisis, and feels as though the whole experience is unreal. This phase can last from a few hours to one or two weeks. Rape victims characteristically display two emotional styles of stress: *expressed* or *controlled*. Some victims express their feelings verbally or through such behavior as crying, shaking, smiling, laughing, restlessness or tenseness. In others, feelings are masked or hidden, and a calm, composed and subdued effect is seen. Both reactions indicate exhaustion, shock, or attempts to deny or repress the violent attack. Almost all victims suffer varying degrees of delayed stress. The amount of suffering each victim endures, as well as the length of recovery time, is largely determined by the support she receives from others.

Phase Two, *outward adjustment*, may last a few months. The victim attempts to get on with life as "usual" and wants to forget the attack.

---

*Men and young boys are victims of rape as well. Wherever "she" is used in the text, the same can be true for males.

Symptoms of this stage include: decrease in anxiety, denial, suppression and rationalization, and reluctance to seek help.

Phase Three, *integration*, begins when the victim develops an inner sense of depression and expresses an urgent need to communicate with those around her. She will make a serious attempt to resolve the feelings that have been aroused by the rape, and will begin to scrutinize the related issues that she has tried to suppress up to this point.[1]

Phase Four, *resolution*, is the final phase and has two distinct stages. The first stage is triggered by an incident that reminds the victim of the assault and a flashback of the event occurs. The symptoms are: regression to the fears they felt in Phase One—anxiety, physical complaints, generalized depression, guilt and shame, nightmares, and isolation. The victim may not associate these feelings with the rape. The second stage leads to an acceptance of the assault as part of her past, and allows her to move on with her life.[2]

Tyler-Jamison says the women who have the most difficulty with rape are those who are young and virgins. "Often young women are struggling with their own sexuality and identity issues. They have had no other sexual experiences with which to compare. In counseling them, it is important to stress the difference between healthy sex and rape. I make a point of telling them, 'You are a victim of a violent crime—rape is not sex.'

"Children under age twelve," she says, "have the best prognosis of getting through the trauma, *if* family members handle it appropriately by focusing on the child rather than the act of rape. Children draw their conclusions from their parents. A child is more in touch with the physical impact—rather than the social impact—of it all."

When the rape victim is married, the social impact can have a devastating effect on the marriage itself. "The entire family is raped and victimized," says Tyler-Jamison; "a spouse becomes the secondary victim. Rape victims frequently become sexually unresponsive to their spouse."

Research supports this claim. Dr. Judith Becker discovered in a study at Columbia College of Physicians and Surgeons that 40 percent of the female rape victims had serious problems with their male partners after being raped.[3]

Why does the crime of rape have such a profound effect on a marriage relationship? One reason is the persistence of myths about rape. Despite the educational efforts made by counselors and agencies, there are engrained beliefs that rape is the victim's fault. Carol Franklin, a psychologist

---

[1]Ronald W. Ramsay, and Rene Noorbergen, *Living with Loss* (New York: William Morrow and Company, Inc., 1981), p. 196. Used by permission of the publisher.
[2]Taken from the brochure, "Rape—A Violent Crime, Not a Medical Diagnosis," produced by Family Resources, Inc., Davenport, Iowa. Used by permission of the agency.
[3]Susan Crain Baker, "Rape—A Couple's Tragedy," *Quad-City Times Sunday Woman* (October 21, 1984), p. 6.

who worked with rape victims, says, "Unfortunately, there are still people who believe a woman can't be raped against her will—especially by someone she knows." Those attitudes engender doubts and plague the lives of those victimized by rape. "Some men feel as though they failed to protect their wife; other men unconsciously still think of their wife as property," adds Tyler-Jamison.

In the past, U.S. courts were prone to set rapists free after the defense proved to the jury the victim was a sexually experienced woman who wore provocative clothing. Great strides have been made in changing state laws and the attitudes of law officials. Still, much work needs to be done to eliminate these deeply ingrained attitudes.

Myths and Facts about Rape

Myth: Sexual assault is primarily motivated by the sexual needs of the rapist.
Fact: Rape is an act of violence. Many rapists have access to sex. What they wish to express is power, dominance, control and anger.

Myth: It is easy to identify a rapist by his bizarre behavior and/or appearance.
Fact: Rapists come from all socio-economic levels. There is no external identifying character trait for rapists.

Myth: The rapist is generally unknown to the victim.
Fact: Frequently the victim and the rapist have a *casual acquaintance* relationship—"the friend of a friend" or even a close relative.

Myth: Rape is an impulse act.
Fact: The rapist's attack is planned and is generally preceded by some conversation or contact with the victim.

Myth: Many rape charges are false.
Fact: About 2 percent of all rape charges are false—the same as in other crimes.

Myth: Most rapes occur in dark alleys or to persons who hitchhike.
Fact: Only a small percentage occur in open spaces. Most rapes occur in the home. [About 36 percent are committed in the victim's home.]

Myth: People cannot be raped against their will.
Fact: Sexual assaults are generally accompanied by the threat of great bodily harm or death.

Myth: Many victims provoke the rapist.
Fact: No one asks to be threatened, brutally attacked, or violated as a person. The motive for rape is not sexual fulfillment; therefore, the

degree of "provocative" apparel is not a factor in the rapist's decision to assault.

Myth: Many people actually enjoy being raped.
Fact: Rape is a physical and severe emotional trauma for all victims.

Myth: Men are not victims of sexual assault.
Fact: Not only can men be actual victims of sexual assault, but they also can be victimized when those persons they care about become victims.[4]

Institutional Victimization

Although attitudes are changing, another form of victimization can be the result of insensitive treatment by medical professionals and the police. Due to the nature of the crime, the manner in which the medical examination is performed is of extreme importance to the well-being of the victim. It is vital for doctors and medical staff to realize just what effect the rape examination has on the victim's recovery process. When the examination is performed in a warm, caring, nonjudgmental and supportive climate, the recovery process will be greatly enhanced. The attitude of the medical staff during the exam will affect decisions that the victim must make. The support given victims during this crucial time may give them the courage to seek help from other support systems rather than succumbing to shame, embarrassment, or guilt. The compassionate care of an understanding staff can minimize the victim's emotional stress.[5] Tyler-Jamison offers these suggestions to medical professionals and police officers investigating the crime:

• *Extend common courtesies.* Introduce yourself to the victim and explain who you are and why you are there.

• *Let the victim know you are there to help.* If you are uncomfortable with the questions you must ask, admit it. Expressing your discomfort will humanize you and help the victim overcome the "uniform barrier" (a uniform is a symbol of authority which can create a communication barrier).

• *Understand that at some time during the attack, the victim thought she might be murdered. Assure her she is safe now.*

• *Ask the victim for permission to proceed with the examination.* This will give back some of the feeling of control lost during the attack.

• *Explain procedures carefully and in a calm, soothing manner.* This will calm the victim's fears.[6]

---

[4] Taken from a brochure produced by the Quad Cities Rape/Sexual Assault Counseling Center for Rock Island and Scott County. Used by permission.
[5] Ibid.
[6] Ibid.

Why?

Tyler-Jamison warns, "Some rape victims will ask, 'Why did God let this happen to me?' Others will take a more fatalistic attitude saying, 'If this wasn't supposed to happen, God wouldn't have allowed it to happen.' "* If this becomes a major issue for the victim, she refers them to the clergy for spiritual counseling.

The question of *Why* cannot be answered apart from some understanding of the forces of evil in this world and how they oppose God's will. Serious theological misconceptions can result if the victim concludes God willed the assault or abandoned her. A pastor needs to assure the victim that he believes in her innocence and of God's love for her as an individual.

In her article, "The *Unmentionable* Violence," Betty Gibb points out that "in struggling with the question of why an assault occurred, it's natural for victims to seek religious explanations which, all too often, are inadequate and simplistic. Unfortunately," she adds, "some churches have encouraged this by seeming to promise that if a person prays and lives a good life, she will never experience suffering."[7]

The victim needs to be reassured that such acts are as offensive to God as they are to the victim.

Both the victim and support persons should understand that anger is a healthy response. Tyler-Jamison says, "Whenever I see a victim in the hospital emergency room and she's angry, I know she's going to be all right . . . anger is an appropriate response to being victimized."

Ultimately, after the fears and the rage and the grief work have dissipated, the Christian woman must face the issue of forgiveness. "The only way to get rid of bitterness is surrender it," says Corrie ten Boom, a Dutch survivor of Nazi concentration camps whose family members were murdered. "Forgiveness is not an emotion," she says in *Tramp for the Lord*; "forgiveness is an act of the will, and the will can function regardless of the temperature of the heart. He [she] who cannot forgive others breaks the bridge over which he [she] must pass, for every man [woman] has the need to be forgiven."[8]

Betty Gibb explains, "God must be allowed to work through the victim to enable her to forgive herself and the rapist. For a human being such an act may be impossible, but God's grace, through prayer and the power of the Holy Spirit, can empower the victim to forgive."[9]

---

*Private interview September 19, 1985.
[7]Betty Gibb, "The *Unmentionable* Violence," *Today's Christian Woman* (July/August 1986), p. 47.
[8]Corrie ten Boom and Jamie Buckingham, *Tramp for the Lord* (Old Tappan, N.J.: Christian Literature Crusade and Fleming H. Revell Company, 1974), p. 51, 57; Corrie ten Boom, *Each New Day*, (Minneapolis: World Wide Publications, 1977), April 25.
[9]Ibid., p. 71.

Advice to Offer Rape Victims

1. *Go to the nearest hospital emergency room.* Do not shower, douche, or change clothes; evidence can be destroyed by doing so. If the rape occurred in your home, do not clean or straighten the room. Evidence needs to be left intact.
2. *Avail yourself of any local resources such as a local rape crisis center.* Your local hospital should have these numbers readily available. The crisis centers usually have an advocate who can be called to be with you during the examination to offer support and answer your questions. These services are usually free.
3. *Reporting the rape and prosecuting your attacker is your decision.* Regardless of whether you report the crime or not, the collection of evidence and medical examinations are imperative because of the threat of venereal diseases.
4. *Give your account of the attack, including as many details as possible, while it is fresh in your memory.* Reporting it to the police maintains your option to prosecute. You may fear the attacker will seek revenge if you report it; then again, you may wish to report him so he can be apprehended to prevent him from attacking you or other women. *The decision is yours.*
5. *Face the issue squarely with your loved ones.* Keeping it secret or acting as though it never happened can cause serious problems later. For example, by not telling your parents, spouse, or male friend, your silence may be construed as consent or guilt if and when the truth is revealed at a later date.
6. *Deal with your feelings.* You are the victim of a violent crime. *You are not to blame for what happened.* You are no more to blame than if you had been robbed by a thief. Self-condemnation is misdirecting the blame on an innocent victim—you. Don't rely on hindsight to evaluate what you did at the time of the attack. You are alive. Your response to the act was right for you.
7. *Seek professional counseling.* Remember your spouse and family are victims also. Dealing with feelings in the safety and impersonality of the protected environment of counseling can be more helpful than trying to deal with sensitive issues of sexuality alone in your bedroom where doubts and myths may creep in.
8. *Resume your lifestyle as much as possible.* You may no longer feel safe if the attack happened in your home or apartment. Discuss these fears with your loved ones.
9. *Understand that it will take time to work through the grief process.* Something very precious was stolen from you—your self-esteem and pride, your sense of well-being and independence, your feelings of self-worth and self-assuredness, your trust of men. It will take time to

recover from these losses, so don't be too hard on yourself if you don't recover as rapidly as you might expect.

10. *Reach out to an empathic, trusted friend who will listen to your feelings.* Because they are less involved emotionally, it may be easier to discuss your feelings with someone who will listen nonjudgmentally.

11. *Ask God for the healing of memories.* Ultimately, healing will occur if you surrender the anger to God and decide to grow from the experience. Through an act of the will and with the help of God, you can choose to grow.

12. *Suggested scriptures for reflection:* Ps. 143:1–12; 140:1; 55:22; Isa. 41:10; 1 Pet. 5:7.

Advice to Caregivers

For Parents:

1. *Refrain from blaming your daughter.* Rape is a traumatic experience, and blaming her for the sexual assault will only add to her emotional and spiritual pain. Remember, it was very difficult for her to tell you. Your daughter is the victim of a crime. She is alive; some rape victims never live to tell about it.

2. *Take her to the nearest hospital emergency room.* Seek the aid of a local rape crisis center if one is available in your community.

3. *Stand by her.* Your warm, caring, nonjudgmental support is vital to her recovery.

4. *Understand that it will take time for her to get over it.* Headaches, nightmares, anxiety, sleeplessness, fear—and in time, anger and depression—are the most common reactions. Don't expect or encourage her to "get over it" or act like nothing happened. Repressing these feelings delays the process of healing and may mean she will never reach the resolution phase.

5. *Explain the difference between rape and healthy sex.* A good sexual relationship is pleasurable, one in which love and caring are shared, and one in which there are choices. The rapist gave her no choice.

If you are the spouse:

1. *Examine your own biases.* If you believe the myths rather than your spouse, these beliefs will hamper your providing the support she needs from you.

2. *Understand the fears she overcame by telling you about the experience.* Some of the most common fears are: you won't believe her, you will blame her, you won't want her anymore, you will think her less worthy, or that you may seek revenge causing more harm, especially

if the violator is a mutual acquaintance or member of the family. The most stressful fear for most women is rejection, loss of respect, and loss of your love for her as a person.

3. *Be warm, caring, and nonjudgmental.* Allow her to set limits in how much of the experience she shares with you. It may be extremely painful for her to tell you all the details. Don't press her beyond these limits.

4. *Don't lose sight of your spouse's emotional and spiritual needs by concentrating on the details of the assault.* Don't criticize her for not resisting the rapist.

5. *Let her set the pace in resuming sexual intercourse.* Ask permission to touch her, and be understanding of her need to regain control over this aspect of her life. Some women want and need to resume having sex soon after the attack; others are sexually inhibited for a longer period of time. Be patient with her. It is difficult for her to trust men. She must regain trust, and your patience and gentleness can permit this to happen.

6. *Assure her of your love and respect for her.*

7. *Seek professional counseling together.* Rape is a crime unlike any other. You are a victim also. A trained counselor can assist with the resolution of this traumatic event in your lives.

8. *Deal with your own emotions.* You will have intense feelings of anger and hatred that must be faced and worked through. Ignoring or denying these feelings will not make them go away. Repressed feelings surface later and cause more harm.

9. *Refrain from seeking revenge.* Vengeful acts only complicate matters. Support your wife if she decides to prosecute, allowing the due processes of law to work in your best interests. "Never avenge yourselves, but leave it to the wrath of God . . . 'Vengeance is mine, I will repay' says the Lord" (Rom. 12:19, RSV).

For a friend or relative:

1. *If called, go to be with the victim immediately after the attack.* You may be of more help because you are less involved emotionally. A parent, spouse, or male friend may be too upset to provide the emotional support she needs.

2. *Respect the victim's privacy.* If she chooses to tell you about the experience, listen nonjudgmentally. Validate her feelings by saying, "This has to have been a horrible experience for you."

3. *Keep confidences.* You may be the one friend she tells about the experience. Don't betray her confidence in you.

4. *Don't accuse her of being partly to blame.* No one asks to be violated or physically assaulted. She needs you to help her sort out her own

feelings of guilt. For example, she may say, "I should have known." An appropriate answer would be, "How could you have known?"

5. *Don't discourage her from reporting the crime or prosecuting the perpetrator.* This must be her decision. She may choose to not prosecute because she fears talking about the assault in a courtroom. She could feel vulnerable to the comments and thoughts of persons who have their own biases. Or she may have a compelling need to report and prosecute the perpetrator.

6. *Do not give easy, simplistic untruths such as, "It's God's will."* The Bible teaches us that God abhors such violent crimes.

7. *Assure her of God's love for her and His presence.* Her trust in a loving God and an understanding Savior will help her through this ordeal. Reassure her that God can heal her of painful memories, but this takes time.

8. *Encourage her to seek professional counseling.* It will hasten resolution and healing. Don't expect her to get over it in a short time. It takes months, sometimes years. Recovery often hinges on the amount of support the victim receives during this crisis.

9. *Secure a copy of the book and encourage her to read* If You Are Raped *or* Recovery.

Additional Reading

Benedict, Helen. *Recovery.* Garden City, N.Y.: Doubleday & Co., 1985. (How to overcome fear, anger and despair caused by rape, where to get help, and a directory of rape crisis programs, shelters, and victim services nationwide.)

Burgess, Wolbert Ann, and Lynda Holstrom. *Rape: Crisis & Recovery.* Englewood Cliffs, N.J.: Brady Communications Co., 1979.

Fortune, Marie M. *Sexual Violence: The Unmentionable Sin.* New York: Pilgrim Press, 1983.

Johnson, Kathryn M. *If You Are Raped.* 1984. Available from Learning Publications, Inc., P.O. Box 1326, Holmes Beach, Fla. 33509.

McEvoy, Alan W., and Jeff Brookings. *If She Is Raped.* (A Book for Husbands, Fathers, and Male Friends.) 1984. Available from Learning Publications, Inc., P.O. Box 1326, Holmes Beach, Fla. 33509.

Roberts, Deborah. *Raped.* Grand Rapids: Zondervan Publishing House, 1981. (A Christian woman's personal experience)

Strom, Kay Marshall. *Helping Women in Crisis.* Grand Rapids: Zondervan Publishing House, 1986. (For caregivers)

The Rational Woman's Guide to Self-Defense. Department of Physical Education, California State University at Los Angeles, 5151 State University Drive, Los Angeles, Calif. 90032.

Teaching Film

Common Sense Self-Defense is a teaching film which shows easy-to-learn self-defense techniques. It is available from:

Department of Physical Education
California State University at Los Angeles
5151 State University Drive
Los Angeles, CA 90032

Local Agencies

To find the telephone number of your local rape crisis center: Check your telephone directory under Social Service Agencies, call your local hospital emergency room, or call your local police department.

◇ **13** ◇

WHEN A MARRIAGE BREAKS UP

The Pain of Divorce

Liz Hunt kept hoping things would get better. Instead, the tension mounted and things grew steadily worse. She and her husband couldn't communicate. It was impossible to straighten things out when there was no willingness or desire to do so. *It takes two persons to work it out*, Liz conceded. She couldn't go on like this; she knew her health would break if she didn't do something. And if her health deteriorated, she would be unable to give of herself or care for their three children. They were hurting, too. Her close involvement with their preteen and two teenagers had widened the rift between Liz and her husband, but there were other more serious problems.

Finally, they agreed to a separation.

After they parted, Liz began to deal with her feelings. She was filled with guilt, self-recrimination, resentment, anger—even hatred. She examined herself and found parts of her personality she didn't like—it was hard to like herself with such powerful, negative thoughts and emotions swirling around in her head and heart. She felt "cut off" from friends, some of her relatives, and the church. After a year's separation, Liz and her husband divorced.

The hardest adjustment, according to Liz, was the change from *loneliness to aloneness*. "You immediately find yourself a single parent, having to do a lot of things you've never done before. You're afraid. You don't know what you're going to do and how you're going to make it, especially if you've never worked outside the home.

"You also go through a process of redefining who you are; you have to deal with this new image of yourself."

The usual response to a socially awkward situation is avoidance. Liz found that her presence among married friends was not only an inconvenience, but a threat. "I felt alienated from my married friends," she said. "It was like I was socially 'invisible.' My friends were uneasy and didn't know what to say to me. One said, 'I see your life situation is changing,' which made me laugh, and she was glad I could laugh about it."

For Nell Browne, being divorced after twenty-one years of marriage was "worse than death." In the beginning, marriage for Nell and her husband had been a sacred venture. Unresolved emotional differences widened the gulf between them, however, causing their marriage to end in divorce.

"I felt like an utter failure," said Nell. "We grew up in an era when you hid your feelings; you just acted like they didn't exist. A lot of feelings pile up when you're not able to talk things through. Despite our differences, divorce, at first, was not a viable option for either of us. We didn't believe in divorce. An outburst of anger one day precipitated a rapid decline in our relationship. These feelings and our deep-seated problems became irreconcilable. Yes," said Nell, "I felt like a failure. My whole self-image was shattered.

"My husband and I were both very active in church," she went on. "In fact, I was in a prayer group; we called it our 'love group.' I felt terribly let down by the church during our divorce. *It seemed as though my church friends were unable to perceive me as a person in pain.* Churches are very couple-oriented, so immediately I felt out of place. My social life literally ended. Later, I became suicidal and required counseling. I felt very alone, and I had to rely totally on God's promise to never leave me. Faith in a loving, forgiving God was all I had to depend on," Nell concluded.

Terry Bird, now the father of three young sons, was brought up by a mother who thought crying was a weakness. His father had deserted the family when he was five years old, so he had no paternal role model. His mother seldom expressed any physical affection, and Terry realizes this became a real problem for him as well. He also knows he probably married for the wrong reasons. "I really didn't know what love was," said Terry. "I had never felt loved, and I couldn't tell my wife I loved her." His marriage ended after nine and a half years.

Since Terry's divorce, he's taken a good look at himself, and he says he's grown a lot. "You have to make yourself Number One for a while after a divorce. It's important to understand what you're going through. Before you can love another person, you have to be able to love yourself. I'm not the same person I was when I first married."

Children Hurt, Too

"At first the boys were terribly confused," said Terry, who sees his sons on weekend visits. "One evening while driving them to their mother's home, the eleven-year-old said, 'Dad, see that shining star? Every night I make a wish and pray that you and Mom will go back together.'" Like most children of divorce, this boy yearns for a reconciliation. Terry says that will never happen.

Liz Hunt was not able to discuss the divorce with her children. They would not open up until four years after the divorce. "I knew our oldest son was angry with me, and that was difficult to take," said Liz. "My children took over the role as head of the house. For example, my teenagers would urge me to go out and not stay at home all the time. When I would go out, they would tell me what time to be in at night. They worried about me a lot."

Sensitive younger children often assume they did something which caused the divorce.

A recent two-year study done by John Guidubaldi, chairman of the Early Childhood Department at Kent State University, finds that boys fare worse than girls after a divorce, and this fact grows as the children approach puberty. Guidubaldi found that fifth grade boys suffer the most from divorce—both academically and socially. He theorizes that older boys may have more difficulty adjusting to divorce because 90 percent are living with their mothers. Girls have the same sex parent with them; many boys do not.[1]

Midlife divorce—a divorce after twenty or more years of marriage—is more upsetting for the couple's grown children than experts once believed. The first study of grown children was done by Penn State. Researcher Michael Smyer, associate professor of human development, found that because they were more mature, children experienced much the same emotions as their parents. Many made such statements as "before we divorced." Most reported a great deal of anger—80 percent of the women, 50 percent of the men. Forty-three percent of the women blamed their father, while the men's anger was directed at no particular parent.[2]

Each year in the United States, more than 1.2 million divorces occur. Research studies are finding that 20 to 30 percent of the children involved in divorces will have serious emotional problems as a result.

Three-fourths of Americans who divorce, later remarry, and four million of those marriages involve children. Step-marriages fail at an even greater rate than first-time marriages. Experts claim that a child born in the 1980s has a 20 percent chance of experiencing, before reaching the age of eighteen, not just one, but two divorces of his or her parents.[3]

Anger That Won't Go Away

"Some assert that the loss in divorce is worse than the loss in death. After death, one recalls good things about a person. After a loss through

---

[1]Barbara Zigli, "Pre-teen Boys Suffer Most from a Divorce." *USA Today* (April 18, 1984), p. D-1.

[2]Felicia Lee, "Grown Children Also Stung by Trauma of Divorce," *USA Today* (April 13, 1984), D-1.

[3]*NBC White Paper—Divorce Is Changing America* (June 3, 1986).

divorce, one tends to remember unhappy, hostile experiences. Divorce is a death that is never complete; it tends to recur with each family contact, after which the relationship dies all over again."[4]

Divorced parents stay angry. Constance Ahrons of the University of Southern California in a study confirmed that more than half of divorced parents continue to have angry relationships that may be harmful to their children as long as five years after they split up. Fifty-eight percent of divorced parents are either constantly arguing or else dragging one another back to court five years after their divorces. These findings, said Ahrons, differed only slightly from one year after divorce, when 63 percent of parents remain very angry with each other.[5]

The Church and Divorce

When couples who were once relatively active in church divorce, many times either one or both partners stop attending. Sometimes the divorced person erects internal barriers; other barriers have to do with the response, or lack of response, from the church family. Some denominations' teachings and interpretation of the Scriptures pertaining to divorce may engender a sense of superiority and judgmental attitudes that permeate the thinking of members of the fellowship of Christ.

But Christ viewed all persons as having worth in the sight of God. Just as He ministered to the woman who had five husbands (John 8:1–11), the gospel He proclaimed speaks to us wherever we are in our lives. We are warned in the Bible to be careful in our judgments about the lives of others (Matt. 7:5; John 7:24), perpetuating the stigma associated with divorce.

Some divorcees report that because they are so filled with intense feelings of shame, resentment, hostility, rejection, and anger, they feel estranged from God and the church. Others feel they have failed—not only themselves and their families and friends, but God as well. At a time in their lives when they need the church the most, they feel unworthy. Many fear judgment and rejection.

These people also soon discover, judging by the reactions of members, they are not accepted as they once were. An identity crisis occurs in divorce, aggravated by the awkwardness or avoidance a divorcee may experience in a couple-oriented fellowship. They no longer fit into the same circles they once enjoyed.

"When a spouse dies, the obligations of friends and relatives are clear and certain rituals can be a comfort to all concerned. But there is no

---

[4]Kenneth A. Erickson, *Please, Lord, Untie My Tongue* . . . (St. Louis: Concordia Publishing House, 1983), p. 35.
[5]"Divorced Parents Stay Angry," *The Argus* (AP), Rock Island, Ill. (October 24, 1986), p. 14.

cleansing ritual for burying a dead marriage. In part, divorce from community occurs because society has not developed accepted behavior for either the divorced or those interacting with them."[6]

In short, people don't know what to say or how to act toward the divorced person, so there are "invisible barriers" the individual experiences in the community of believers. Thus, disillusionment grows as divorcees do not experience the warmth and nonjudgmental acceptance they so desperately need. Lacking substantial support and finding themselves unwelcome, they often stop attending church services and fellowship group meetings.

Only in recent years have churches seriously considered the needs of divorced people and single parents. Unfortunately, too few organized, church-based programs exist. What should be a *constant*—reaching out to those with special needs—is the exception rather than a rule.

To minister to the needs of divorced individuals, the church should concern itself with the physical as well as the spiritual needs of its members—and their children—whose lives have been disrupted by divorce. Divorced women and men who have custody of the children, for example, frequently need affordable child care.

These are ways the church can use its resources to assist divorced persons:

A pastor can put the newly divorced individual in dialogue with another divorcee in the congregation who can truly understand what he or she is going through. An empathic pastor can provide the counseling important to the faith journey as he or she guides the individual through penitence, forgiveness, and rediscovery of hope that leads to healing and wholeness.

By surrounding them with acceptance and love, the church as a caring, supportive family of believers can do much to help divorced individuals. Healing takes place in a loving atmosphere where tangible evidence of God's love is conveyed through human caring.

Advice for the Newly Divorced

1. *Don't deny or suppress your feelings.* You will need to do "grief work." Keep in mind that mourning the death of a relationship is a process that leads to healing. Give yourself time to heal.
2. *Keep busy.* Force yourself back into the mainstream of living.
3. *Seek out other divorced persons and build new relationships.* They can understand what you are going through and will often offer the best advice.

---

[6]Diane Barnhill, "Divorce . . . Must One Be a Lonely Number?" *Menninger Perspective*, Vol. 2, No. 2, p. 6.

4. *Refrain from rushing into another intimate relationship on the rebound.* The breakup of another relationship before you have worked through your divorce can be doubly devastating.
5. *Pray for your former spouse and pray for strength each time you may encounter him or her.* Encounters may thus become less painful for you if tempered by God's love in your heart.
6. *Seek counseling.* If you or your children are experiencing pain so great you can't live with it, seek out a pastor or professional counselor to help you deal with it.
7. *Surrender to God the anger and resentment you feel.* These emotions are devastating if harbored continually. Ask God's forgiveness.
8. *Ask God's guidance as you redefine your personhood.* As you pick up the pieces of your shattered life, God alone can lead you from the valley of despair to a new sense of self, and give purpose and meaning to your life as a single person. Growth is not only possible, but exciting.
9. *Plan new activities for the painful holidays.* Perhaps family gatherings will not be the same as they were before the divorce. Planning new experiences will create memories unrelated to former celebrations.
10. *Reach out and help other people.* By helping others, you learn to like yourself and love again.
11. *Stay close to your children.* Communicate, be attentive to their grief.
12. *Suggested devotional reading:* Ps. 5:22; Jer. 29:11–13; 2 Cor. 1:3–5; Eph. 4:23, 24, 30–32; 1 Pet. 5:7.

How to Help Your Child with Divorce

1. *Tell your child how you feel even if you can't fully explain the feeling.* It's okay to let your child see you cry. Say, "I'll talk about it when I'm able."
2. *Give gentle explanations, but tell the truth.* When children are not given facts about the divorce, their imaginations will fill in the missing pieces and they may blame themselves for the divorce.
3. *Don't weaken the child's relationship with the other parent.* Don't use your child as a go-between or a means of getting even with your former spouse. Parents shoot an arrow through a child's heart when they talk negatively about each other.
4. *Don't try to make the child open up.* Be available, accepting, and nonjudgmental. Most importantly, LISTEN. Love is the most important healing factor.
5. *Be open to your child's need for physical warmth.* Touching will comfort and reassure a child of your love.
6. *Encourage the child to talk about his or her feelings with a trusted*

adult. Don't tell the child what these feelings should be. Their confusion and pain are real.

7. *Keep the lines of communication open with your children.* They are working through some of the same intense feelings you are.

8. *Encourage the family to accept God's love and yours.* Divorce in a family does not necessarily mean the parents do not love God.

9. *Don't assume that a child who has experienced divorce in the family is destined to have emotional problems later.* Be attentive, however, to your child's spiritual life and mental health.

10. *Expect the feelings in a divorce to be similar to those when there is a death in the family.* Realize though, that a family often receives more support after a loss by death.

11. *Seek professional help if the child is highly upset.* For most young children, healing after a divorce takes about one year. Time doesn't necessarily heal all wounds.[7]

Advice to Caregivers

1. *Be loving, offering total acceptance of the person.* Avoid conveying feelings of superiority or judgment. Only the heart of God knows what the divorced person has gone through, and God alone fully understands.

2. *Be open.* Avoid assigning blame to either partner. Blaming helps no one. Don't take sides. Each partner has unique needs and is hurting in his or her own way.

3. *Avoid hollow or cliché expressions of condolence.* Don't say, "I'm sorry." They are already feeling sorry. Also avoid saying, "I know just how you feel," or "You shouldn't feel this way."

4. *Greet the divorcee the same as you always did, with no more or no less enthusiasm than before.* Recognize and acknowledge his or her presence.

5. *Allow the person to express visible feelings of pain in your presence.* By saying, "Don't cry," you deny them permission to grieve, thus causing suppression of these painful feelings.

6. *Offer the gift of self.* The newly divorced person may need someone to talk to who will listen nonjudgmentally. You may begin a conversation by saying, "I know you are hurting, and I really care about that—and if you want to talk about it, I'll listen."[8]

7. *Keep confidences.* Assure the divorcee that you can be trusted and will not divulge what has been said in confidence.

---

[7]Adapted from the book *Please Come Home* by Doris Sanford, illustrated by Graci Evans, copyright 1985 by Multnomah Press, Portland, Ore. 97266. Used by permission.
[8]Erickson, op. cit., p. 39.

8. *Keep in touch.* You may have to initiate contacts with your friend. Though they resist, they may appreciate your continued concern for them.
9. *Offer practical assistance.* Be willing to provide child-care. Invite the single parent and children to your home, remembering their own family gatherings may no longer be possible. If the divorcee is seeking a job, inform her of job openings. Remember to call after painful court proceedings to reassure your friend that someone cares.
10. *Help the divorced person learn to trust life again and engender the hope that life can be beautiful.* God can heal painful memories and feelings. The divorcee needs to be reassured there is hope for the future.

Additional Reading

Allen, Charles L. *When a Marriage Ends.* (Soothing Words for the Pain of Divorce.) Old Tappan, N.J.: Fleming H. Revell Co., 1986.

Barnes, Robert J. *Single Parenting—A Wilderness Journey.* Wheaton, Ill.: Tyndale House Publishers, 1986 (fourth printing).

Benham, Arliss R. *The Long Way Back.* Grand Rapids: Baker Book House, 1977.

Biddle, Perry H., Jr. *Marrying Again—A Guide for Christians.* Nashville: Abingdon Press, 1986.

Buchanan, Neal C., and Eugene Chamberlain. *Helping Children of Divorce.* Nashville: Broadman Press, 1981.

Buscaglia, Leo. *Loving Each Other.* New York: Fawcett Crest, 1985.

———. *Personhood.* New York: Fawcett-Columbine Books, 1978.

Coleman, William L. *What Children Need to Know When Parents Get Divorced.* Minneapolis: Bethany House Publishers, 1983.

Colgrove, Melba, Ph.D., Harold H. Bloomfield, M.D., and Peter McWilliams. *How to Survive the Loss of a Love.* New York: Bantam Books, 1976.

Elliot, Elisabeth. *What God Has Joined...* Westchester, Ill.: Good News Publisher, 1983. (Booklet)

Fordham, Kate. *No Pit Too Deep.* (The Diary of a Divorce.) England: Lion Publishing, 1982.

Fisher, Bruce. *Rebuilding.* San Luis Obispo, Calif.: Impact Publishers, 1981.

Gardner, Richard A., M.D. *The Parents Book About Divorce.* New York: Doubleday, 1977.

Goldstein, Sonja, and Albert J. Solnit, M.D. *Divorce and Your Child—Practical Suggestions for Parents.* New Haven: Yale University Press, 1984.

Green, Carol. *I Am One.* Prayers for Singles—Minneapolis: Augsburg Publishing House, 1985.

Hensley, J. Clark. *Coping with Being Single Again.* Nashville: Broadman Press, 1978.

Johnson, Nancy Karo. *Alone and Beginning Again.* Valley Forge, Pa.: Judson Press, 1982.

Krantzler, Mel. *Creative Divorce.* New York: A Signet Book, 1973, 1974.

Krebs, Richard. *Alone Again.* Minneapolis: Augsburg Publishing House, 1978.

Miller, Keith, and Andrea Wells Miller. *The Single Experience.* Waco, Tex.: Word Books, 1981.

Mumford, Amy Ross. *When Divorce Ends Your Marriage It Hurts.* Denver: Accent Expressions, 1982.

Morgan, Richard Lyon. *Is There Life After Divorce in the Church?* Atlanta: John Knox Press, 1985.

Naifeh, Steven, and Gregory W. Smith. *Why Can't Men Open Up?* New York: Bantam Books, 1982.

Petri, Darlene. *The Hurt and Healing of DIVORCE.* Elgin: David C. Cook Publishing Co., 1976.

Smith, Harold Ivan. *Positively Single.* Wheaton: Victor Books, SP Publications, Inc., 1986.

———. *I Wish Someone Understood My Divorce—A Practical Cope Book.* Minneapolis: Augsburg Publishing House, 1986.

Smoke, Jim. *Growing Through Divorce.* Irvine, Calif.: Harvest House, Publishers, 1976.

Stearns, Ann Kaiser, *Living Through Personal Crisis.* Chicago: Thomas More Press, 1984.

Steward, Suzanne. *Divorced!* Waco, Tex.: Word Books, 1974.

———. *Parent Alone.* Waco, Tex.: Word Books, 1978.

Wallerstein, Judith S., and Joan Berlin Kelly. *Surviving the Breakup.* New York: Basic Books, Inc., 1980.

Weising, Edward F. and Gwen. *Singleness.* Springfield, Mo.: Gospel Publishing House, 1982.

Young, James J., C.S.P. *Divorcing, Believing, Belonging.* Ramsey, N.J.: Paulist Press, 1984.

For Children:

Gardner, Richard A., M.D. *The Boys and Girls Book About Divorce.* New York: Bantam Books, Inc., 1970.

Krementz, Jill. *How It Feels When Parents Divorce.* New York: Alfred A. Knopf, 1984.

Phillips, Carolyn E. *Our Family Got a Divorce.* Ventura, Calif.: GL Publications, 1979. (For ages 7–11)

Richards & Willis. *How to Get It Together When Your Parents Are Coming Apart.* New York: Bantam Books, 1977. (Excellent for Adolescents)

Ryan, Trevor. *What to Do When Mom and Dad Divorce.* Nashville: Abingdon Press, 1986. (For 8- to 12-year-olds)

Sanford, Doris. *Please Come Home.* Portland, Ore.: Multnomah Press, 1985. (For young children)

Organizations

Parents Without Partners, Inc.
7910 Woodmont Avenue, Suite 1000
Washington, D.C. 20014
(301) 654–8850

Has 1000 Chapters across the country for single parents. Publishes a magazine for parents, custodial and non-custodial, called *Single Parent.* Subscription: $15 per yr. Address: 8807 Colesville Road, Silver Spring, MD 20910.

America's Society for Divorced Men
575 Keep Avenue
Elgin, IL 60120

14

PART OF ME IS GONE

Mastectomy, Disfigurement, or Disability

Betty* believed the pea-sized lump she felt in her breast would go away. *Probably just a cyst*, she thought. When it was still there weeks later, she had a mammogram done. In August, after getting a second opinion, a biopsy was done.

"Cancer," the doctor said following the biopsy.

Betty and her husband, Bob, both agreed. "Do what you have to do," they told him. Surgery was scheduled for a few days later.

Betty's thoughts immediately flashed back to seven years before—in August—when her mother had died of cancer. She was tense, anxious, and numb with worry. It was hard to believe this was really happening to her—at age thirty-seven! She wondered if she would ever stop crying. She dreaded telling anyone, especially her father.

"Don't get crazy, Betty. You don't have all the answers yet," advised one friend. But it was hard not to jump to conclusions. What if the cancer had spread into the lymph nodes? She felt out of control, angry, sad—most of all, scared! Betty tried to keep busy and her mind on the present.

Sensing her needs, Bob put his arms around her and held her. "Talk to me. I want to know what you're thinking and feeling. I know I can't fix it, but I want you to tell me what it's like for you," he told her. "I'm scared, too, but this is happening to us as a couple. We will face it together; we have no choice."

During those troublesome worry-filled days, Betty appreciated the way Bob was able to accept her wavering moods.

Her prayers were questioning pleas. "Why did you let this happen to me, God? Why are you punishing me? What have I done?" She was angry with God. Bargaining, she promised to be a better person, to change. Ultimately, her prayers ended with just one request: *"God, be with me!"*

In the space of a few panic-filled days, she discovered it was okay to be angry with God. Her anger toward Him did not mean she loved Him

---

*Names of the women having mastectomies have been changed.

less, and she sensed God's ability to understand her anguish. In the past, the Christian faith had taught her God would be with her regardless of what happened. Now, she would have to rely on what her head was telling her, not her emotions.

On the day of surgery, Betty's father and sister flew in from out-of-state to be with her at the hospital, and waited along with other friends and relatives. "You're a strong person, you can get through this. I'm going to be in your corner," her father told her.

Betty was glad the waiting was over. She would get some sort of answer and would no longer have to wonder what this loathsome intruder in her body was going to do to her.

After surgery, her doctor's big grin was a welcome relief. "No nodes is good nodes," he announced. He had performed a modified radical on the right breast and there appeared to be no involvement in the lymphatic system.

Betty felt as if an albatross had dropped from around her neck. But the next morning, she began crying and couldn't stop. It was the beginning of a phase that lasted for more than six weeks, a phase she later referred to as the "close-call syndrome." Relief was replaced with a new set of worries and anxieties. She was angry it had happened and afraid the cancer would come back.

Every time she undressed, she was faced with her disfigurement. How did Bob honestly feel about her now? She couldn't imagine herself being very attractive to her husband. Her breasts were no longer symmetrical, and she hated the idea of a prosthesis. She had heard of husbands who couldn't bear to look at or make love to their wives after a mastectomy.

But Bob was different. He asked to see the scar, wondered how it felt to her, and watched as she did the painful arm strengthening exercises.

"I really feel ugly," she said one day, revealing her embarrassment and shame to her husband.

"Those are just your battle scars," he replied. Betty needed his constant and genuine reassurances that he loved her as a person. He was sensitive to her needs. She was also thankful he was patient with her unwilling-ness—at first—to have sex. All she wanted was to be held. But even that was painful.

"I'm ready when you are," he said lovingly.

As time passed, friends reminded Betty she should be grateful to be alive. But she had other things on her mind. "I was still so worried about whether the cancer would come back that I couldn't think of anything else," says Betty. "Gratitude and counting your blessings comes later."

Vicki's Reach to Recovery

Vicki was thirty-two when she had her mastectomy; her daughter was only twenty-three-months old. When faced with the choice of living or not living, Vicki felt the decision was simple. "I've got to be here for her," she said with determination.

Her husband, Peter, was also supportive. "There is no question about how I will feel about you. The important thing is that you'll be here with us," he told her.

One of Vicki's first concerns after her mastectomy was how others would react. She went back to work ten days after the surgery. Her friends were supportive, but curious. "Will you have to have chemotherapy or radiation?" they questioned. She knew they were really asking, "Are you going to die?"

She particularly remembers an elderly neighbor who came to her door one day. After a fleeting glance to see which breast was missing—something she eventually became accustomed to—he tearfully said he was glad she was home and doing well. His visit touched her deeply, for it showed he really cared about her.

While in the hospital, Vicki had been visited by a Reach to Recovery volunteer who, like herself, had had a mastectomy. Seeing another woman who had fully recovered and who could offer practical information and give moral support was invaluable. During the volunteer's visit, she was given an information kit with appropriate literature for her and her family, and a temporary prosthesis to wear. After her recovery, Vicki, too became a trained volunteer reaching out to other women experiencing the trauma associated with losing a breast.

Mastectomy Grief

Authors of *Living With Loss*, Dr. Ronald Ramsay and Rene Noorbergen, claim:

> While every physical loss is dramatic, few losses are as shattering as the removal of a woman's breast as the result of breast cancer. In our culture, the female breast is a prime symbol of feminity, and often its size and form determine a woman's sex appeal. Because they are also a natural life-support system for the offspring, they fulfill a vital physical as well as a symbolic role in the life of a woman. A woman knows that if there is a mastectomy, her life and entire future will undergo a dramatic change. She may perhaps feel mangled, disfigured, grotesque—even unwanted. The surgeon's knife has struck far beyond mere flesh. He has cut deep into the psyche of a defenseless woman, and only time will tell how well she survives. Some patients, they claim, take as many as eight years after the operation to get over their loss—and even then, the process is not finished.[1]

---

[1] Dr. Donald W. Ramsay, and Rene Noorbergen, *Living with Loss* (New York: William Morrow and Company, Inc. 1981), pp. 154, 155, 157, 159.

According to Ramsay and Noorbergen, the following phases of grief are common to many women:

Shock—Felt from the first moment she knows she has cancer. It remains with her until after the operation and one or both breasts have actually been removed.

Disorganization—She experiences an avalanche of conflicting and confusing emotions.

Searching behavior—Known as a phantom experience. Some patients report "feeling" the nonexistent breast at least once per day, others once per month. This may persist for years. These phantom experiences can be regarded as part of the searching for the lost breast.

Fear—The fear that she will be losing her breasts and may die holds her in an iron grip, sometimes from the moment of discovery until final reintegration. She may also fear her husband will not think of her as an adequate sex partner, and that her children no longer appreciate her. This can lead to feelings of inferiority.

Embarrassment or shame—She no longer feels like a "complete woman." She may turn her back when undressing, make love with a blouse on and the lights off, and may be unable to look at herself in the mirror while bathing. She may also be embarrassed when friends press for details of the operation, or when meeting close friends for the first time after surgery.

Desolate pining—Crying, feeling that life has ended, a desperate feeling of "not belonging anymore" and that no one cares are typical in this phase. Deepening feelings of loneliness, sorrow, hopelessness, helplessness and inferiority often lead to increased use of tranquilizers, sleeping pills and alcohol.

Despair—She may feel a sense of hopelessness best described as "a broken vase that cannot be repaired." Feelings that life is now without meaning and that suicide may be the best way to end her prolonged emotional crisis can occur during this stage.

Guilt—Based on the feeling that the mastectomy might not have taken place if medical help had been sought earlier, guilt may arise. She may also ask, "What have I done to my marriage?"

Jealousy—She may have a feeling of jealousy toward other women who still have their breasts. "I was once that way—but look at me now."

Protest and aggression—She may turn on the family as if they are to blame, may aggressively react to limited clothing, her inability to perform tasks that were once routine, and she may be angry with friends who regard her as a permanent patient.

Denial—She may exhibit a stubborn refusal to admit she has undergone a mastectomy and refuse to look at herself in the mirror. For example, she may hide the scar from her husband and undress in a dark closet.

Resolution and acceptance—When the emotions mentioned previously have been worked through and resolved, they give way to a total acceptance of the new reality. Then life for her once again becomes manageable.

Reintegration—This phase depends more on those who have been unable to give her the full understanding and the emotional support she has needed. Only when both sides work toward bridging the gap that has been created by the surgery can a conscious attempt at total reintegration become a fact.[2]

The Pain of Being Different

Disfigurement

Living in a society and culture that values beauty almost above all else, few of us—unless we ourselves have experienced it—can understand the pain associated with "being different." Added to the trauma of physical injury, disfigurement, or disability is the pain of being the object of obvious stares, the brunt of thoughtless statements, or avoidance because some (rather than risk saying the wrong thing) will say nothing to the victim, thus contributing to a sense of isolation and loneliness.

Michele McBride was a victim of the Our Lady of the Angels School fire which occurred December 1, 1958, in Chicago. The blaze claimed the lives of ninety-two children and three nuns. Michele was thirteen at the time. In her dramatic and sensitively written book, *The Fire That Will Not Die*, she gives numerous accounts of the thoughtless, sometimes devastating, comments people made that added to her severe physical and psychological pain:

> It was embarrassing for me and my friends when a stranger stopped me on the street to ask what happened to my face. This startled all of us, and everyone felt bad—and I never knew exactly what to say. People were crude and said things like "Are you contagious?" and "Should you be out in public?" Once someone told me I should stay at home and not frighten people on the streets. I tried to force myself into believing these people did not mean to be cruel . . . .
>
> Another time I was in a store with my girlfriend and we stood paralyzed in horror as a man grabbed the scarf off my head to display my facial scars to another person. The hurt I was experiencing from these onslaughts was worse than all the pain I endured in the hospital when all the bandages were pulled off my body.

---

[2]Ramsay and Noorbergen, op. cit., pp. 197–203.

Michele went on to say, "When people told me how brave I was, I always resented it. Bravery is a matter of choice, and I never volunteered for my position in the disaster."[3]

Julie Breuninger, founder of *Face to Face*, a support group for parents of children with cranio-facial disfigurements, relates her experiences. Julie's son, Jonathan, has Crouzon syndrome, a malformation of the skull and face caused by premature closure of the skull's suture lines. "Our society places so much value on beauty that people just couldn't accept Jonathan. We would go to McDonald's, and kids would ask why he looked so funny or parents would look away. When they'd hear him talk, they'd act surprised. They assumed he was retarded."[4]

Why do we react that way? How should we react? Again, the answers come from those who know best: the persons who are disfigured. In a newsletter article published by The Phoenix Society, a national organization providing self-help services to burn survivors and their families, these answers were given by Alan Breslau:

"It is perfectly normal to be alarmed at something or someone who looks out of the ordinary because it or they might present a threat . . . . The disfigured person is going to be cautiously examined to ascertain if there is any threat being presented. The other reason is that no one has taught us how to deal with people who are disfigured. When a child stares and the mother says, 'Don't look at him like that!' she is giving the wrong message. Not noticing disfigurement is as bad as staring, because if the disfigurement is obvious, then by looking away you are sending the message: 'discomfort.' "

Breslau adds, "As a disfigured person, I feel much more comfortable when people are direct, and ask, 'What happened to you?' By facing the reality, I can satisfy their curiosity, put them at ease, and probably make a friend. To the mother with the little child, I confront her and say, 'It's all right for her to look because I do look different, and it is normal to be curious.' Then I tell them both how it happened. Now I have two new friends.

"If we had some way of telling everyone how to deal with the disfigured, neither party would then feel uncomfortable again."[5]

Disability

Husband and wife, Patrick and Kathy Doherty were among the last persons in this country to contract polio. Both acquired it shortly before

---

[3]Michele McBride, *The Fire That Will Not Die* (Palm Springs, Calif.: ETC Publications, 1979), pp. 154, 147, ix. Used by permission.

[4]"Seeing with God's Eyes," *Today's Christian Woman* (March/April 1986), p. 31.

[5]Alan Jeffry Breslau, "How to Deal with the Disfigured and Disabled," *The Icarus File*, Vol. 4, No. 2 (Winter 1983) p. 1. Used by permission.

the Salk vaccine was introduced in the early fifties. Kathy was two years old; Patrick, six.

Today, though paralyzed from the waist down, Kathy walks with the aid of straight-leg braces and Canadian* crutches, using a wheelchair for longer distances. Patrick walks with a decided limp and occasional assistance of a cane or Canadian crutches.

Kathy and Patrick have a family, and are full-time health care professionals. Kathy is the director of a day program for the chronically mentally ill; Patrick is a rehabilitation counselor in a hospital.

Kathy cites one of the reasons she was able to accept her disability and adjust to normal living was her parents' attitude. They treated her as normal as possible. "I was expected to do household chores along with my sister, and they never restricted my activities. My parents wondered how I would survive on a college campus alone, but I always seemed to manage. When my wheelchair would get stuck in the snow, a couple of fellows would come along and lift my chair out of the rut, then be on their way. Generally, people want to be helpful. But I've been pushed a lot of places I didn't want to go," she said jokingly.

During her teen years, Kathy said the statement she resented most was made to her by someone who challenged her faith. "If you pray hard enough, you can throw those braces and crutches away." Kathy was pragmatic enough to know that just wasn't so. Her faith did not hinge on walking or not walking.

She can now look back and laugh at some of the things people have said to her over the years. "One person was bold enough to ask me how I got pregnant. Sometimes, I know things were said in ignorance. When one of my babies was born, someone asked, 'Do you suppose this baby will have to use a wheelchair or cane?' "

Comments made to Kathy vary greatly. "One person told me, 'You'd be pretty if that hadn't happened to you.' Another said, 'I'd rather be dead than have it like you have it.' It's not uncommon when we're out in public, in a restaurant for example, for a waiter to ask Patrick, 'What does she want?' People will address able-bodied persons rather than the disabled person.

"A lot of people tend to attribute a handicapped person with super-human qualities; we are extremely good, or very courageous. My sister once called me 'superwoman.' I just think of myself as having the same problems as any working wife and mother. People also tend to equate disability with sadness.

"My disability has never kept me from doing the things in life I really wanted to achieve, although it might be different if I didn't have the use

---

*Elbow to floor length.

of my hands. I would love to be able to dance—but, then, a lot of able-bodied persons don't dance, either.

"Many times my clients will ask why I can't walk. After I tell them, we can quickly come to grips with the fact that life isn't always fair, a feeling common to them, too," said Kathy.

In his job as rehabilitation counselor, Patrick works with some patients who have had head or spinal cord injuries, or are stroke victims. Others are amputees, or have debilitating illnesses such as Lou Gehrig's disease or rheumatoid arthritis. Unlike Kathy and Patrick, who have adapted to their disabilities over a period of years, many of these patients *suddenly* become disabled. One day they are fine, able-bodied workers; the next day, because of an accident or catastrophic illness, some are para- or quadri-plegic and will spend the rest of their lives in a wheelchair.

"At first, patients who have had a catastrophic injury often go through a period of denial and disbelief," said Patrick. "They think in a short time, their life will be back to normal and they'll recover. We live in a 'fix-it' society, so we tend to believe anything or anyone can be fixed."

Patrick says one of the most frequent questions they ask is, "Why is God punishing me?" They recall something they did and feel that God is now getting even. To that Patrick answers, "God doesn't work in that fashion!"

Some patients, he says, keep hoping for a miracle. "I try not to destroy hope; we all need hope. But I try to help them set realistic goals for themselves. Usually, their Number One goal is walking. If that is not possible, I try to help them set goals attainable within their limitations."

Patrick feels that it is normal for the person who has suddenly become totally helpless, dependent on others, and whose whole life has been changed overnight, to grieve those losses.

A disabled man may lose his job, and thus his role as breadwinner for his family; he may experience a loss of bodily and sexual function, athletic abilities, sometimes manual dexterity, and his self-esteem. A woman loses her role as a fully functioning wife and mother, sometimes her professional role, as well as her sexual and bodily functions. Most traumatic of all is their loss of control over their lives and feeling dehumanized. They have an "altered body image," a term used to describe the difficult inner thought process that the newly disabled or disfigured person experiences.

Patrick explains that while they are being treated as patients during the critical phase of their illness, victims are given passive care; nurses and doctors do everything for them. Once they become rehabilitation patients, the person is expected to participate in his or her therapy and work very hard to regain the use of what body function is left. He claims it's difficult for some patients to make that transition.

"Our goal is to make that individual as independent as possible and help him or her achieve an optimum level of function." That, says Patrick, often requires falling back on whatever coping skills the individual has acquired in the past—and a fierce determination. *"The ones who cope best are those who have a good emotional support system.* If they want to participate in life, the patients must rely on their inner coping mechanisms. The ones who make it are able to say to themselves, 'I don't like this. I don't know why it happened, but it happened. This is the way it is—but life goes on!' "

Patrick adds that patients have to become desensitized to the stares and the new ways people react to them, and this is often very difficult. It makes re-entry into society an even more painful adjustment. "For the rest of their lives, they are faced with the added burden of explaining what happened. Some resent having to do that."

Advice to Offer

Mastectomy Patients:

1. *Expect to feel sad.* Feelings of fear, anger, and loss are normal reactions. Allow yourself to grieve.
2. *Think in the present; take one step at a time.* Don't let your imagination run wild with fears for the future.
3. *Share thoughts and feelings with your family.* Families are usually very supportive and loving. This experience can draw you closer together. It is also a time for reordering priorities and discovering anew what is really important in life.
4. *Reach out to others.* Those who can help you most are those who have experienced similar pain. Friends may want to help but often don't know what to say. If you open the discussion, friends are usually relieved and eager to talk about the subject.
5. *If you have small children, be honest with them.* Explain the reasons for the surgery.
6. *Seek counseling.* If your spouse cannot accept these changes in your personal appearance and it's becoming a real problem for both of you, seek the aid of a qualified counselor. Ask your husband to go with you.

The Disfigured and Disabled:

1. *Openly discuss your thoughts and feelings with your loved ones.* Giving vent to feelings helps dispel them.
2. *Accept the fact that people are curious.* Explaining will be less of a burden if you project an image of self-assurance and comfort within

yourself.[6] Once the unknown is dealt with, persons are usually free to relate to you as a person from that point on.

3. *Ask for help when you need it.* Friends and relatives (and strangers) are usually eager to help, but often need specific suggestions on how they may do so. Some refrain from offering for fear of offending you.

4. *Mainstream friendships.* Maintain friendships between both able-bodied and disabled persons. You need them both.

5. *Try to keep your sense of humor.* It will help you over the rough spots and handle the absurdities that occur in life.

6. *Rely on God as a source of strength for daily living.* God has promised to be with us regardless of what happens to us. Draw from His strength as you meet each new crisis. Believe that God understands your anger, fears, and frustrations.

7. *Suggested devotional reading:* Ps. 139:7–12; 109:21, 22; 23:1, 2, 4; Isa. 43:1, 2; Heb. 4:15, 16; 13:5, 6.

Advice to Caregivers

1. *Give as much love and emotional support as possible to the newly disabled or disfigured person.* A person's physical, emotional, and spiritual survival is often dependent on the support given by caregivers. Remember your friend frequently with cards and letters. Visit your friend; don't abandon him or her. Keep the person informed about the work-a-day world and mutual friends.

2. *Love as God loves; relate to the person.* Do not ignore the disabled or disfigured person.

3. *Tactfully ask what happened if not knowing prevents you from relating to a disabled or disfigured person.* Most persons would prefer your asking, rather than being avoided, stared at, or misunderstood. For example, a burn victim wearing a Jobst body garment on his face (to reduce scarring) was once mistaken for a bank robber.

4. *Don't pretend it didn't happen if the incident is recent.* Acknowledge the loss and expect the individual to be fearful and sad. Give permission to grieve over their losses.

5. *Learn to emphathize.* Try to put yourself in their situation and imagine how you would want to be treated. *Listen* when and if they want to talk about the deep concerns that may weigh on their hearts and minds.

6. *Let the newly disabled do as much for themselves as possible.* Doing too much can be harmful to the person's adapting to life and this new reality.

7. *Be willing to assist when it is obvious help is needed.* Barriers, such

---

[6]Breslau, op. cit., p. 1.

as heavy doors or other obstacles, often prevent the disabled person's entry into a building.

8. *Take the time to listen to difficult speech.* Don't stand or sit in a place that makes the disabled person strain to see or hear you.

9. *To shake hands, extend your left hand if the patient's right hand is disabled.* This gesture is usually appreciated.

10. *Don't even hint that what happened to them is the will of God.* Rather, have confidence in their deep inner strengths. Affirm their faith and the fact that God helps us through whatever life may bring.

11. *Don't think of the amputee, disabled, handicapped, or the disfigured person as an object of pity.* They don't want or need your pity. They want and need to be heard, to be respected as a person with a voice and with rights the same as you.

12. *Don't equate disability with sadness or mental incapacity.* Many persons adjust quite well and have come to accept and enjoy life. Speak directly to the person; don't speak to someone else on their behalf.

13. *Lend your efforts in eliminating physical barriers.* Many older church structures, city buildings, and movie theaters are still not accessible to the handicapped.

Additional Reading

Brandt, Leslie. *Why Did This Happen to Me?* St. Louis: Concordia Publishing House, 1977.

Cox-Gedmark, Jan. *Coping with Physical Disability.* Philadelphia: The Westminster Press, 1980.

Eareckson, Joni, with Joe Musser. *Joni.* Minneapolis: World Wide Publications, 1976.

————, and Steve Estes. *A Step Further.* Grand Rapids: Zondervan Publishing House, 1978.

Hale, Glorya. *Sourcebook for the Disabled.* Philadelphia: W. B. Saunders, 1979.

Kushner, Harold S. *When Bad Things Happen to Good People.* New York: Schocken Books, 1981.

Lasser, Terese. *Reach to Recovery.* New York: Simon & Schuster, 1972. (For mastectomy patients)

Learning to Live With Disability: A Guidebook for Families. Available from the National Rehabilitation Information Center (address below).

Roth, William. *The Handicapped Speak.* Jefferson, N.C.: McFarland and Co., 1981.

Standhardt, Robert T. *Journey to the Magical City.* Nashville: Abingdon Press, 1983. (A quadriplegic person's reflections on suffering and love)

Whipple, Lee. *Whole Again*. New York: Caroline House Publishers, Inc., 1980. (For amputees)

Yancey, Philip. *Where Is God When It Hurts*. Grand Rapids: The Zondervan Corporation, 1977.

For Burn Victims

Bernstein, Norman R., M.D. *Emotional Care of the Facially Burned and Disfigured*. Boston: Little Brown & Co., 1976.

Bernstein, Norman R., M.D. Jean Ann Graham, Ph.D., and Alan Jeffry Breslau, M.S.Ch.-(Eds.). *Coping Strategies for Burn Survivors and Their Families*. New York: Praeger Publishing Company, 1987.

Breslau, Alan Jeffry. *The Time of My Death*. New York: E.P. Dutton & Co., 1977.

Bringgold, Diane A. *Life Instead*. Ventura, Calif.: Howard Publishing Co., 1976.

McBride, Michele. *The Fire That Will Not Die*. Palm Springs, Calif.: ETC Publications, 1979.

Rothenberg, Marie, and Mel White. *David*. Old Tappan, N.J.: Fleming H. Revell Company, 1985.

Snitker, David. *I Can Make It One More Day*. Newell, Va.: Bireline Publishing Company, 1983.

Sonnenberg, Janet, R.N. *Race for Life: The Joel Sonnenberg Story*. Grand Rapids, Mich.: Zondervan Publishing House, 1983.

Ton, Mary Ellen. *The Flames Shall Not Consume You*. Elgin, Ill.: David C. Cook Publishing Co., 1982.

Womach, Merrill & Virginia. *Tested by Fire*. Old Tappan, N.J.: Fleming H. Revell Company, 1976.

(The above books written by burn victims are available from The Phoenix Society, Inc., 11 Rust Hill Road, Levittown, PA 19056. Write for more information.)

Organizations

The *Reach to Recovery* program is affiliated with the American Cancer Society. For more information, contact your local chapter.

For more information about the *Face to Face* support group, write: Julie Breuninger, 431 Hawthorne Avenue, El Cajon, CA 92020.

The Phoenix Society (address listed above) has a newsletter for burn victims and their families who are members of the society called, "The Icarus File." Write for more information.

The National Rehabilitation Information Center has resource publications for the disabled person and their families. More information can be obtained by writing: 4407 8th Street, N.E., Washington, D.C. 20017, (202) 635–5826.

15

BY ONE'S OWN HAND

Death by Suicide*

Sharon quickened her step as she heard the commotion ahead. Loud, angry shouts tore at her heart: It was Dan's voice. A small crowd was gathering as she neared the scene. A male clerk was holding Sharon's twelve-year-old son's arms in an attempt to prevent him from hitting his younger sister again. Amy was dazed and crying.

Sharon had left them in K-Mart for only thirty minutes while she bought Dan's Christmas present in a nearby store. Like his father, Dan was becoming more and more abusive; she could no longer control him. Hurriedly, she thanked the clerks for separating them and hustled her troubled son and bewildered ten-year-old daughter out of the store.

"You can't come back to visit us," Sharon stormed at her son as she drove them both to her mother's home. "I don't even like you anymore."

Sharon and her husband, Roger, were divorced. Their eldest, Melanie, 15, and Dan lived with their father. She and Amy were living with Sharon's mother. Dan and Melanie visited her on weekends only. Melanie felt sorry for "poor daddy who was all alone," so she chose to stay with her father.

Few people knew why she had left Roger—most wouldn't believe her if she told them. Roger had a good-paying job. He was good-looking, well-educated, and was active in church and civic affairs. But at home, he was volatile and abusive. Once he had hit her. "Don't ever hit me again," she warned him. A minister-counselor had once told her to try to be a better wife, and she tried. But being a better wife didn't solve their problems. Roger had begun taking his anger out on the children until Sharon couldn't stand it anymore.

Sharon was the director of a social service agency and taking courses toward her master's degree. Her salary was not sufficient to support all three children. And Roger had contributed a mere thousand dollars that year toward Amy's support.

---

*Based on an interview with a mother whose twelve-year-old son committed suicide. Names have been changed.

As Christmas neared, Sharon relented and invited Dan to visit her. "I love you, Mom," he told her, embracing her. Sharon and Dan spent the weekend playing the new computer game she had bought for him. She loved him so much, and her heart ached for him. She was so grateful for those rare moments when the loving child in him came through. Dan had always been a very sensitive child, but over the years, his father's frequent verbal assaults had destroyed the boy's self-esteem. Sharon had witnessed her blonde-haired, good-natured youngster become more and more insecure. Now he was troubled and easily agitated and his behavior resembled his father's. Dan was taking his bottled-up anger out on his younger, smaller sister, Amy. He seemed depressed: his father said he was going to work abroad.

"What will happen to me?" Dan asked his mother. It was then that Dan first mentioned suicide.

The night it happened, Sharon was at class. After coming home, she answered the phone. Roger's voice was strained as he began, "Sharon, something terrible has happened. Dan hanged himself."

When she arrived at the emergency room, Dan was dead.

Melanie was tearless, staring at the wall. She and Dan had been home alone. Her father had gone to a church meeting. Melanie was doing her homework when she heard a thumping noise downstairs. Dan's body was suspended from a makeshift rope with a bandana tied loosely around his neck. Melanie immediately knew where he had gotten the idea—it was something they had seen that same evening on TV.

"I *tried* to save him, Mom. I shouted, 'Dan! Get up!' but he didn't move. I—" Her voice broke and she turned away.

Sharon lay in bed that night with Amy snuggled close beside her. Tears flowed, but she controlled her sobbing carefully so as not to awaken her daughter. Guilt began creeping in. Did I really say: *Don't come back. I don't like you anymore?* Yes, she had. *Oh, God, Dan talked about suicide and I didn't take him seriously!*

The community was stunned. Friends began filling the house that had once been Sharon's home. Among them was the Episcopal priest, the one person with whom she could share her pain and frustrations. Taking her in his arms he said, "Sharon, you can't look back and analyze all that you did or didn't do, and sit in judgment upon yourself. If we do, there's no end to the possibilities of where we came short of the very best. We have all failed at points in our relationships, but there is forgiveness for us, even now." His words comforted her and, later, she found herself going back to them again and again.

Mechanically, she and Roger made funeral plans. Sharon asked the minister to read Eph. 4:32 (TLB):

"Be kind to each other, tender-hearted, forgiving one another, just as God has forgiven you because you belong to Christ."

If only our home had been filled with kindness, thought Sharon.

Melanie sat stone-faced, refusing to cry through the entire service. Sharon could not cry, either. She was too numb.

She went back to work the day after the funeral.

The Emotional Aftermath of Suicide

In the days that followed Dan's death, Sharon found the words of one of her son's favorite songs running through her mind—"Hey, Jude, don't be afraid . . ." She found reassurance in the words. A review of all the things she had done for him passed through her mind: the time she spent her last five dollars to take him to the circus, the backpacking trips she took with him, all the good things . . . Sharon considered it the work of the Holy Spirit, God's way of comforting her.

As months passed, Melanie never cried about her brother. She moved into his room, wore his clothes, and wanted a baby to name after Dan. She met and became infatuated with a divorced man nine years her senior. Sharon didn't know how to get through to her.

Sharon faithfully read from her Bible. It had been the one source of comfort in her chaotic life. She had been reading from the Book of Job when Dan died. Her heart now cried out to God: "You had every right to allow this to happen because you are God. You just have to help me get through this."

At her job as executive director of the social service agency, Sharon had to be in control. But inside, she felt weak and helpless.

Things were falling apart in Sharon's world. Melanie had become suicidal and wanted to drop out of high school. Sharon's mother had a heart attack. Dealing with job pressures and public controversy involving an issue affecting her clients was getting to her. She had virtually no support system; others relied on her for strength, but few could nurture her in return. Now, cruel "if onlys" were haunting her. Sharon herself began entertaining suicidal thoughts.

Melanie's anger and depression deepened and her mood was becoming evident to everyone. Her outbursts were more violent and more frequent. One day, triggered by an exchange over the phone with her father, Melanie lashed out at Sharon, "I hate you! I hate you all!" she screamed, "I want to be with my brother."

Sharon's heart was breaking as she prayed, "Lord, I don't know what to say anymore. Melanie is a stranger to me."

Entering Melanie's room after the outburst, Sharon found her crying so hard she thought her daughter would choke.

"I couldn't save him. If only I had gone down sooner . . ." she began. Sharon enfolded her daughter tightly in her arms, crying with her. The grief that had separated them for many months was now drawing them closer.

Sharon read again and again from Isaiah 54: *Enlarge the place of your tent, stretch your tent curtains wide, do not hold back; lengthen your stakes* (v. 2).

Though the mountains be shaken and the hills be removed, yet my unfailing love for you will not be shaken (v. 10). As she clung to the passages in the months that followed, her understanding of its message became clear: *Sharon, choose to grow from this experience! Fill your mind with faith-filled, positive thoughts.* With God's help, Sharon and Melanie have survived and are building new lives for themselves.*

Teen Suicides Increase

More than 5,500 teenagers commit suicide each year; it is the third leading cause of death among teenagers. Among the causes of teen stress are family discord, disruptions, separation or divorce; excessive academic and social pressures; a painful loss such as a broken romance or the death of someone close; or relocating to a new city. Depression is a very common illness, even among teenagers. Adolescents who consider suicide generally feel alone, helpless, and rejected.

Other experts claim some types of rock music plant the suggestion of suicide in the minds of teenagers. In their book, *Why Knock Rock?*, Steve and Dan Peters with Cher Merrill write that often when things go wrong and a teen feels hopeless, then "rock music is most likely to have a major affect by convincing him death is the only answer to his pain."[1]

They tell Steve Boucher's story. Steve was a normal thirteen-year-old who was average in school and obedient to his parents. His interest in rock music began when the group *KISS* became popular in this country. As his absorption in rock music grew, he became defiant and began to stay in his room for hours. His mother thought it was a phase that would soon pass. Then he began smoking pot. They had no idea what influence his newly adopted rock "heroes" were having on him. They had no idea "that *KISS'S* LP'S were filled with songs about drugs and rebellion, and that *AC/DC* sang of revolt and self-destruction. . . . Neither parent recognized the connection between Steve's actions and his music." On March 27, 1981, Steve Boucher propped a 30–30 hunting rifle against the floor, leaned over it, and put the barrel to his forehead.

---

*It has now been four years since Dan's death. Melanie finished her education and is married. Sharon is finishing her master's degree, has run for public office along with holding down her agency job, and is energized by her ever-growing faith. She has also broadened her talents to include a writing ministry.

[1] Dan and Steve Peters, with Cher Merrill, *Why Knock Rock?* (Minneapolis: Bethany House Publishers, 1984), pp. 153. Used by permission of authors.

After his death, his parents were baffled. What had caused it? What thoughts had been going through his mind? Then they began to listen to the tapes and lyrics of the songs Steve had heard night and day. What his mother discovered astounded her.

In the lyrics of *AC/DC*'s "Shoot to Thrill," Sandee Boucher found some answers. The song goes, *"Are you willing? Keep it coming, and put your head up to me. I'm gonna pull it, pull it, pull the trigger. Super thrill, way to kill . . . I've got my gun and I'm ready and I'm gonna fire at will. . . ."*

"Anyone would have to be a fool to think that it had no influence," said Steve's father.[2]

"If a child was running for the road," Sandee reasons, "and a car was heading down on him, the parent would get the child out of danger. Also, if a child were reaching for fire, the parent would grab his hand and keep it away from fire. Music is as dangerous. We have an obligation to screen it . . . and get rid of it if it's dangerous."

The Peters brothers add, "Many groups play music that is best understood, and in some cases only makes sense, when the listener is on a mind-altering drug. And, of course, while in the suggestible frame of mind that drugs induce, the lyrics are free to wreak havoc on the listener's subconscious. That is why drugs and rock music are often accomplices in the suicide conspiracy."[3]

An Unspeakable Loss

There is also an alarming increase in the rate of suicides among the elderly—especially white males over sixty-five—in our society today. Men have been conditioned to keep feelings bottled-up; they do not willingly seek counseling. The white male in particular loses his identity, status, and economic security upon retirement, for we live in a society that says, "Who you are is what you do." Illnesses, poverty, and the loss of a spouse also contribute to the loneliness and hopelessness of elderly persons.

Mourning the loss of a suicide victim is often complicated and of longer duration than other losses. "Suicide is the most difficult bereavement crisis for any family to face and resolve in an effective manner," says Richard McGee, director of a suicide prevention center in Florida.

Though guilt is normal after any type of death, it is even more intense in cases of suicide. "Why didn't I see the warning signs? Could I have prevented it?" are questions that cry aloud for answers. These questions haunt friends of the suicide victim as well as relatives.

Suicide carries with it a stigma and leaves behind a bitter legacy of

---

[2]Dan Peters, and Steve Peters with Cher Merrill. op. cit., pp. 156–159.
[3]Ibid., p. 161.

shame, humiliation and embarrassment. It is the ultimate rejection, so survivors are often angry with their loved one for publicly rejecting them. Feeling abandoned is one of the most devastating and extreme feelings, for the suicide victim *has chosen* to end all relationships with those who loved him or her. Suicide is a powerful means of communication, and its message to survivors is devastating.

Thus, distorted thinking often occurs in survivors, and as a result, distorted communication can develop in families. William J. Worden in *Grief Counseling and Grief Therapy* describes what happens:

> The family creates a myth about what really happened to the victim and if anyone challenges this myth by calling the death by its real name, they reap the anger of the others, who need to see it as an accidental death or some other type of natural phenomenon. This kind of distorted thinking may prove helpful on a short-term basis, but it is definitely not productive in the long run.[4]

Some experts claim the ego strength in some families is so fragile that they must hang on to the myth created to survive, and friends and counselors should not try to shatter the myth.

In the event of death by natural causes, there is an openness which allows caregivers to respond naturally. This is not true in the case of suicide. Sometimes suicide is suspected but not confirmed publicly. Survivors may tell a few close friends; others can only speculate. Some families keep it a secret and allow friends to assume their loved one's death was the result of natural causes. Some suicides, however, make front page news.

The uneasiness sensed by friends manifests itself in ways that can later cause isolation for suicide survivors. Chris McCormick-Pries, A.R.N.P.*, says, "The supportive network drops off even more quickly for suicide survivors than it does for others. For the death of a child or spouse, the support given by friends and relatives usually lasts two to four weeks. With suicide, friends pull back even more quickly."

As in Sharon's case, survivors themselves may in time entertain suicidal thoughts. As one survivor has said, "A suicide in the family brings it into your experience and consciousness."

The role of the caregiver for survivors cannot be underestimated. Caring friends and relatives can play a key role in the survivor's mental health

[4]William J. Worden, Ph.D. *Grief Counseling and Grief Therapy: A Handbook for the Mental Health Practitioner* (New York: Springer, 1982), p. 82. Used by permission.
*Advanced Registered Nurse Practitioner, Chairperson of the Adolescent Suicide Prevention Task Force and member of the Mental Health Task Force on Suicide for Scott and Muscatine Counties, Iowa, and Assistant Director & Coordinator of Adolescent Outpatient Department at Vera French Mental Health Center, Davenport, Iowa. Private interview September 3, 1986.

and healing. In some instances, a sensitive and caring friend or relative can prevent further tragedy.

Causes and Warning Signals

"The only people who kill themselves are those who have lost all hope," says Marv Miller, executive director of The Information Center in San Diego. Dr. Miller conducts training workshops for social workers, medical and mental health professionals throughout the country. He claims that "95 percent of them do not want to die. The 'typical' suicidal person wants to be rescued. What these persons are seeking is relief or escape from an intolerable situation in which they are experiencing more stress, pain, grief, anguish, alienation, anger, frustration, disappointment, guilt, or illness than they can bear. There is no single cause of a suicide— only *causes*. Suicide is a permanent solution to what is usually only a temporary problem." Because of "tunnel vision," the suicidal person can no longer see other alternatives. Dr. Miller adds, "Suicide is usually the result of a gradual wearing away of the person's ability to cope."[5] Possible warning signs at any age include:

• Prolonged depression. Depressive symptoms include: sleeping and eating disturbances, lethargy, withdrawal and rebelliousness, tearfulness, sadness and discouragement, carelessness or recklessness, inability to tolerate frustration, inability or unwillingness to communicate, has difficulty concentrating, inactivity and boredom.

• Verbal statements such as "I'm going to end it all," "Life isn't worth living," or "I can't go on any longer." Many of the persons who commit suicide have told someone they were thinking of doing it.

• Abrupt changes in behavior and mood or work performance. This can include a sudden improvement in mood that may indicate the person has decided on suicide as a means to end his or her pain or solve his or her problems.

• Giving away personal belongings such as cherished possessions, which is a means of divesting interest in life and making final arrangements.

• Previous suicide attempts.

If a loved one or friend is threatening suicide:

1. *Take any suicide threat seriously.* Talk to the individual about it, reassuring him or her you will listen.
2. *Be direct. Ask feeling-oriented questions.* Say, for example, "Have your

---

[5]Marv Miller, *1985 Training Workshop Manual* (The Information Center, San Diego, Calif.), pp. 1, 3, 5. Used by permission.

problems been getting you down so much that you're thinking of harming yourself?" Remember, most people don't want to die; they merely want to end the pain.

3. *Be aware that the more specific the plan, the greater the risk of suicide.* If the individual has a gun or bottles of pills, and can tell you how he or she plans to harm him or herself, intervention is imperative!

4. *Reassure the individual that depression and suicidal tendencies can be treated.* Don't lecture or point out all the reasons the person has for living—it doesn't help.

5. *Be highly directive.* Don't ask people who are suicidal what they would like to do. Tell them what they must do—seek help. Be firm.

6. *Don't take on the job of counseling a suicidal person.* This is a job for trained professionals.

7. *Never promise to keep suicidal intentions a secret.* This is a secret you can't keep. Tell parents, a teacher, a school counselor, a spouse or other persons who need to know and who can take appropriate action.

8. *Refer your friend or relative to a clergyperson, school counselor, or mental health professional.* Explain that seeing a counselor or psychiatrist does not mean that he or she is crazy. Seek information from local mental health services or crisis hotlines. If none are available, call the *NATIONAL HOTLINE: 1–800–621–4000.*

9. *Engender hope.* Hope is light at the end of the tunnel.

10. *Be aware that it is not unusual for suicides to have a "cluster or ripple effect."* Others may imitate the behavior of teens or well-known persons who commit suicide. Teenagers tend to intensify and overreact to perceived relationships. A teenager may think, "If my hero or role model can't make it, how can I?"

11. *Parents, be aware!* Give careful attention to what your teenagers are eating, what time they get to bed, who their friends are, what influences their thinking, how things are going at school, and any kind of erratic behavior. Communicate your love and concern for them. *LISTEN TO THEM.*

If your friend or loved one has committed suicide:

1. *If you're not comfortable relating the circumstances about your loved one's death, don't.* You don't need to share the complete story with those not close to you.

2. *Don't try to deny or hide the anger you feel.* It is a natural consequence of the hurt, rejection, and abandonment you have experienced. Find someone with whom you can talk about this anger. If you are angry with God, share your feelings with a sympathetic clergyperson. Tell God. He can handle your anger. Ultimately, anger needs to be healed

through a willingness to forgive your loved one or friend for taking his or her life. You also need to forgive God for allowing it to happen, yourself for the things you may have done or not done while the loved one was alive, and life for being cruel.

3. *Try not to judge or criticize yourself too harshly for your behavior toward the person while he or she was alive.* Most persons feel guilty no matter how their loved one died. Accept the fact that no one person can take responsibility for another person's actions; there are limits to one's power.

4. *Seek professional counseling and/or a self-help grief group.* If your feelings are more than you can handle alone in working through the grief process, seek help from others.

5. *Attend worship. Reach out to caring, empathic friends, and return to your normal routine.* Share your time and understanding with someone else who is hurting.

6. *Trust God to give you strength one day at a time.*

7. *Communicate with children in the family.* Let them know the suicide victim was very unhappy—but don't give the impression that death is the answer to being sad. Let them know that taking one's life is a bad decision. They need to understand that the reasons behind the suicide may never be known.

8. *Children need to be told the mode of death.* It makes it more difficult to discuss the death if this is kept secret. A child's imagination is worse than actually knowing.

9. *Assure the child that you will be with them a long time.* Allow the child to express his or her feelings. Children need touching and much reassurance that they or their behavior are not the reason for the suicide. See Chapter 9 for additional information on talking with children about death.

10. *Suggested scripture readings:* Ps. 119:169, 170, 174–176; 130:1, 2, 5–7; 139:1, 2, 7–12; Ps. 141:1, 2; Matt. 5:1–12; Heb. 4:14–16.

Advice to Caregivers

1. *Acknowledge the death the same as you would the death of any friend.* Don't pry for information about the circumstances. Don't shy away if you do not know what to say. Your phone call, card, letter, or presence conveys acceptance and love.

2. *Acknowledge the bereaved person's pain.* Say, for example, "I know this is painful for you now."

3. *Show you care.* Weep with them, use the touch of a hand, a hug, an arm around the shoulder to say you care.

4. *Offer the gift of self.* Say, "I'm here because I care about you and I'm

concerned for you. I know that you've had a death in the family. I don't know all the circumstances but I want you to know I'm here for you and your family. Are there things I can do for you? Can I sit with you?" When you offer self, and when it is sincere, you seldom will sit in silence; you will have given your friend permission to grieve in your presence.

5. *Give them permission to be angry.* Say, "It's okay to be angry." When the survivors can verbalize anger, they can *externalize*, rather than *internalize*, the anger and put a name to it. Once it is external, they can better deal with it.

6. *Don't try to make them own up or admit to anything.* Most people don't want to say the word "suicide."

7. *Avoid asking questions or making statements that will cast blame on survivors.* They are already overburdened with guilt.

8. *Give them permission to talk about their loved one.* Don't be afraid to mention their loved one's name or to recall pleasant memories you shared with the deceased.

9. *Listen.* Don't analyze. Don't change the conversation. Don't make it heavier or lighter than it is. Don't rationalize suicide. Listen.

10. *Encourage the survivors to avoid judging yesterday with the knowledge of today.* They did the best they could with what they knew at the time. Help them assess how much of their guilt is valid.

11. *Stay in touch.* Telephone the survivors, remembering them on the painful anniversaries and holidays. Meaningful letters can be read over and over at difficult times.

12. *Watch for warning signs of unhealthy, morbid grief.* If after six weeks to three months, you see the following symptoms, there is reason to believe the survivor is experiencing complicated grief. The person will

    —be withdrawn, less emotionally accessible to friends and family.

    —be irritable, expressing other depressive symptoms.

    —have steadily deteriorating work, job, or school performance rather than returning to a fairly normal level.

    —be obsessed with details of the death.

    —continue to talk about the suicide victim as though he or she were still alive.

13. *Express your concern.* Do it in a manner that conveys genuine caring. Don't begin by saying, "You need counseling." In a private, well-timed moment free of distractions, begin by saying, "I am concerned about you. I've watched you during the past several months. I want to share my concern with you."

14. *Share your observations.* Give concrete examples: "You've withdrawn from your friends. You tell me all you think about is death. You've

even said you're not doing as well with the kids as you used to do. It's hard for you to go to work." Conclude by saying, "It's important you listen to yourself and recognize these symptoms are warnings that you are having trouble with grieving."

15. *Suggest that it is more than you or they can handle.* Say, "It would be helpful for you to speak to someone who knows how to help someone grieve."

16. *Help them find a counselor or support group.* Offer options, such as the clergy, a hospital chaplain, a mental health therapist, a private practitioner, or a self-help or support group.*

Additional Reading

Anderson, Luleen S. *Sunday Came Early This Week.* Cambridge, Mass.: Schenkman, 1982.

Baker, Don, and Emery Nester. *Finding Hope and Meaning in Life's Darkest Shadow.* Portland, Ore.: Multnomah Press, Critical Concern Series, 1983.

Baucom, John Q. *Fatal Choice—The Teenage Suicide Crisis.* Chicago: Moody Press, 1986.

Blackburn, Bill. *What You Should Know About SUICIDE.* Waco, Tex.: Word Incorporated, 1982. (Especially helpful for anyone living with a suicidal person or friend.)

Bloom, Lois A. *Mourning, After Suicide.* New York: The Pilgrim Press, 132 W. 31 St., N.Y. 1986. (A booklet)

Bolton, Iris. *My Son . . . My Son . . .* Atlanta: Bolton Press, 1983.

Cain, Albert C., ed., *Survivors of Suicide.* Springfield, Ill.: Charles C. Thomas, 1972. (Good for parents)

Coleman, William L. *Understanding Suicide.* Elgin: David C. Cook Publishing Co., 1979.

Davis, Creath. *Lord, If I Ever Need You, It's Now.* Palm Springs, Calif.: Ronald N. Haynes.

Elkind, David. *The Hurried Child: Growing Up Too Fast Too Soon.* Reading, Mass.: Addison-Wesley, 1981.

Grollman, Earl A. *Suicide.* Prevention—Intervention—Postvention. Boston: Beacon Press, 1971.

Grollman, Earl A. and Sharon H. *Talking About Suicide*, 1985. Creative Children, P.O. Box 1212, Polson, Mont. 59860. (A guide for youth)

Hewett, John H. *After Suicide.* Philadelphia: The Westminster Press, 1980.

Horton, Marilee. *Dear Mamma, Please Don't Die.* Nashville: Thomas Nelson Publishers, 1982.

---

*Advice to caregivers is information based on the interview with Chris McCormick-Pries.

Hyde, Margaret O., and Elizabeth H. Forsythe. *Suicide: The Hidden Epidemic.* New York: Franklin Watts, 1978.

Klagsbrun, Francine. *Too Young to Die: Youth and Suicide.* Boston: Houghton Mifflin, 1984.

National Institute of Mental Health. *Adolescence and Depression.* DHHS Pub. No. (ADM) 84–1337, Rockville, Md. 20857: The Institute, 1984. (Free single copy)

National Institute of Mental Health. *Depression. What We Know,* DHHS Pub. No. (ADM) 84–1318, Rockville, Md. 2–857: The Institute, 1984. (Free single copy)

Mack, John E., and Holly Hickler. *Vivienne: The Life and Suicide of an Adolescent Girl.* New York: NAL, 1982.

Madison, Arnold. *Suicide and Young People.* Boston: Clarion/Houghton Mifflin, 1981.

McCoy, Kathleen. *Coping with Teenage Depression: A Parent's Guide.* New York: NAL, 1982.

Page, Carole Gift. *Neeley Never Said Goodbye.* Chicago: Moody Press, Sensitive Issues Series, 1984.

Peters, Dan and Steve, with Cher Merrill. *Why Knock Rock?* Minneapolis: Bethany House Publishers, 1984.

Rosenfeld, L., and M. Prupas. *Left Alive: After a Suicide Death in the Family.* Springfield, Ill.: Thomas, 1984.

Ross, Eleanora "Betsy." *After Suicide: A Unique Grief Process.* Iowa City: Ray of Hope, Inc., 1986. $13.95 available from author.

———. *After Suicide: A Ray of Hope.* Iowa City: Ray of Hope, Inc.

Stone, H. W. *Suicide and Grief.* Philadelphia: Fortress Press, 1972. (Especially helpful after suicide occurs)

White, John. *A Christian Physician Looks at Depression and Suicide.* Downers Grove, Ill.: InterVarsity, 1982.

Wrobleski, Adrina. *Suicide: Questions and Answers; Suicide: The Danger Signs;* and *Suicide: Your Child Has Died—For All Parents.* 5124 Grove St., Minneapolis, Minn. 55436–2481.

Films

Teen Suicide, produced by MTI Teleprograms, Inc., a Simon and Schuster Communications Company, 108 Wilmot Road, Deerfield, IL 60015. 23 minutes. #4882MV. To rent or purchase 16mm. film or video, call collect (312)940–0208.

> Related Films:
> *A Last Cry for Help*
> *Amy and the Angel*
> *Everything to Live For*
> *Hear My Cry*

In Loveland: Study of a Teenage Suicide
Suicide: But Jack Was a Good Driver, CRM Films Collection as part of
their Conflict and Awareness Series, McGraw-Hill Films. 1974. 16 minutes.

Organizations and Newsletters

Suicide Prevention Center, Inc.,
184 Salem Ave., Dayton OH 45406
24-hour hotline: (515) 223–4777
Business phone: (513) 223–9096

Has publications available at reasonable cost and a quarterly newsletter, *The Ultimate Rejection.* Write to Wanda Y. Johnson, Editor, at the
above address for subscription. $5 yearly.

AFTERWORDS is another newsletter for people who are grieving a
suicide death. Send $5 to AFTERWORDS, Adrina Wrobleski, Box 53, Dept.
T., 5124 Grove St., Minneapolis, MN 55436–2481.

Ray of Hope
P.O. 2323
Iowa City, IA 52244
Eleanora "Betsy" Ross (founder)
Phone: (319) 351–0330
Offers guidelines for establishing support groups.

The Information Center
6377 Lake Apopka Place
San Diego, CA 92119

Maintains an updated list of materials on suicide and suicide prevention. Will send a free list of books, cassette tapes, articles and bibliog-
raphies. Enclose a stamped self-addressed envelope when writing for the
list.

More helpful information about suicide can be obtained by writing:

National Mental Health Association
1021 Prince Street
Alexandria, VA 22314–1932
Phone: (703) 684–7722
Ask for "Teen Suicide Can Be Prevented" prepared by the Kansas City,
MO, MHA, and lists of agencies which offer material.

American Psychiatric Association

1400 K Street, N.W.
Washington, D.C. 20005
Ask for "Facts About Teen Suicide"

To obtain a list of 100 centers and hotline numbers, write:

Contact USA
Pouch A
Harrisburg, PA 17025
Phone: (717) 232–3501

NATIONAL SUICIDE HOTLINE NUMBER: 1–800–621–4000

◇ **16** ◇

WITHOUT WARNING

Sudden Catastrophic Death

Lawrence Apple unwrapped the Christmas gift from their son Lowell, 37, his wife Jeanne, and son Shawn, living in Spring Lake Park, a suburb of Minneapolis.

"Look, Ann! It's a family picture!" he said as he gazed lovingly at the happy threesome. Lawrence Apple loved his five children more than anything or anyone else in the world—with the exception of his wife, Ann.

Unlike the short note in other years, this year their son had written a newsy letter and enclosed it with the Christmas card and gift. His words and thoughtfulness warmed Ann's heart.

Four days later, Lawrence and Ann could not bear to look at the picture. Lowell's letter was the last Ann and Lawrence would ever receive from their son.

On December 31, 1981, at 5 p.m., the phone rang at the Apple household. It was Jeanne's brother-in-law. He reported there had been a terrible accident. Jeanne had been killed, and Lowell and Shawn were both in critical condition in North Memorial Hospital in Minneapolis. Could they come?

Anxious to learn more, Lawrence immediately called the hospital. "It's a matter of time," the chaplain told him.

Lawrence then called the doctor assigned to their case. "I want the truth," he began. "I don't want to be told 'they're doing as well as can be expected.' I want the truth so we can begin coping with it."

"Your son has an open skull fracture," he began. "His left arm was mangled, so we had to amputate above the left elbow. He's been given nineteen pints of blood. Shawn has a closed skull fracture. There's not much hope for either of them," the doctor ended.

One by one, Lawrence and Ann called their other children—Joyce, and Dennis, Ron, and Frank—to break the news. Dennis, living near Chicago, made immediate plans to go to the hospital.

Lawrence and Ann are members of our congregation. My husband went to their home as soon as he heard and prayed with them. He then offered assistance in making travel arrangements. But Lawrence needed something to do; he preferred doing it himself. Numbly, he made flight arrangements for the next day.

As they disembarked from the plane, the stewardesses' cheery greeting, "Have a Happy New Year," fell heavily on their breaking hearts. Neither Ann nor Lawrence could respond.

The accident happened on snow-covered Interstate 94 at midday. The driver of a semitrailer truck braked to avoid an accident ahead, and his truck jack-knifed across the median strip to collide with three vehicles. Unavoidably, Lowell's car had driven under the trailer, shearing off the top of their car. Jeanne had been thrown from the car and killed outright. A passenger in another car was killed also.

At the Hospital

Ann still had hope; Lawrence did not after hearing the severity of their injuries.

Up to this point, it had all seemed unreal for Lawrence. His first glimpse of his son's room in the intensive care unit hit him hard. This was flesh of his flesh, a son too precious to lose. Shawn, 13, was in the bed next to Lowell's.

"I suggest you don't lift the towel covering your son's face," the chaplain warned. "Talk to them, touch them," he advised.

Ann whispered tearfully, "I love you," to her son and grandson while the respirator rhythmically beat, forcing air into their still bodies.

How can I wish life for them as a vegetable, if neither can live a full life? she thought. Ann put their lives in God's hands. There was nothing else they could do.

The next day, Lowell was declared brain dead. Would they consent to donate his organs? If so, it meant an autopsy and keeping him on the respirator.

"There's got to be some good out of this tragedy," Ann responded. They agreed, and signed consents.

Returning to the hospital to see Shawn the next morning, they found Lowell's bed empty. Lawrence prayed for strength not to break down. He couldn't stay in the room.

That afternoon, Shawn died.

A memorial service had been held for the Apple family in the United Methodist Church they attended in Spring Lake Park. Funeral arrangements were made in Wisconsin Dells, Jeanne's hometown.

Three closed caskets stood before the altar of the United Presbyterian Church, and beside them, the parents and grandparents of a family that once was, but who now lived only in the memories of loved ones and friends. It was a funeral few would ever forget.

Lowell Apple had been a highly skilled memory design engineer for Control Data Corporation. Once he had been sent to Paris to correct a faulty computer; another time, to the Internal Revenue Service Center in Kansas City as a trouble-shooter. He was given an Award of Excellence by his company. Jeanne worked as a computer technician at the same company. She had a marvelous sense of humor and loved life. Lowell had adopted Shawn as his own when they married six years earlier. Shawn was active in basketball and baseball, and Lowell had been his coach. They were a happy, vital family who had everything to live for.

Their gravestone reads, "Together Forever."

Inventory

The day after the funeral, Lawrence and Ann returned to Lowell and Jeanne's home. The immediate business at hand was taking a thorough inventory of all the family's belongings for tax purposes. Friends Terry and Yvonne Royle, the family lawyer, and Dennis and his wife assisted. Dennis was asked to serve as administrator of the estate. Every item, every piece of furniture, every tool was recorded.

Among their things, Lawrence found a puzzle-type block of wood on which was mounted the name, J-E-S-U-S, a Christmas gift from Jeanne's father. He studied it carefully, for he loved working with wood. And the name Jesus has special meaning for him, for he confesses Jesus as the Lord of his life.

Tearfully, Ann took down their two Christmas trees. It was hard, knowing Lowell, Jeanne and Shawn were never coming back to their home. Their shoes still stood by the front door where they removed them each time they entered.

Lawrence and Ann kept the things of worth only to them: picture albums, Lowell's Award of Excellence, his diploma from the University of Illinois School of Engineering, a watch that had belonged to Lawrence's father, and a few Christmas tree ornaments Ann had made for them.

The money they eventually received from the estate was given away as memorials. "That money was dearly bought. We don't feel right keeping it," says Ann.

For Lawrence and Ann, Christmases are tinged with a lingering sadness and longing.

Open Arms

The Apples returned to their home in Rock Island, Illinois, ten days after the accident. Knowing they would come home to an empty house, members of our church, Mildred Lamp and Marg Snyder, greeted them soon after their arrival with a hot meal and warm, loving embraces.

The next morning was Sunday. "I just have to go to church," Lawrence told Ann, "but the car won't start. I'll call the church to see if someone will pick us up." Soon a horn sounded outside their home. It was Peter Hong; he came to pick them up.

"We were greeted with open arms. That's the only way I can describe it," said Lawrence.

"For months afterward, often it was just a touch on the arm or a squeeze of my hand, an embrace, or just a 'How are you?' to acknowledge our need. It was comforting to know so many people cared," said Ann.

"Since the accident, I've had an even stronger desire to attend worship. My life just isn't complete without it," said Lawrence.

"I don't know how people go through such tragedies without faith," adds Ann.

"I've never blamed the truck driver. It couldn't have been helped. I heard later he didn't want to drive a truck any longer."

Blocking and Work Therapy

Ann had to take yet another Christmas tree down when she got home—their own. A year later, she could not find the ornaments.

"I had blocked it out," said Ann.

"We didn't talk much about the accident," Lawrence added. "We were trying hard to avoid dwelling on it."

"I would close my eyes and see them in the hospital beds, side by side," says Ann.

"We both had to keep our hands busy. I crocheted a rug, which I gave away when finished—it had served its purpose. Lawrence spent his time woodworking, making the JESUS plaques and clocks to give away as gifts," she explained.

"We would have gone crazy had we not kept ourselves busy," adds Lawrence. "You're just numb at first. Your mind and body form a shield to guard against any extra hurt. If we wouldn't have had each other to lean on, I don't think we would have made it."

The Plane Crash

"Do you have to go today?" Charlotte Graeber asked her husband, Vance, 53. It was Memorial Day—May 25, 1981.

"When I come home, we'll go out for supper," he replied appeasing her.

Charlotte thought nothing of it. Vance and his friend, Bob O'Day, often went flying on weekends. An experienced pilot, Vance was practicing for an upcoming competition in Cincinnati for single-place experimental aircraft. Charlotte understood her husband's love for flying, for she knew he craved adventure. She always thought of Vance as being special. And she felt special, too, for she gave him the freedom to pursue his interests. The week before they had looked at sailboats; he wanted to try sailing next.

Charlotte and Vance had been married eighteen years. Each had been married before, and each had two children from a previous marriage.

To pass the day, Charlotte and her daughter decided to go to the mall. When they returned from shopping, Bob O'Days' black van was parked in front of her house. *Oh, there's Bob,* she thought. Maybe Vance invited him back to the house. Bob followed Charlotte and her daughter inside.

"There's been an accident, Charlotte," Bob announced, his voice unsteady, his hands shaking.

Vance had crashed once before, landing in a soggy cornfield, escaping with bruises. "What hospital is he in now?" Charlotte asked.

Bob's behavior puzzled Charlotte. He was evasive, and he wasn't making sense. Clearly, he was distraught. She wished he would tell her what hospital Vance was in so she could go to her husband.

Soon, the doorbell rang. A police officer accompanied by a minister stood in her doorway. A memory flashed through Charlotte's mind. When she was eighteen while visiting her grandmother in Iowa there had been a similar incident; a police officer had come to the door and told her grandmother that her son had been killed. Suddenly it struck Charlotte— a police officer! A minister! Vance was dead!

"How did it happen?" she managed to ask.

"He went into a roll and never came out of it," Bob stammered.

The police officer and minister were strangers; Charlotte wanted them to leave. She went into her bedroom and wouldn't come out.

"I wanted very much to be alone. I was in limbo. I felt my body walking and talking but my mind didn't take it in; it refused to accept. I just wasn't there *except* when I was alone," said Charlotte. "I wanted to be alone with [thoughts of] my husband. I had the feeling that I didn't say goodbye."

On Center Stage

"I marveled that people—relatives and friends—needed to share my grief and my feelings. They were in their own grief, but they wanted to hear my feelings. I felt as if I were on stage," said Charlotte.

"My son called and wanted to be alone with me. We sat quietly for a long time. Finally, he said, 'You know, Mom, so many things Dad told me were really important to me. I wish I could tell him.' "

Where Are You?

For Charlotte, the question *why* was not a pressing issue.

"He was flying his plane and doing what he wanted to do. I knew it was an accident. He claimed that most plane crashes were due to pilot error. It was either that or he blacked out. I was just sorry he didn't get to do all the things he wanted to do.

"Vance had once said, 'When I go, I want it to be in my plane.'

"I did wonder: Did he know? Was he conscious? What was he feeling? When he crashed before, he told me he didn't have time to think; he was too busy trying to pull the plane out of the dive.

"Vance wanted to be cremated. I never saw his body, and I have never regretted that. It was his life, his body. How could you change what somebody wants for himself?"

John Monnett, designer of the experimental plane Vance flew, read a tribute to his friend at the funeral service. It touched Charlotte deeply. She longed to read a poem she had written for him, but others discouraged her, thinking it would cause her to break down. Later, she regretted not having done so.

At John's house following the service, Charlotte wandered among the relatives and friends, greeting and thanking them for coming.

"All the while, I kept saying to myself, 'Vance, you're dead! You're dead! You should be here. Where are you? Will you tell me where you are?' "

Forgotten Grievers

"One of the saddest things of all is that few people allowed or acknowledged my mother's grief. My mother was very close to my husband. Nobody knew how much she loved him. Nor did most people acknowledge my son's or daughter's grief for their stepfather, even though he'd raised them. People gave their condolences to Vance's children. My daughter said later, 'I'm his daughter, too. Why doesn't anybody know that?' My son expressed similar sentiments."

The Better Place

Charlotte presents creative arts programs for school children, and two weeks prior to Vance's death, she presented a program for second graders. She told the children how much her husband loved to fly in his plane. A few days after the crash, a large manila envelope arrived for her. It was filled with pictures second graders had drawn.

"I sat down on the floor and read them. They wrote from the heart; they drew pictures of planes in the air, planes crashing and going to heaven. On one, the cloud said, 'The Better Place.' Several drawings showed his plane with angel-like wings going up into the sky.

"I was so grateful the teacher didn't edit the pictures, but just sent them. It was a good thing to do."

Let Me Feel Grief

"My mother wanted to take all my hurt away. Others wanted me to take sedatives. I got very little sleep. But it was important for me to experience grief. I didn't want to hide or run away from it. I knew those moments wouldn't come back and Vance seemed so close.

"His work boots stood near the back door. It had been a struggle to get him into the habit of leaving them there. I put my feet into his empty boots and plodded around the house. I sat in his chair. I would go to the closet and press his clothes against my face so I could recall the smell of his body. These things made me feel good and sad and mad. I was angry and sorry that I hadn't said more of the things I felt about him. If we knew someone was going to die, we would say those things. Of course, had I said them, Vance would have asked, 'Why are you being so soppy?' "

"I would play music all night. I found Elton John's *Funeral for a Friend* very comforting.

"I was drawn toward stories on television of plane crashes. Although I had seen pictures of Vance's crash on television, those seemed unrealistic to me. I wanted what was left of the plane. Vance built it and it was something he loved. I asked my neighbor, Earl, to retrieve what he could. My children wanted something, too.

"A friend discouraged me by saying, 'Are you sure you want to do that?' But Earl never questioned. A part of the plane's propeller hangs above my bedroom window."

A Circle of Love

"The first week in June shortly after my husband died, I was out walking with my dog. I had been crying. Our neighbors, the Arizmendis, were in their yard and they saw that I had been crying and sensed my need. Little Anna Marie could never pronounce my name so she called me 'Jar' rather than 'Char.'

" 'Come, Jar,' " she said to me. Instinctively, Marie and Sergio, and their four children encircled me with their arms. They patted me, but said very little. I knew I was in the midst of a loving circle.

"It is the warmest memory I have."

The Saddest Dream of All

Before her husband's death, Charlotte sometimes had bad dreams after which she would wake up crying. Her husband would hold her, allow her to tell it, and comfort her until she could fall back to sleep. Following Vance's death, she had a dream that seemed particularly real to her.

"It was the saddest dream of all; it was about my dreaming. In my dream, I had fallen asleep. I woke up and Vance was not in our bed. And I was terrified . . . he was not there. *Maybe it's true, he is dead*, I thought. I ran out in the living room and he was there on the sofa. He was awake. I ran and threw myself in his arms. I cried and cried, and he asked, 'Another bad dream?'

" 'Oh, this is the worst. You're dead. You crashed in your airplane. It was terrible! It was real and I know it.'

"He held me and said, 'It's only a bad dream. You can stop crying.' Then I woke up and it was true.

"I value that dream. It was like he was reaching down to have a conversation with me. *He was there*. I felt his body and his arms. I smelled his scent. It was him; I heard his voice."

The Quiet People

"I am most grateful for my children's simple quietness and for the people around me giving in to my demands to be alone.

"I could see in my neighbor Earl's face a longing to help me. His concern was expressed in quiet, sensitive ways. He would say, 'I'm just going to check the oil in your car. Okay?'

"Least helpful were comments such as 'You should have stopped him from flying,' or 'He shouldn't have taken such chances.' Others wondered out loud whether Vance had a fatal disease and committed suicide. I knew that wasn't true.

"The quiet people helped me most."

The Impact of Sudden Death

Circumstances surrounding the unexpected death of a loved one often add to the traumatic impact upon the bereaved and those left in death's wake.

Danny goes off to school on his bicycle and is struck by a car and killed. Normally, his mother drives him to school. "*If only* I had not let him ride his bicycle!" cries the mother.

One morning, Betty and Carl have a quarrel because the checking account is overdrawn. He leaves for work angry. She is defensive and calls after him, "If you made more money . . ." Suddenly at work, Carl has a heart attack and dies. *"If only* I could tell him I'm sorry," says Betty.

Mother and teacher-astronaut, Christa McAulifffe, along with six other astronauts, is killed as the nation watches the Challenger explode a minute after take-off on Jan. 28, 1986. Her daughter's plea, "Don't go, Mom," seen on TV haunts the memories of children and parents the nation over.

A four-year-old boy is killed during a Mother's Day outing at a cemetery, crushed by a 500-pound headstone that toppled from a grave. "The boy was walking behind his parents when the monument just fell over," said the police.

Fourteen postal workers are shot by a crazed gunman in Edmond, Oklahoma. Innocent victims. All tragedies.

In some instances, sudden deaths are made public by news coverage, and involve law enforcement agencies. Public speculation may add to the family's bereavement and become an invasion of their right to mourn in private.

The impact of sudden death is devastating, for it happens without warning or a chance to anticipate what lies ahead. It allows no time for goodbyes, no time to make amends or ask forgiveness for harsh words spoken in trivial quarrels, and no time to express the love one feels but doesn't verbalize. The unfinished business of the day can never be transacted—it remains unresolved. It is like an unfinished song, the melody stopped in mid-phrase that longs for completion.

Weizmaan and Kamm describe the tremendous impact it has on a survivor:

> There is nothing to compare with the impact and profound shock of sudden unexpected death. The assault is a jolt to the system. After a sudden death the period of shock and disbelief is long lasting. Those who have suffered the sudden death of a loved one will experience a long period of numbness and denial.[1]

In *Grief, Dying, and Death*, Therese A. Rando says about sudden death:

> At least when a death has been anticipated, even though it puts tremendous emotional demands on the individuals involved, coping capacities are directed toward an expectable end. When the loss occurs, it has been prepared for. When this preparation is lacking, and the loss comes from out of the blue, grievers are shocked. They painfully learn that major catastrophic events can occur without warning. As a result, they develop a chronic apprehension that something unpleasant may happen at any time. It is this lack of security, along with the experience of being overwhelmed and unable to grasp the situation, that accounts for the severe postdeath bereavement complica-

---

[1]S.G. Weizman and P. Kamm, *About Mourning, Support and Guidance for the Bereaved* (Human Science Press, Inc., New York, 1985), p. 101.

tions that occur in cases of sudden death.[2]

William Wordon in *Grief Counseling and Grief Therapy* identifies seven special features that tend to complicate the grief process for survivors.

1. Sudden death usually leaves the survivor with a sense of unreality that may last a long time.
2. Sudden death fosters a stronger-than-normal sense of guilt expressed in "if only . . ." statements.
3. In sudden death, the need to blame someone for what happened is extremely strong.
4. Sudden death often involves medical and legal authorities.
5. Sudden death often elicits a sense of helplessness on the part of the survivor.
6. Sudden death leaves the survivor with many regrets and a sense of unfinished business.
7. In the event of sudden death, there is the need to understand why it happened. Along with this is the need to ascribe not only the cause but the blame. Sometimes God is the only available target and it is not uncommon to hear someone say, "I hate God."[3]

The devastating experience of sudden death, complicated by these unique factors, can frequently lead to negative behaviors, thoughts, and feelings which Parks and Weiss have labeled the "Unexpected Loss Syndrome."[4]

Sudden deaths are more likely to involve violence, accidents, mutilation, destruction and killing, stirring the worst imaginations in the bereaved. In some circumstances, the survivor cannot see the body, thus adding to the problem of failing to accept the finality of the loss.[5]

God-Given Grief Reactions

Most persons view grief as a negative experience. If, however, we view grief as a process one goes through to regain health and experience healing, then it takes on a more positive note.

Dr. Kenneth Moses sees grief as a natural, healthy, self-corrective process. He defines grieving as the ongoing, continuous, highly fluid process

---

[2]Theresa A. Rando, *Grief, Dying, and Death: Clinical Interventions for Caregivers* (Champaign, Ill.: Research Press, 1984), p. 52. Used by permission.
[3]William Wordon, *Grief Counseling and Grief Therapy* (New York: Springer Publishing Company, 1982), pp. 84–85. Used by permission.
[4]C.M. Parks and R.S. Weiss, *Recovery from Bereavement* (Basic Books, Inc., New York, 1983), pp. 93–94.
[5]Beverley Raphael, *The Anatomy of Bereavement.* (New York: Basic Books, Inc., 1983), p. 223.

whereby an individual can separate from someone or something that has been lost. "If you can't separate yourself from it, then a part of you dies with it," he warns. Grief is unlearned; it is a spontaneous, automatic process. The survivor needs the time to find within him or herself ego strength to deal with it and time to find the external system to deal with it. *Denial buys the time* that permits the survivor to deal with loss, to find ego strength, and gain a support system. Dr. Moses also believes that grieving is a social process. "You cannot grieve alone," he adds. "Grief requires a relationship with another significant human being. The problems with grieving are social."[6]

Advice to Offer Survivors of Sudden Death

1. *Allow yourself to grieve.* Give vent to your intense emotions. This sudden death has allowed you no opportunity to prepare yourself; therefore, you will be going through all the stages of grieving *after* the death. It is better to express—rather than suppress—these feelings. Tears give release to sorrow.
2. *Though you feel God has deserted you, the Bible assures us God has promised the Holy Spirit as your Comforter* (Heb. 13:5; John 14:16). God is as saddened as you are right now.
3. *Your body's grief reaction is normal.* You may experience disturbing physical symptoms. (See Summary for "Physical Symptoms of Grief.")
4. *Follow what feels right for you.* Don't let others dissuade you from doing what is meaningful for you.
5. *Tell friends and relatives how you want to be treated.* At times, say, "I want to be alone," if that is your wish.
6. *Share your troublesome thoughts and feelings with an understanding, nurturing friend.* Giving vent to feelings with a friend who can listen with acceptance helps dispel their intensity.
7. *Join a support group or grief recovery program.* Call your local hospital or ask your pastor if such groups exist in your community. Seek counseling with a pastor or psychologist if you feel continually overwhelmed.
8. *Keep busy, but not to the point you stop the grieving process.* Take time to mourn and let go. (See Summary for "Letting Go.")
9. *Give meaning to your life through helping others.* Try to do things that you feel are worthwhile so you can have good thoughts and feelings about yourself.
10. *Keep active in a church where Christian friends will continue to show support.*

---

[6]Kenneth Moses, "Grief Counseling and Mourning Therapy," Macomb, Ill., 1980. Address presented at Western Illinois University. Used by permission.

11. *Recognize there will always be a void.* The pain will lessen as time and life go on, but you may always feel your loved one's absence and have the feeling your family is incomplete.
12. *Recognize that suffering engenders growth.* On your own timetable and with God's help, you will survive and eventually heal.
13. *Scripture for Reflection:* Deut. 33:27; Ps. 46:1–2, 7; 91:14–15; Isa. 54:1–7; John 14:1–7, 15–21.

Advice to Caregivers

1. *Someone should stay with the survivor for the first twenty-four to forty-eight hours after learning of the sudden death.* Stay with the family, allow them to cry on your shoulder, to question God or the hospital staff without trying to temper the emotions and without discouraging them from using angry language.[7]
2. *Contact the family if you are a close friend.* You become a member of the vital support system your friend needs to cope with the disaster. Cards, letters, and personal visits help them realize how many friends they have.
3. *Ask a family member, rather than the bereaved, what needs to be done.* Notifying relatives, overnight accommodations for out-of-town relatives, and care of siblings can be of invaluable assistance. Don't *assume* someone else is doing it.
4. *Simply say, "I'm so sorry." Remember that touch—a handshake, a caress—can communicate tenderness and compassion.* Words are not always necessary.
5. *Never say, "Don't cry" or "You've got to hold up."*
6. *Refrain from saying, "I know how you feel."* You really don't know how it feels unless you've gone through a similar tragedy.
7. *Avoid telling them about similar accidents.* Statements that usually begin, "When such and such was killed . . ." only add to their burdens.
8. *Don't second-guess God's will or try to give explanations as to why it happened; just quietly be with your friend.* Saying a tragic accident is God's will can be cruel, as well as untrue.
9. *Avoid platitudes, clichés, and trite expressions.* "Everything will be all right," "You'll get over it," "Time heals all wounds," "At least he didn't suffer," or similar phrases do not comfort.
10. *Help your friend actualize their loved one's death by using the word dead or death.* It will help to affirm the finality of death. Trite phrases such as "It all seems like a bad dream," or "It's hard to believe he's

---

[7]Elisabeth Kubler-Ross. *Questions and Answers on Death and Dying* (New York: The Macmillan Publishing Co., 1974), p. 140.

really gone" don't serve to acknowledge this finality.

11. *Understand the survivors' need to talk about many of the same things repeatedly.* The repetition of the same things over and over again helps mourners convince themselves that the death has really happened.

12. *Comfort and acknowledge the grief of "forgotten" mourners.* Children, stepchildren, in-laws, grandparents, cousins, aunts, uncles, best friends—need your love and compassion also.

13. *Don't tell the survivors how lucky they are to have other loved ones or children who are still alive.*

14. *Assure the survivors that they are not going crazy and that they are experiencing normal grief reactions.* Feelings of disorganization and the inability to concentrate cause the bereaved ones to feel they are "losing their mind." They need reassurance that they are not crazy and that these are normal feelings.

15. *Understand your friend's need to be alone at times.* But don't allow the griever to remain socially isolated for long periods. Those who are left to grieve alone may move toward despair instead of acceptance.[8]

16. *Help your friend separate realistic from unrealistic guilt by asking questions.* "How could you have known that?" "Are you expecting yourself to have known things that couldn't have been known with any certainty?" Point out all the ways the bereaved is not to blame.[9]

17. *Allow your friend to talk about the deceased and don't be afraid to mention the loved one's name.* Conversation will be strained and unnatural if you decide that not mentioning his/her name is best for your friend. Such acts deny the loved one's existence.

18. *Understand the grief process is long-lasting.* Don't try to force your friend to "get over it" because of your own discomfort in dealing with his or her depressed state.

19. *Remember your friend on painful anniversaries and holidays.* A phone call letting them know you remember and care is helpful.

Additional Reading

Cato, Sid. *Coping with Grief—Healing Life's Great Hurts.* Chicago: Chicago Review Press, 213 West Institute Place, Chicago, Ill. 60610, 1983.

Colgrove, Melba, Ph.D., Harold H. Bloomfield, M.D., and Peter McWilliams. *How to Survive the Loss of a Love.* New York: Bantam Books, 1976.

---

[8]Randall Perry, "Care of the Bereaved," *Thanatos,* Vol. 6, No. 4, p. 3.

[9]Ann Kaiser Stearns, *Living Through Personal Crisis* (Chicago: The Thomas More Press), 1984, p. 39.

Grollman, Earl A. *Living When a Loved One Has Died.* Boston: Beacon Press, 1977.

Henry, Iona, with Frank S. Mead. *Triumph over Tragedy.* Westwood, N.J.: Fleming H. Revell Company, 1957.

Holmes, Marjorie. *To Help You Through the Hurting.* New York: Bantam Books, 1983.

Kreis, Bernadine, and Alice Pattie. *Up from Grief—Patterns of Recovery.* Minneapolis: The Seabury Press, 1969.

Price, Eugenia. *Getting Through the Night.* New York: Ballantine Books, 1982.

Stearns, Ann Kaiser. *Living Through Personal Crisis.* Chicago: The Thomas More Press, 1984.

Westberg, Granger E. *Good Grief.* Philadelphia: Fortress Press, 1962, 1971.

Wolff, Pierre. *May I Hate God?* New York: Paulist Press, 1979.

Wiersbe, Warren W. *Why Us? When Bad Things Happen to God's People.* Old Tappan, N.J.: Fleming H. Revell Company, 1984.

Williams, Philip W. *When a Loved One Dies.* Minneapolis: Augsburg Publishing House, 1976.

17

LIVING ON BORROWED TIME

Life-Threatening or Terminal Illness

During the summer of 1984, Ed Westendorf noticed a twitching in his left arm and a weakness in his shoulder. He went to a chiropractor who treated him for a pinched nerve. But when his condition didn't improve, he went to a medical doctor, who in turn, referred him to a neurologist. Tests revealed he had amyotrophic lateral sclerosis (ALS), commonly known as Lou Gehrig's Disease. By December, the right arm was affected and Mayo Clinic gave him the same diagnosis—ALS.

Despite years of research, the cause of ALS remains uncertain. It is characterized by the progressive deterioration of the motor nerve cells that control skeletal muscles. This deterioration results in increasing weakness and atrophy of muscles. Victims lose the use of arms and legs, and have difficulty swallowing, coughing, and deep breathing. ALS is a form of muscular dystrophy, a progressive neuromuscular disease, terminal in about three years. It primarily afflicts persons within the forty to seventy age bracket, the average age being sixty.

Ed was only thirty-eight.

Ed and his wife, Linda, were disbelieving. They read everything they could find, hoping it was something else. But by June 1985, the disease had progressed to the point where he had to quit his job as a truck driver with Roadway Express.

He could no longer do simple things such as work the zipper in his Levis or dress himself. "People don't realize what it is like to lose the use of your hands. You lose a lot more. I felt rejected, as if my manhood had been taken away. I was angry toward everybody. It was hard to get over, but you have to learn not to take your anger out on yourself or anybody else."

"I knew I couldn't cope with it all. I just couldn't," said Linda. "There was nothing I could do about it *except* turn it all over to God. I was able to do that before Ed could. We prayed a lot, and finally, Ed was able to do the same. We both have more peace of mind now."

Linda said the first year of her husband's illness, their children's school grades dropped drastically. Their son Joel, 18, and daughter, Skye, 12, had a lot of difficulty with anger and resentment. "They were very bitter," said Linda, "but we've never hidden anything from them. Ed and I believe in leveling with our children. It's been that way since the children were small—we go through things together. Now that they see us handling it, they have an easier time dealing with it."

Linda's personality is warm and loving, although she claims she is, by nature, a very impatient person. She and Ed laugh about her impatience, among other things. But she is sensitive to Ed's needs. His speech is slurred, and talking requires great effort for him. Linda allows him time to express himself and refrains from speaking for him.

The Shift in Roles

When Ed had to give up his $40,000 a year job, Linda was faced with compensating for the loss of income, in part by applying for Social Security Disability. "We went through a lot of red tape. I learned that it is important to have your birth certificates for all members of the family, marriage license, discharge papers—any legal documents—available at all times. We've made a will and I have also made funeral plans.

"It is hard for me to be independent when I'm still very dependent on Ed," says Linda, who is feeling the strain of carrying additional role obligations. On off hours, after working full time as a sales clerk, she finds herself doing all the odd jobs Ed or their son once did. Joel is now married and has his own family. Nurses stay with Ed while Linda works—up to sixteen hours a day.

What Helps the Most

"The thing that helped me most was finding out that there were a lot of people who cared and loved me *for who I was and am.*" Ed was once very muscular and well-coordinated. He and Linda taught dance for five years. Many of those acquaintances maintain contacts with them. "I can't go anywhere without having people ask me, 'How's Ed doing?' " Linda added.

"I once heard that if you make one good friend in a lifetime, you are rich," said Ed. "Well, by that standard I am independently wealthy. We all have people close to us who have their own way of showing how they care for us. It takes a disease or some other tragedy for people to express how they feel toward one another."

"But some friends avoid coming," said Linda. "Some can't stand seeing him the way he is. They tell me, 'I want to remember Ed the way he was.'

If they can't handle it, I suppose it is better they don't come and break down in front of Ed. People have to know their own strengths. I think it causes them to say to themselves, *That could be me.* But I would like for them to call and ask about him or send a note. It's the thought that counts."

Ed advises friends to *act natural as if nothing were wrong.* "All I care about is hearing how and what my friends are doing. I'd like to discuss with them the same things we used to talk about. My interests haven't changed. It bothers me to dwell on my own sickness.

"Linda needs encouragement. A good word from friends helps her a lot. The pressures can tear her down. The family needs support, too," he adds.

Their pastor calls on them every two weeks and gives Ed and Linda communion. "I appreciate his regularity, and his prayers help," said Ed.

Borrowed Time

When asked how it feels to be living on borrowed time, Ed replied, *"We're all living on borrowed time.* Those of us who know that the end may be soon know you live *one day at a time.* Some days are pretty hard to live through, but all you can do is reach for the top and hang on.

"If I had known the disease would progress this fast, I would have quit work a long time before and done a few things I always wanted to do. Linda and I would have traveled. I would advise anyone to *do all he can while he can*!

"Emotionally, I have a hard time—like most men—saying what I really feel. I used to think about how I felt toward people, but when it came to telling them face to face, it was very hard. Having ALS has made me realize what I should have done a long time ago—tell them *now* that I love them. After having done it, I found 'it ain't all that hard.' "

A Foretaste of Heaven

Ed's breathing is labored. He suffers from headaches and pain in his lower spine and is confined to bed.

In December 1985, and again in February 1986, he had two experiences that he feels were a foretaste of heaven.

"Whether I stopped breathing, then started again, I don't know," said Ed. "I had the feeling I was falling down a long tunnel. All I can remember was it was easy to breathe and I felt as if there was nothing wrong with me. A voice at the end of the tunnel told me to 'go home.' They weren't ready for me yet. It had a very calming effect on me."

The second near-death experience was just as vivid for him.

"I was told 'no more pain,' " said Ed. "Three years ago, my uncle died of cancer . . . he was there waiting. Again, I was told to 'go back, not yet.' " Ed's eyes grew moist and he had to pause a moment before continuing. ". . . It was even more beautiful there than the Bible describes. I used to be afraid of dying; now I'm not. It's real simple," he ended.

People Die as They Live

The day Bill was diagnosed as having cancer, he and his wife Alice decided never again to say the word "cancer" or discuss his illness.

The day Tom was diagnosed as having a terminal rare blood disease, his wife Margaret began talking about his impending death to him, and in front of him with everyone she encountered.

Some persons choose never to tell; many are conditioned to avoid intimacy with others. Others choose to discuss it openly and seem to come to some acceptance of their fate, making it easier for friends and relatives to relate to them. Others are obsessed by it.

"People die as they live," says Carol Paper, Executive Director of Hospice Care in Scott County, Iowa. She had observed that if people live a certain way, they often die the same way. Some persons need to believe they're not going to die and refuse to deal with it. Others are angry and that anger becomes a source of energy. "And some truly have this eternal hope that something can happen, that doctors can be wrong. They will say, 'They don't know everything!' Who can counter that? It is their way of maintaining energy and hope to deal with the situation," says Paper.

Some tell her they would much rather be ignorant about what is happening to them, that way they would not have to be depressed all the time. They feel helpless because no one can do anything about it.

Paper reports that most people find it hard to know what to say to a person who's been diagnosed as having a terminal illness. To say nothing is to appear indifferent and uncaring. She suggests, if it is someone you know reasonably well, open a conversation by saying, "I understand you've been ill lately." *Then take your cues from the person.* If he wants to talk about it, he will. Tune into his feelings. If he chooses not to discuss his illness, then it is his choice. At least you will have acknowledged his illness and let him know you care about him.

Paper adds. "The ill person often thinks that friends are going to think less of them because they're ill. The patient thinks, 'They're going to see me undesirable as a friend.' People don't want to deal with it because they have to think about the possibility of their own death. They don't know what to say, so they avoid."

Anita Siegel, whose thoughts about cancer and living are recorded in the booklet, *The Sky Is Bluer Now*, says, "Cancer patients are often subjected to a social death long before a physical one. In the beginning, the attitudes of my family and friends had changed. They were uneasy around me, afraid they would say the wrong thing. Some people deal with this problem by not telling the truth, by denying their cancer. I think that's the biggest mistake that could be made. Even when people are not told, they know anyway. Being truthful from the start saves the energy you'd spend keeping secrets, although I can tell you that being honest won't always be easy."

A safe rule to follow is to *deal with the now and the person's present experience* without projecting an anticipated end or imposing a time limit on their lives.

Making the Most of What's Left

"Between the initial diagnosis and death, there's a lot of living to do," said Siegel, who discovered anew the meaning of life.

"In a way, I'm happy I got cancer. It changed my whole concept of what life is all about. My goals became different. My interests changed. The last eight years of my life have been much different from what they could have been if I hadn't been faced with the fact that my life might be coming to an end. I've accomplished more and I've experienced more than I could have imagined in an entire lifetime.

"When I drive down the street, I don't see the endless pavement anymore. I see the buildings and the beauty of their architecture. I see children—all kinds of people—even more for the individuals they are. The trees are greener now. The sky is bluer, and the planes seem to fly lower. I suppose you could say I have become more interested in the details of life.

"I want people to know that just because you are a cancer patient, you don't have to be sad or sullen all the time. You can have happy moments. You can have joy. If you look around, there are still things to get excited about."

Anita Siegel resents being called a "victim" or "terminal."

"I am a cancer patient. Victim sounds hopeless and helpless. I am neither. I also resent being called 'terminal.' Everyone is terminal, so that word really doesn't describe my condition at all."[1]

As The Family Assumes Homecare

One of the problems that plague families of the terminally ill is isolation, both for the patient and his or her family. This separation results mainly from withdrawal from familiar social contacts to commit time to the dying person.

---

[1]Anita Siegel, *The Sky Is Bluer Now* (Evanston, Ill.: Self-Help Center, 1981), pp. 3–4, 13, 15. Used by permission of Penny Siegel Swartz.

Isolation is also brought about by well-meaning friends who assume the family would prefer to be alone. And, of course, most persons are uncomfortable in the presence of death and dying, and fear not knowing what to say or do should the subject of death come up.

Caring church members, friends, and hospice volunteers can do much to alleviate the sense of isolation and abandonment for both the patient and family members by providing emotional support and bridging the gap between the outside world and the family that suffers the agonizing, gradual loss of a loved one.

Anticipatory Grief

The dying grieve about all their impending losses: the people close to them, as well as the ability to do things they once did. These anticipated losses engender a profound sadness, a process of separating themselves in preparation for death. In like manner, loved ones also begin this "anticipatory grief" or separation process.

"If the condition of the ill family member progresses gradually toward death, family members slowly get in touch with what is happening," says Barbara Giacquinta. "They begin to recognize the defeat and loss they feel, the strain of carrying additional role obligations, and their need to change sights, to find satisfactions with life as it is evolving, and to plan more realistically for their life together. Grieving usually begins at this phase."[2]

Because of this period of anticipation, when death finally comes, loved ones may display less public grief, and may find themselves expected to show emotion they have already worked through. Survivors may feel guilt and shame as a reaction to their own less-than-expected feelings, and the disapproval of others.

"Mourning is seldom complete, and significant grief work remains,"[3] says Therese A. Rando in her book, *Grief, Dying and Death*. Studies have shown that grief following anticipated loss is no less painful. But the anticipatory grief process has lessened the assault on the survivors adaptive capacities, unlike the grief associated with sudden death.

Why Can't They Fix My Daddy's Pain?

"Small children ask a number of impossible questions," says hospice director Carol Paper. They ask: What does it mean now that he's dead? Why didn't he take his body with him? What does God do with his body?

---

[2]Barbara Giacquinta, R.N., Ph.D., "Helping Families Face the Crisis of Cancer," *American Journal of Nursing,* Vol. 77, No. 10 (October 1977), pp. 1587–1588.
[3]Therese A. Rando, *Grief, Dying, and Death*, (Champaign, Ill.: Research Press Company, 1984), p. 38. Used by permission.

What is this heaven they tell me about? What do angels look like? How can you tell me it's real and how can you tell me he's really there?

"When you have a little child looking to you for an answer, it hurts so much, and you deal painfully with his questions. Children think adults know everything," says Paper. When an adult answers, "I don't know; nobody does," the inquirers tend to ask the same questions again and again, thinking eventually they'll get an answer.

"One young child kept asking me, 'Why can't they fix my daddy's pain?' and I had to answer him truthfully, 'They don't know how. I wish I knew how, and I wish it would be different.'

"It's important to let children know there are things in life even adults don't understand. In those cases, I assure the child he or she will be taken care of. Generally, *those are the questions they're really asking: 'Who's going to take care of me? Am I going to be okay?* Let them know that whoever is left is going to take good care of them. It's important also to reassure them that what happened to their parent won't happen to them. If you can't answer the impossible questions, answer those basic questions," Paper advises. "By doing so, you're rebuilding the sense of security they had established in both parents—or whoever the caregiver might be. Kids don't have a lot of control; their control rests in their parents. So long as that appears to be in order, they can continue to grow and build their own identify."*

Does Suffering Have Meaning?

We all fear pain; yet from infancy it serves as a warning mechanism within our bodies to protect us from the hot stove or alert us to an inflammatory process within. But when it ravages our bodies, or the body of a loved one, it sears the soul and torments us physically, emotionally, and spiritually. *Why does God allow suffering?* we ask. *Does suffering have meaning?*

Daniel Simundson, in *Where Is God in My Suffering?*, reminds us that "when we cry out to God in our times of suffering, we know that we will be heard by one who truly knows what we have gone through. It is a great comfort for a sufferer to know the presence of an understanding and compassionate God, who not only invites our very human prayers but also knows what it is like to be in so much pain. God hears. God understands. God suffers with us. The lament is heard by One who has been there."[4]

Fostering Hope

Hope is the basic ingredient of human strength, without which our souls cannot survive. Until the day we die, we need hope—our final hope

---

*Private interview September 25, 1985.
[4]Reprinted by permission from WHERE IS GOD IN MY SUFFERING? by Daniel Simundson, copyright © 1983 Augsburg Publishing House, pp. 28, 29.

of heaven and a continuing relationship with those who have gone before us and with God. Without hope, we despair.

Maurice Finkel in *Fresh Hope with New Cancer Treatments*, says, "Above all, what the cancer patient needs is hope. Hope to give him [her] the energy to struggle with his [her] illness—even if his [her] struggle fails. . . . The quitter always dies, the fighter has a chance of surviving."[5]

During the course of illness, hope cannot be sustained without the support of significant others. Both the patient and family members are very perceptive to the attitudes of hopefulness or hopelessness of the people around them. Hope allows the patient and the family to imagine a future.[6]

Hope means different things to the patient as he moves through the different stages of the illness. At first, of course, the hope is that he will get well or a miracle will happen. When he realizes that that is not going to occur, then his hope might be to finish uncompleted tasks. As time progresses, his hope might be to live long enough to see a son's wedding; and near the end, he hopes that the pain can be controlled. The day before he dies, the patient may hope to live long enough to say goodbye to his grandson who is coming home Saturday from college.

Caregivers need to concentrate on the person's needs and state of mind now, to encourage, understand, and foster his need for hope.

"No one wants to talk about it. People won't let cancer patients talk about dying, but they're all thinking about it," said a woman in the *Make Today Count* support group in Alton, Ill.

Yet the dying need to talk openly about the concerns they have. "Open dialogue is so vital and so necessary when you're talking about having a little time left. Communication is our greatest responsibility," says nurse thanatologist, Vickie Lannie.*

Advice to Those Who Are Ill

1. *Be realistic and face the issue.* Don't let denial engulf you.
2. *Live a day at a time and consider each day as a gift from God.* Cherish the moment. Make the most of the time you have left.
3. *Do all you can while you can.* If there are places you want to go and things you want to accomplish, do them while strength allows. Set goals for yourself. Life without meaning is empty.
4. *Keep your mind active.* Though physical limitations may become nec-

[5]Maurice Finkel. *Fresh Hope With New Cancer Treatments*. Englewood Cliffs, N.J.: Prentice-Hall, Inc., 1984, pp. vi, vii.
[6]Giacquinta, op, cit., p. 1586.
*Coordinator of palliative care services at Methodist Medical Center in Peoria, Ill., who speaks nationwide to health care professionals. Lecture May 30, 1984.

essary, your intellectual life need not be ended. Read, write letters, keep a journal, learn new projects. Use this time to prepare yourself spiritually.

5. *Maintain a positive attitude.* Self-pity is self-centered and self-destructive. You help those you love by your positive attitude.

6. *Retain your sense of humor and the ability to laugh at yourself.* It lightens the load for you and those who love you.

7. *Talk about your illness and your feelings with your spouse and loved ones.* Try to keep the lines of communication open. Understand that anger is a natural part of facing loss. Your spouse and loved ones may be angry because of your illness and you may feel that anger. Discuss these feelings; don't keep them bottled up. Bringing hidden anger out in the open helps dispel it. Understand it is a natural part of the grief process.

8. *Get professional help* if the stress of your illness affects your relationships and you cannot seem to regain good feelings about yourself.

9. *Seek out other persons with a similar illness,* someone who is going or has gone through it. A sharing of information and feelings can be very helpful for you personally. Join a support group.

10. *Help your friends support you.* Some friends will say nothing rather than risk saying the wrong thing. You can dissolve the barrier by bringing the issue of your illness up. When they see you are dealing openly and honestly, they are more at ease. Most friends are grateful if there is something concrete they can do to show their friendship. Tell them your needs.

11. *Write a will; consult your lawyer.* Protect your loved ones by having legal matters in order. It will spare them needless worry, stress, and legal entanglements.

12. *Let go.* Discover an unexpected strength which flows out of this experience . . . a new kind of strength which will allow you to admit your weakness to yourself, and sometimes to others, and live with the weakness of being human.

13. *Rely on God.* Take things as they come and you will discover God will give you strength to cope one step at a time.

14. *Tell your loved ones how much you love them and how much you appreciate their care.* Nothing is more difficult to bear than ingratitude or feeling unloved.

15. *Recognize that illness is exhausting for everyone.* Your loved ones may need time away from you to regain their strength and perspective on life.

16. *Investigate hospice services.* Trained hospice staff can be of invaluable support to you and your family, as well as assisting with pain management. Call the social services department of your local hospital for information about hospice services offered in your locale.

17. *Suggested devotional readings:* Ps. 39:4–5; 42; 139:1–18, 23–24; 2 Cor. 4:16–17; 5:2, 5, 8; 1 Pet. 5:7.

Advice to Caregivers

1. *Don't avoid me.* Be the friend . . . the loved one you've always been.
2. *Touch me.* A simple squeeze of my hand can tell me you still care.
3. *Call me to tell me you're bringing my favorite dish and what time you are coming.* Bring food in disposable containers, so I won't worry about returns.
4. *Take care of my children for me.* I need a little time to be alone with my loved one. My children may also need a little vacation from my illness.
5. *Weep with me when I weep.* Laugh with me when I laugh. Don't be afraid to share this with me.
6. *Take me out for a pleasure trip,* but know my limitations.
7. *Call for my shopping list and make a "special" delivery to my home.*
8. *Call me before you visit, but don't be afraid to visit.* I need you. I am lonely.
9. *Help me celebrate holidays (and life!)* by decorating my hospital room or home or bringing me tiny gifts of flowers or other natural treasures.
10. *Help my family.* I am sick, but they may be suffering. Offer to come stay with me to give my loved ones a break. Invite them out. Take them places.
11. *Be creative!* Bring me a book of thoughts, taped music, a poster for my wall, cookies to share with my family and friends . . . an old friend who hasn't come to visit me.
12. *Let's talk about it.* Maybe I need to talk about my illness. Find out by asking me, "Do you feel like talking about it?"
13. *Don't always feel we have to talk.* We can sit silently together.
14. *Can you take me or my children somewhere?* I may need transportation to a therapist . . . to a clinic for a treatment . . . to the store . . . to a doctor.
15. *Help me feel good about my looks.* Tell me I look good, considering my illness.
16. *Please include me in decision-making.* I've been robbed of so many things. Please don't deny me the chance to make decisions in my family . . . in my life.
17. *Talk to me of the future.* Tomorrow, next week, next year. Hope is so important to me.
18. *Bring me a positive attitude.* It's catching!
19. *What's in the news?* Magazines, photos, newspapers, verbal reports, keep me from feeling the world is passing me by.

20. *Could you help me with some cleaning?* During my illness, my family and I still face ordinary tasks: dirty clothes, dirty dishes, dirty house.
21. *Water my flowers.*
22. *Just send a card to say "I care."*
23. *Pray for me and share your faith with me.*
24. *Tell me what you'd like to do for me and, when I agree, please do it!*
25. *Tell me about support groups so I can share with others.**

Additional Reading

For the Person Who Is Ill:

Becton, Randy. *The Gift of Life.* Abilene, Tex.: Quality Publications, 1979.

Biegert, John E. *Looking Up While Lying Down.* New York: The Pilgrim Press, 1978, 1979. (Booklet)

Cousins, Norman. *Anatomy of an Illness.* New York: Bantam Books, 1979.

Davidson, Glen. *Living with Dying.* Minneapolis: Augsburg Publishing House, 1975.

Hubbard, David Allen. *Why Do I Have to Die?* Glendale, Calif.: Regal Books, 1978.

Johnson, Paul A., as told to Larry Richards. *Who Can I Turn To?* Portland: Multnomah Press, 1980.

Kubler-Ross, Elisabeth, and Mel Warslow. *To Live Until We Say Goodbye.* Englewood Cliffs, N.J.: Prentice-Hall, 1978.

————. *Death—The Final Stage of Growth.* Englewood Cliffs, N.J.: Prentice-Hall, 1975.

Moster, Mary Beth. *Living with Cancer.* Wheaton: Tyndale House Publishers, 1979.

Simundson, Daniel J. *Where Is God in My Suffering?* Biblical Responses to Seven Searching Questions. Minneapolis: Augsburg Publishing House, 1983.

Nolen, William A., M.D. *Surgeon's Book of Hope.* New York: Coward, McCann & Georghegan, 1980.

Swartz, Penny Siegel. *The Sky Is Bluer Now: Thoughts on Living with Cancer.* To obtain a copy, write: Self-Help Center, 1600 Dodge Avenue, Suite S 122, Evanston, IL 60201 or call (312)328–0470. Enclose $1.00

Tsongas, Senator Paul. *Heading Home.* New York: Alfred A., Knopf, 1984.

Watson, David. *Fear No Evil.* (One man deals with a terminal illness.) Wheaton, Ill.: Harold Shaw Publishers, 1984.

Rosenthal, Ted. *How Could I Not Be Among You?* New York: Braziller, 1973.

(*Taken from the brochure, "25 Tips to Help Those Facing a Serious Illness," Saint Anthony's Hospital, Alton, Ill. Special thanks to Saint Anthony's Hospital and *Make Today Count* for reprint permission.)

Yancey, Philip. *Where Is God When It Hurts?* Grand Rapids, Mich.: Zondervan Publishing House, 1977.

About Hospice Services:

Buckingham, Robert W. *The Complete Hospice Guide.* New York: Harper & Row, Publishers, 1983.

Callari, Elizabeth S., R.N. *A Gentle Death: Personal Caregiving to the Terminally Ill.* Greensboro, N.C.: Tudor Publishers, Inc., 3712 Old Battleground Rd., Greensboro, N.C. 27408.

Duda, Deborah. *Coming Home.* A Guide to Home Care for the Terminally Ill. Santa Fe, N.M.: John Muir Publications Co., 1984.

Hamilton, Michael P., and Helen F. Reid, Editors. *A Hospice Handbook* Grand Rapids: Wm. B. Eerdmans Publishing Co., 1980.

Stoddard, Sandal. *The Hospice Movement: A Better Way of Caring for the Dying.* New York: Steinard Day, 1978.

For Survivors:

Bozarth-Campbell, Alla, Ph.D. *Life Is Goodbye—Life Is Hello.* Grieving Well Through All Kinds of Loss. Minneapolis: CompCare Publications, 1982.

Colgrove, Melba, Ph.D., Harold H. Bloomfield, M.D., Peter McWilliams. *How to Survive the Loss of a Love.* New York: Bantam Books, 1976.

Elliot, Elisabeth. *Facing the Death of a Loved One.* Westchester, Ill.: Good News Publishers, 1973. (Booklet)

Grollman, Earl A. *When Your Loved One Is Dying.* Boston: Beacon Press, 1980.

Holmes, Marjorie. *To Help You Through the Hurting.* New York: Bantam Books, 1983.

Lewis, C.S. *A Grief Observed.* New York: Bantam Books, 1961, 1976.

Means, James E. *A Tearful Celebration.* Portland: Multnomah Press, 1985.

Mertzlufft, Nancy. *Gift of Life.* Kansas City, Mo.: Sheed & Ward, 1985.

Shepard, Dr. Martin. *Someone You Love Is Dying.* New York: Harmony Books, 1975.

Stearns, Ann Kaiser. *Living Through Personal Crisis.* Chicago: The Thomas More Press, 1984.

Thompson, Virginia. *Help Me, Lord—I Hurt.* Irvine, Calif.: Harvest House Publishers, 1978.

Vail, Elaine. *A Personal Guide to Living with Loss.* New York: John Wiley & Sons, Inc., 1982.

Westburg, Granger E. *Good Grief.* Philadelphia: Fortress Press, 1962, 1971.

Wiersbe, Warren W. *Why Us? When Bad Things Happen to God's People.* New Jersey: Fleming H. Revell Company, 1984.

For Children:

Krementz, Jill. *How It Feels When a Parent Dies.* New York: Alfred A. Knopf, 1981.
For additional books on explaining death to children, see Chapter 9.

For Caregivers:

Becker, Arthur H. *The Compassionate Visitor.* Minneapolis: Augsburg Publishing House, 1985. (Resources for ministering to people who are ill)
Burnham, Betsy. *When Your Friend Is Dying.* Grand Rapids: Chosen Books, 1982.
Dobihal, Jr., Edward F. and Charles William Stewart. *When a Friend Is Dying—A Guide to Caring for the Terminally Ill and Bereaved.* Nashville: Abingdon Press, 1984.
Dulany, Jospeh P. *We Can Minister with Dying Persons.* Nashville: Discipleship Resources, 1986. (Booklet)
Kopp, Ruth, M.D. *When Someone You Love Is Dying—A Handbook for Counselors and Those Who Care.* Grand Rapids: Zondervan Publishing House, 1980.
Richards, Larry. *Death and the Caring Community.* Portland: Multnomah Press, 1980.
Ryan, Juanita R. *Standing By.* Wheaton, Ill.: Tyndale House Publishers, 1984.
Taking Time. Support for people with cancer and the people who care about them. U.S. Department of Health and Human Services, Public Health Service, NIH Publication NO. 832059.
Yancey, Philip. *Helping the Hurting.* What You Can Do for Those in Pain. Portland: Multnomah Press, 1984. (Booklet)

Educational Materials

Full Circle Counseling, Inc., has booklets and tapes available often used for volunteer and professional training by hospices, high schools, colleges, hotlines, hospitals, etc.

Do You Want to Help Me?—The Art of Relating by Steve Henderson is a 24-page handbook.

Living with Life-Threatening Illness: A Patient Tells What It's Like. The experience of one man who is both patient and counselor.

Coping with Loss (Illness, Death and Grief). 60-minute lecture by Morgan and Steven Henderson recorded on cassette. Side one: "The Feelings of the Patient"; Side two: "The Feelings of a Family Member."

For more information, write Full Circle Counseling, Inc., Box 2726, Staunton, VA 24401

Ministering to the Terminally Ill is a set of three cassette tapes produced by David C. Cook Publishing Company of a unique seminar led by Joseph Bayly at which persons shared from their own experience, and three Christian doctors explore a difficult subject and offer help. Topics include: What Is Dying Like?, Why Is Dying Harder Today Than Ever Before?, What Do You Say to Someone Who Knows He Is Dying?, What About the Death of Children?, How Can a Christian Help? and How Can We Handle Grief? Check with your local Christian bookstore.

The National Hospice Organization has working papers and publications available concerning the hospice movement. Write:

The National Hospice Organization
301 Maple Avenue West, Suite 506
Vienna, Virginia 22180
Phone: (703) 938–4449

Videotapes and Films

How Could I Not Be Among You? by Ted Rosenthal, a young American poet who succumbed to Leukemia. It is available through Benchmark Films, 145 Scarborough Road, Briarcrest Manor, NY 01510.

Dying is a documentary film series that follows the last months' activities of several terminally ill patients including the Reverend Mr. Bryant, a Protestant minister ill with cancer, who terms his illness "the happiest time of my life." It is available through PBS Video, 475 L'Enfant Plaza S.W., Washington, D.C. 20024.

The University of Texas System Cancer Center in Houston, Texas, has scores of motion pictures and videotapes covering every aspect of cancer. For a complete listing write:

Department of Medical Communication
The University of Texas System Cancer Center
M.D. Anderson Hospital and Tumor Institute
Texas Medical Center
Houston, Texas 77030
Phone: (713) 792–6746

Make Today Count
P.O. Box 303
Burlington, Iowa 52601
Has 300 chapters and publishes a newsletter available for $10 a year.

I Can Cope education programs are offered through some hospitals for persons diagnosed with cancer. Contact your local or state office of the American Cancer Society or write:

American Cancer Society
Director of Service and Rehabilitation
777 3rd Avenue
New York, NY 10017

Information about cancer self-help groups nationwide may be obtained from:

Self-Help Center
1600 Dodge Avenue, Suite 3122
Evanston, IL 60201
Phone: (312) 328–0470

18

ALL ALONE

The Death of a Spouse

Bob McFarland always said he'd die young. And he said it would be from a heart attack—it ran in his family. That day came far sooner than either he or his wife, Rita, had anticipated. At the age of thirty-five, Bob died, leaving his wife and five children ranging in ages from two and a half to eleven.

Bob was devoted to his family. He made friends easily and his friends loved and admired him. His sudden death triggered an avalanche of kindnesses that overwhelmed Rita. Rather than giving flowers, friends gave generously to an education fund for the children. One friend stayed at the house during the funeral to assure their home would not be robbed. Others gave special attention to the children. A business associate stayed at their home several days following up on Bob's unfinished company business answering letters and doing whatever needed to be done. Rita felt as though their friends had "stopped" their lives to help her. And many did.

Just two weeks prior to his death, Rita and Bob had attended their first Marriage Encounter, an uplifting experience for both of them. Bob had written a letter explaining to their children all about this special weekend and what their marriage meant to him. Little did he know that, one day, his letter would be circulated around the world to other couples participating in similar Marriage Encounters.

Several weeks before he died, they had had a family portrait taken. "You can only pick one," Bob told Rita. What he didn't tell her was that he had selected other poses and had them gaily wrapped and marked for Christmas presents for his children, members of their family, and friends.

But Rita felt as if her whole world had collapsed when Bob died. She experienced a whirlwind of emotions. Unlike herself, but typical of many widows—especially young widows—she hated those she had once loved. She hated Bob for dying and leaving her all alone. She hated the children, for they reminded her of Bob, and they forced her to keep going when she really didn't want to go on living—not without Bob. She hated her friends, for they were couples, and she was now single, a misfit living in a coupled world. At times, she hated God, too. She felt cheated.

Then a near-miss accident with her aunt and uncle and the children during Thanksgiving holidays forced Rita to wake up and say to herself, "I want to live."

"As I look back over the months before his death, I can see where God was preparing us. But I still ask, 'Why did God let it happen?' "

Rita sought help by attending a Grief Recovery Group sponsored by a local hospital. She later joined and became actively involved in Widowed Persons Service, and over the years, has helped other widows and widowers who have experienced similar losses. It has been ten years since Bob died. To support her family, she resumed her job as a nurse.

A Summer He'll Never Forget

Russ Munn remembers the summer of 1977 as the worst summer of his entire life. His wife, Kay, a social worker, had died of cancer in May at the age of thirty-five, leaving him with a seven-year-old son to raise. Russ had lost his best friend, for he and Kay had had a good marriage.

"Losing Kay was like someone had carved something right out of the middle of me," said Russ. "I would find myself talking to Kay. And it wasn't inconceivable to me that she could hear me."

In the months that followed Kay's death, Russ was short-tempered and easily upset. His nerves were on edge. He would awaken often at 3 a.m. or 4 from a fitful sleep. He got up in the mornings exhausted.

He had worked hard to be "in control" of things during Kay's illness. This sense of disorganization and confusion he was now experiencing was stressful for him. But Russ never once denied his role as a father. Their son was a much-wanted, much-loved child from the start, and Russ took his responsibility for his son seriously. The boy was his anchor, his reason for living, for going on. Russ's job as a freelance designer allowed him the freedom to arrange his schedule so he could deliver and pick up his son from the day care center. But even the smallest tasks required giant efforts.

"I couldn't work," said Russ; "it wasn't important to me. All I could think of was Kay, and how alone and insecure I felt."

Russ found it helpful to consult with a psychologist during that summer. "There are things, like nightmares, you don't feel comfortable talking about with a friend," said Russ. After six sessions, he felt much relieved. Primarily, he learned that what he was experiencing was all part of the normal grief reaction.

He came to value those friends who stuck by him. "I needed those people," said Russ. "You wonder if anybody cares. I wanted to talk about Kay. Not about the grim details of her illness; I wanted to talk about the happy person that used to be in my life." He found one friend especially helpful—another widower like himself.

That fall, a friend in the advertising business asked Russ to spend half-days working for him. Structuring his time around a new job helped put an end to the agonizing physical symptoms he had been experiencing.

Russ is still a freelance designer and has not remarried. His son Alex is now in high school, and he and his father enjoy a very close relationship.

Asking the Hard Questions

Jim Terry owned and operated the *Geneseo Republic*, a small-town newspaper, for many years. His love for the newspaper and the community endeared him to the hearts of its townspeople. Jim always had a big smile for everyone. His pursuit of excellence commanded the respect of his employees, many of whom he had trained himself.

When he was diagnosed as having terminal cancer, his wife, Bettie, felt that she and Jim had to face the reality that time was running out. One day, mustering all the courage within her, she asked, "Jim, do you know you're dying?"

Jim had not known death was imminent.

His impending death involved the family business and certain legal issues had to be dealt with while Jim was able to do so. A lawyer was called in assigning Power of Attorney to Bettie.

Bettie's ability to deal with reality created a bond of trust between them that eased decision-making. She saw to it he was given the opportunity to participate in decisions about his care and the treatments he was given. They discussed whether extraordinary means or CPR to sustain life should be used. Jim said no. Funeral arrangements were discussed. Bettie never shrank from using the hard words like "death" and "dying."

She promised him that she and the doctor would help eliminate the pain as much as possible. As the end neared, Betty continually affirmed her love for Jim.

She told him, "You'll always be in my heart."

Each time she left his hospital room that last week, she said goodbye, knowing she might not see him again. One Sunday morning, Jim greeted her with his usual big smile . . . it was his last. He died shortly after she left the hospital.

"When they told me Jim had died, I actually had the feeling of joy, a lightening of my heart and spirit. The suffering—the terrible strain—was over for him. And for me, too."

Bettie kept a journal during his illness. She now looks back through it and feels good about helping Jim die with dignity.

"One thing I wanted most of all was to maintain my love and patience with him, and I was able to do that. I felt it was important, also, to release him. I learned that you have to give a loved one permission to die. I assured Jim time and again I would be okay."

Bettie is grateful they faced the hard issues together. She feels, by doing so, she eased her husband's dying, as well as preparing herself for the inevitable.

Work Therapy

Ruby and William Armstrong did everything together; they had been married forty-nine years. His death at seventy-six came as a surprise, even though she knew he had heart trouble and diabetes and had been in and out of the hospital during the summer of 1986.

After his death, Ruby was devastated. If only she had been with her husband when he had gone to the doctor! She could have made sure he reported more of his symptoms. They were never able to talk about his dying, and there wasn't time for goodbyes.

Ruby wasn't able to sleep in their bed for some time after his death— she slept on the couch. Sensing her grandmother's loneliness, her teen-aged granddaughter Kim curled up on the floor beside Grandma to keep her company. Ruby appreciates the love by which she was surrounded.

"Without my family and friends, I could not have made it through those first few weeks," says Ruby.

Eight months after her husband's death, Ruby is still tearful and finds it hard to talk about him. Ruby treasures the cards and letters she received, but reading them brings back the pain.

"Gradually, the good memories are beginning to come back," said Ruby.

To keep her mind occupied, though nearing seventy, Ruby found work in a doctor's office where she does filing and other duties. "Some days I come home so tired I'm ready to drop, but it's a good tired. It keeps me from dwelling on my thoughts." She adds, "It isn't good to sit home and feel sorry for yourself all the time."

But she realizes many friends in her age group are dying, and "It's scary feeling you'll be left alone."

A Gaping Wound

Few losses, with the exception of the loss of a child, impact an adult as intensely as the loss of a spouse. The years of shared memories, physical sexual bonding, and complex interactions create an entwining of lives that—when severed—threaten the remaining partner's purpose for living.

To measure stress, researchers T. H. Holmes and R. H. Rahe designed the Social Readjustment Rating Scale.[1] The loss of a spouse receives the highest stress rating of all life events on the scale.

Lynn Caine, whose husband died in his forties, says in her book *Widow* that she wishes someone would have explained the nature of grief to her. She writes:

> If only someone whom I respected had sat me down after Martin died and said, "Now, Lynn, bereavement is a wound. It's like being very, very badly hurt. But you are healthy. You are strong. You will recover. But recovery will be slow. You will grieve and that is painful. And your grief will have many stages, but all of them will be healing. Little by little, you will be whole again. And you will be a stronger person. Just as a broken bone knits and becomes stronger than before, so will you.[2]

Doug Manning in *Don't Take My Grief Away* describes grief this way:

> A cut finger—
>   is numb before it bleeds,
>   it bleeds before it hurts,
>   it hurts until it begins to heal,
>   it forms a scab and itches until
>   finally, the scab is gone and
>   a small scar is left where
>   once there was a wound.
> Grief is the deepest wound you have
>   ever had. Like a cut finger,
>   it goes through stages and
>   leaves a scar.[3]

In a home they once loved, the newly widowed now find themselves surrounded by painful reminders of their loved ones. The muddy shoes by the back door, the pipe and tobacco that once caused irritation, a closet filled with clothing that bears a familiar scent, a favorite perfume still on the dressing table—all painful reminders that for them, life will never be the same. Years of emptiness lie ahead.

For many, life seems to have stopped. Jane Seskin in *Young Widow* tells her feelings:

> I awoke the next morning at eight and stared out the window seeing the people on their way to work. It was funny, a slap in the face really, that life went on. The sun didn't stop shining, cars didn't stall on the freeway, people went about the business of living and yet our promising world, our little circle, was shattered. I couldn't seem to under-

[1]Holmes & Rahe, *Journal of Psychosomatic Research*, 1957.
[2]Lynn Caine, *Widow* (New York: William Morrow & Co., 1974), pp. 46, 47.
[3]Doug Manning, *Don't Take My Grief Away* (San Francisco: Harper & Row, Publishers, 1984) p. 68.

stand why the world hadn't stopped.[4]

One of the things most difficult to bear is not having a spouse to tell things to, for no one else is as interested in the everyday happenings of mutual interest to both partners. Some people report that the desire to share with the spouse goes on for years.

Another is the lack of physical touch—reaching across the bed to find it empty. A friend of mine said that after his mother died, he made a special effort to embrace his elderly father each time he greeted him. He recognized his father's need for affection and physical touch, a need once met by a loving partner.

A further difficulty is the desolate pining—the longing—and waiting for the loved one to come home at the end of a day's work. The widowed yearn to hear the familiar whistle or step coming up the walk.

An additional source of pain is the awareness of all the little jobs that a loved one did that the spouse was unaware of or took for granted—fixing whatever is broken or needs mending, sending Christmas cards or shoveling the walks. All these things are left undone once the spouse is gone.

The Young Are More Angry

Rita McFarland's intense anger is typical of the young widow who feels as though she has been cheated from having her spouse for a lifetime, like other couples. The young widow may be enraged also when she is left with young children to raise—especially if she has few job skills. These problems can be compounded by the lack of an accumulation of assets or insurance or the lack of a will clearly giving the wife the rights of survivorship.

In this country, there are presently 11.1* million widows, one-third of whom are under the age of thirty-five.

The Forgotten Man

Widowers, especially young men, often experience the unrealistic societal expectations for him to "be strong" and take it "like a man." The male is expected to be more resilient and able to control his feelings. These expectations may inhibit a man from openly expressing his grief. It should be clearly understood that both men and women experience the shock, the anger, guilt and loneliness, and depression that accompanies bereavement. When forced to suffer in silence, a man's pain can become unbearable for him and produce an inner rage.

---

[4]Jane Seskin, *Young Widow* (New York: Ace Books, 1975), p. 23.
*U.S. Bureau of the Census, *Current Population Reports*.

Traditionally, society has not understood the role, identity, and special plight of the widower. To the contrary, widowers must learn certain life skills such as purchasing children's clothing, doing laundry, buying food, preparing meals, learning household chores, and supporting grieving children. Loneliness is the greatest problem suffered and many widowers admit they are tempted to find a female companion too soon in order to fill the void.[5]

Loneliness is clearly the number-one problem for the widower, both young and old. The older widower may not have children living in the same community and thus finds himself totally cut off from family support systems.

Presently, there are 2.1 million widowers in this country. It is estimated that more than 550,000 are left with young children to raise.

Advice to Offer the Newly Widowed

1. *Allow yourself to grieve.* Don't try to "be brave" or stoic. You have lost the person most intimate and close to you. This intense grief will affect you physically as well as emotionally and spiritually. Manifestations of grief are confusion, depression, insomnia, loss of appetite, dizzy spells, self-recrimination and guilt, fear, anger, social withdrawal, and erratic behavior.

2. *Do not make any major decisions during the first year unless absolutely necessary.* Selling your house to avoid painful memories, moving out-of-state, making large investments, or selling the car are examples of things you might be tempted to do, but decisions you might later regret. Be on guard against those eager to exploit you.

3. *Make a list of the positive things you do to help yourself.* It will give you a sense of accomplishment to measure your successes, however small. Keep a journal. It will help you move forward in a positive way and express your innermost feelings.

4. *Keep in mind it's healthy to let your children remember.* Your unwillingness to talk with them about the deceased parent may close the subject. Keep talking so that they may vent their feelings. Listen to your children to help them work through the grief process. See chapter 9 for suggestions on how to help your child and books on the subject.

5. *Do not let your children control your life.* You do not need to ask your children's permission to date. Remind them you will never forget their parent, but that you need adult companionship.

6. *Understand that your status as a widow or widower may be perceived*

---

[5]Louise A. Allen, "The Forgotten Man: Creative Approaches to Helping the Widower," *Thanatos* (Spring, Vol. 8, No. 1), p. 5.

as a threat to a friend's marriage. For this reason, it would be helpful to develop new friends, especially in organizations for persons who have experienced similar losses.

7. *Understand that grief is long-lasting.* There is no time limit on emotions. Adjusting to life without your spouse is painful. Experts claim the most difficult period is seven to nine months after the death of a loved one.

8. *Seek professional counseling, especially if you feel suicidal.* Families, friends, and employers may not be understanding when they feel you should be over your grief. A clergyperson or psychologist can more objectively understand your needs and offer you counsel free of the personal biases of the untrained.

9. *Avoid the use of drugs or alcohol to deaden the pain.* Use of these substances can only lead to more problems, and in the end, intensify and prolong your grief.

10. *Keep busy.* Work can be very therapeutic. Resume your normal routine when it feels right to do so. Exercise can also be beneficial in overcoming depression.

11. *Rely on God to give you the strength to go on.* As you work through the grief process, you will need to redefine who you are and what you want to do with your life. Ask God to direct you through this process toward healing and a renewed purpose for living.

12. *Remain in the community of Christian friends.* Attending church may be painful; however, it is vital for you to stay in contact with caring Christian friends—and God.

13. *Suggested devotional reading:* Ps. 23; 32:8; 33:18, 19; 34:18; 39:4, 5; 103:15, 16.

Advice to Caregivers

1. *Acknowledge the death with a card or letter.* Letters can be saved and read time and again. Share an incident, story, or admirable qualities about the deceased in your letter. Sign the guest register at the funeral home so the family knows you visited if you cannot attend the funeral. It means a lot; your presence means you care.

2. *Call and visit often.* A significant letdown occurs after the funeral when friends have returned to their own routines. Remember, Sunday is the loneliest day of the week.

3. *Listen with your heart.* The grieving spouse will need to repeat the same things again and again. Ask how he or she feels and listen. Allow your friend or loved one to express feelings of guilt and anger. Listening and sharing his or her pain says you care. Don't be afraid of tears.

4. *Offer practical assistance.* The widow or widower will be assuming new roles and tasks once performed by the spouse. Lending a hand with a casserole, fixing a sink, offering a ride, or caring for the children can be an added boost for the grieving person who barely has enough energy to get through the day.

5. *Don't be afraid to mention the name of the deceased.* The widowed person wants to talk about someone who has been a very important part of his or her life. Tell the spouse you miss the loved one, too.

6. *Avoid clichés and explanations of why this happened.* Don't say things like "It's for the best," or "It's God's will." Your friend really doesn't want an explanation. Just care and listen.

7. *Don't mention remarriage.* Don't say things like, "You're young, you'll marry again." Such comments discount the life of the deceased partner and are not appreciated by a grieving spouse.

8. *Don't assign the role of the deceased parent to the eldest son or daughter.* Don't say, "Now you're the 'man' or 'woman' of the house." Such responsibility burdens a young person with an impossible task.

9. *Take the initiative in inviting your friend out to a specific event.* If your friend refuses, call again on another occasion. Be persistent. Suggest things you can do together rather than asking if they want to do something. Your friend may feel lethargic and may say no. Even if you simply go for a walk together, such contacts will help relieve the loneliness and initiate socialization. Encourage your friend to pursue new interests.

10. *Do not force your friend into relationships before he or she is ready.* The time may come when this person may appreciate your introducing him or her to new friends, but it should be in accord with his or her wishes.

12. *Don't be critical of the widow or widower for dating too soon, according to your standards.* Loneliness and the need for companionship is great and you need to understand his or her need to relate to someone of the opposite sex.

13. *Remember your widowed friend by sending a Christmas card the same as usual.* The bereaved are hurt by being dropped from a list and made to feel that their friendship is no longer valued.

Additional Reading

Brandt, Catharine. *Flowers for the Living*. Minneapolis: Augsburg Publishing House, 1977.

Brite, Mary. *Triumph over Tears*. How to Help a Widow. Nashville: Thomas Nelson Publishers, 1979.

Brooks, Anne M. *The Grieving Time*. A Month-by-Month Account of Recovery from Loss, 1982. For more information write: Delapeake Publishing, P.O. Box 1148, Wilmington, Del.

Burton, Wilma. *Without a Man in the House.* Winchester, Ill.: Good News Publishers, 1978.

Decker, Bea, as told to Gladys Kooiman. *After the Flowers Have Gone.* Grand Rapids: Zondervan Publishing House, 1973.

Grollman, Earl A. *Living When a Loved One Has Died.* Boston: Beacon Press, 1977.

Greenblatt, Edwin. *Suddenly Single: A Survival Kit for the Single Man.* New York: Times Books, 1973.

Holmes, Marjorie. *To Help You Through the Hurting.* Garden City, N.Y.: Doubleday & Company, Inc., 1983.

Jensen, Maxine Dowd. *Beginning Again.* How the Widow Can Find New Life Beyond Sorrow. Grand Rapids: Baker Book House, 1977.

Kohn, Jane Burgess and Willard K. *The Widower.* Boston: Beacon Press, 1978.

Kreis, Bernadine, and Alice Pattie. *Up from Grief—Patterns of Recovery.* Minneapolis: The Seabury Press, 1969.

Lewis, C.S. *A Grief Observed.* New York: Bantam Books, 1961. (Written by a widower.)

Manning, Doug. *Don't Take My Grief Away.* San Francisco: Harper & Row, Publishers, 1984.

Marshall, Catherine. *To Live Again.* New York: McGraw-Hill, 1957.

Means, James, E. *A Tearful Celebration.* Portland, Ore.: Multnomah Press, 1985. (Written by a widower.)

Neal, Emily Gardiner. *In the Midst of Life.* New York: Hawthorn Books, Inc., 1963.

Nudel, Adele. *Starting Over.* New York: Dodd Mead, 1986.

Nye, Miriam Baker. *But I Never Thought He'd Die.* Practical Help for Widows. Philadelphia: The Westminster Press, 1978.

Osgood, Judy. *Meditations for the Widowed.* Can be obtained from the Centering Corporation, P.O. Box 3367, Omaha, Neb. 68102.

Peterson, James A. *On Being Alone.* (AARP Guide for Widowed Persons.) A booklet available from American Association of Retired Persons, 1909 K Street, N.W., Washington, D.C. 20049.

Price, Eugenia. *Getting Through the Night.* New York: Ballantine Books, 1982.

Raley, Helen Thames. *To Those Who Wait for Morning—Thoughts on Being a Widow.* Waco, Tex.: Word Books, 1980.

Seskin, J. *Young Widow.* New York: Ace Books, 1975.

Temes, Roberta. *Living with an Empty Chair—A Guide Through Grief.* New York: Irvington Publishers, Inc., 1977.

Westburg, Granger. *Good Grief.* Philadelphia: Fortress Press, 1962, 1971.

Williams, Philip W. *When a Loved One Dies.* Minneapolis: Augsburg Publishing House, 1976.

For Children:

Krementz, Jill. *How it Feels When a Parent Dies*. New York: Alfred A. Knopf, 1981. (Death of a young parent.)

National Organizations

Widowed Persons Service
c/o Leo Baldwin, Coordinator
National Retired Teachers Assn.
1909 K Street, N.W.
Washington, D.C. 20049
Has groups in 55 U.S. Cities, uses specially trained widows and widowers who reach out to the newly widowed.

THEOS (They Help Each Other Spiritually)
1301 Clark Bldg.
717 Liberty Avenue
Pittsburg, PA 15222
(412) 471–7779
Will provide a list of chapters in your state upon request. Offers the newly widowed a magazine series called *Survivor's Outreach* for $15.00.

Parents Without Partners, Inc.
7910 Woodmont Avenue
Washington, D.C. 20014
(301) 674–8850
Many of the 1000 chapters of this organization of single parents conduct education for remarriage. More socially oriented and includes children in a variety of activities.

◊ **19** ◊

SOMEONE SHE ONCE KNEW

Gradual Loss of a Loved One
to Alzheimer's Disease

Pharmacist Fred Hauerwas looked puzzled as he set the prescription he had just filled on the counter. Beside it was another bottle of the identical medicine for the same person. He had filled the same prescription twice. Fred was forgetting a lot of things these days. In passing, he mentioned it to his doctor.

"We all forget. It's a normal part of aging," his doctor replied. But for Fred it wasn't normal, and it was growing progressively worse.

Five years later, he and his wife, Virginia, went to Mayo Clinic, Iowa City, and UCLA for neurological tests. After ruling out other treatable causes, Fred was diagnosed in 1970 as having Alzheimer's Disease. He was fifty-nine.

Virginia breathed a sigh of relief; at least they knew what it was. She went to the library to read more about the disease. *Merck Nursing Manual* had one paragraph which briefly stated: "Cause and cure unknown, usually attacks middle-age males, terminal in about 5 years, institutionalization required in final stages." No other information was available about the disease, nor could her doctor tell her much more. Virtually no research had been done on Alzheimer's disease.

Virginia was unprepared for what would follow.

At the height of his career, Fred had managed several pharmacies and won management awards. Now, he was unable to practice pharmacy. To keep himself occupied, he found a job that paid fifty cents an hour; he lasted one week. The couple invested in lapidary saws and rock polishers so Fred would have something to do with his time. Eventually, he forgot what to do and how to use the equipment.

Virginia found her husband could not make simple decisions or follow instructions. One day she asked him to heat a casserole for lunch while she finished her work. Soon, she smelled a strange odor. It was burning plastic: Fred had placed a plastic bowl directly on the burner.

"I can't do anything right," he said in disgust. Virginia could see her husband was deeply disturbed and bewildered by his own behavior and forgetfulness. Fred had always been a very private person who seldom revealed his inner thoughts and feelings. One day she found him sobbing. "I don't want to become a zombie," he cried. Virginia tenderly embraced him. The thought horrified her, too.

Few of their friends recognized what was happening to Fred, for he had become quite good at covering up, says Virginia. "His friends would come up and say, 'Remember me, Fred?' and Fred would answer, 'Sure, I remember you.' Unless you were with him for a longer period of time, you would think there was nothing wrong with him. Friends didn't believe me when I told them about his bizarre behavior and memory loss."

"As time passed, Fred became very fearful and suffered hallucinations. He would wake me in the middle of the night and want me to call the police. He thought someone was breaking into the house. This went on night after night," said Virginia. One night she discovered a loaded revolver under his pillow, which she promptly removed, unloaded, and hid. Fred replaced the gun with a stove poker, which he put by his side under the covers.

"Fred had never been a drinking man, but one day I found him in a stupor. He apparently was so disturbed by his condition that he wanted to escape by drinking heavily. That lasted only a couple of months."

Gradually, Virginia stopped going out in public with Fred. It was too embarrassing. She could never be sure what he would do. Friends stopped coming to visit or asking them out. It was no longer safe for him to drive, so she had to take the car keys away from him.

Fred began following Virginia everywhere. Other times, he wandered off and she had to go looking for him. In the evenings, he was anxious and paced incessantly. She had to keep a watchful eye on him twenty-four hours a day. Seldom did she get a full night's sleep. She had to label cupboards and drawers so he knew where things were. Roles changed and she had to look after all of their financial affairs, and care for their home. She consulted a lawyer and got Power of Attorney.

Virginia's own health was deteriorating, and she felt tired all the time. Caring for him was taking its toll on her physically, emotionally, and spiritually. Her daughter lived in California, and there were no other relatives or friends on whom she could call for relief. Some days her anger and irritation mounted after having to answer the same questions over and over again; some days she did explode. Afterward, she would be plagued with guilt.

"I regret the fact that Fred was not more open with me about what he was thinking and feeling in the early stages. I think I could have been more patient and understanding had I known what he was experiencing," said Virginia.

As his illness progressed, Virginia claims her husband became more and more meek. Unlike some Alzheimer's victims, he was never violent. He seemed to need and want more affection. Eventually, he became incontinent and regressed to a childlike, then infantile state. He is now in the terminal stages of Alzheimer's and is no longer verbal, nor does he recognize Virginia. It has been twenty-two years since the first symptoms appeared.

Virginia sold their home and has resided for the past eight years in a life care retirement center where Fred is a nursing center patient. She visits and feeds him faithfully every day. "Living here has probably saved my life. Had I cared for him by myself much longer, no doubt I would have died before Fred.

"I feel as if I am in limbo; I am not single, and yet I don't have a husband. I miss his companionship," Virginia says.

"For so many years I felt so alone. There were no adult day care or respite care centers then, and no one to talk to. Doctors didn't know how to help either of us. Fortunately, they know so much more about the disease and have support groups now."

Alzheimer's Devastates Families

In some ways Virginia is more fortunate than many. Some Alzheimer's sufferers undergo drastic personality changes and become violent as the disease progresses. No two patients follow the same course or speed of progression. From onset to total disability, it may take anywhere from three to twenty years or more.

And some families become virtually penniless. Most savings and resources must be expended before government benefits such as Medicaid can be obtained. When the patient must be confined to a nursing home, those expenses average some $17,000 to $20,000 a year. Neither Medicare nor private insurance pays for these expenses because it is considered "custodial care."

Donna Cohen, Ph.D., Professor of Gerontology and Deputy Director of the Gerontology Center School of Public Health at the University of Illinois at Chicago, estimates that in this country, there are 2.5 million Alzheimer's victims, and 1.4 million nursing-home beds are presently occupied by Alzheimer's patients. By the year 2030, she claims, there will be 9.5 million Alzheimer's victims and they will occupy 5.4 million nursing-home beds. The disease claims 120,000 lives each year.*

Alzheimer's has been known to strike victims as early as in their forties and early fifties, but most commonly in their sixties and seventies.

---

*Donna Cohen, Ph.D., "Practical Aspects of Home, Day and Nursing Home Care." Public lecture at Governor's Alzheimer's Disease Conference, May 18, 1987, Springfield, Ill.

Lewis Thomas, chancellor of Memorial Sloan-Kettering Cancer Center in New York, has called dementia [of which Alzheimer's is the most common form]

> a disease of the century . . . the worst of all diseases, not just for what it does to the victim but for its devastating effects on family and friends. It begins with the loss of learned skills, arithmetic and typing, for instance, and progresses inexorably to a total shutting down of the mind. It is, unmercifully, not lethal; patients go on and on living, essentially brainless but otherwise healthy, into advanced age, unless lucky enough to be saved by pneumonia.[1]

The caregiver, most often the spouse, becomes the "invisible patient" often succumbing to heart problems, high blood pressure, mental illness, cancer, or strokes. These health problems develop as a result of years of around-the-clock physical demands and sometimes emotional abuse from the Alzheimer's patient prior to his or her being placed in a nursing home.

Often, older persons worry about forgetfulness and can be inappropriately labeled as having Alzheimer's when momentary memory lapses occur. The distinction between forgetfulness and memory loss is this: "With forgetfulness, the lost idea will ultimately be remembered. The memory can be 'jogged.' Forgetfulness is not progressive and does not seriously interfere with daily functioning. However, with profound memory loss, when a thought is forgotten it cannot be retrieved with reminders."[2]

What Is Alzheimer's Disease?

Alois Alzheimer, a German psychiatrist and neuropathologist, first described the disease in 1906. It wasn't until 1976, however, that researcher Dr. Peter Davies presented his observation that Alzheimer's-diseased brains have a chemical deficiency. The chemical acetylcholine, a neurotransmitter which brain cells use to send signals to one another, is lacking. Acetylcholine is involved in memory processing, among other functions, and its absence may account for the severe forgetfulness typical of Alzheimer's. On autopsy, researchers have found small nerve fibers in the brain called "plaques and tangles" under the microscope that resemble twisted strands of yarn.

Alzheimer's disease is not hardening of the arteries, a natural course of aging, the aftermath of a stroke, depression, the result of injury to the head, or alcoholism. Nor is it communicable. Dr. Lowell Weitkamp at the University of Rochester has found evidence, however, that indicates some

---

[1]Charles Leroux, "The Silent Epidemic," *Chicago Tribune*, 1981. (First of three-part series)

[2]Carolyn J. French, M.S.W., Nancy Lyon-Morrison, M.Ed., and Eve B. Levine, M.S.W., *Understanding and Caring for the Person with Alzheimer's Disease* (Atlanta Chapter ADRDA, 1985), p. 5.

persons have an inherited predisposition toward the disease.

Presently there is no test to detect it, so other conditions, some of which are treatable, must be ruled out before a diagnosis can be made. Some one hundred reversible conditions may mimic these disorders. At this time there is no known cause, treatment, cure, or single diagnostic test for Alzheimer's disease.

In 1986, however, researchers at Albert Einstein College of Medicine in New York reported finding an abnormal protein, called A-68, in the spinal fluid of patients with Alzheimer's. Dr. Peter Davies and Dr. Benjamin Wolozin suggest that this finding may lead to a diagnostic test for Alzheimer's in the near future. That same year, Dr. William Summers and co-workers reported testing a new oral drug, THA (tetrahydroaminoacridine), on seventeen patients with presumed moderate to severe Alzheimer's. Ten of the seventeen patients showed significant improvement in performance. More testing and research needs to be done before THA's value in treating Alzheimer's patients is confirmed.[3]

In 1987, researchers found a genetic defect on chromosome 21 in studies done on families that had numerous cases of Alzheimer's disease in several generations. Two studies report a marker on chromosome 21 for the gene producing the brain protein amyloid. Amyloid is an important component of the neuritic plaques in the brain—one of the hallmarks of Alzheimer's disease. Scientists claim these breakthroughs will help researchers in their efforts to develop a test to detect the disease among living patients and is an important step in the development of useful therapies.

Grieving the Inevitable

Family members, especially those not in daily contact with the person, sometimes deny the problem, oftentimes adding to the stress, anguish, and isolation of the principal caregiver. The family grieves while watching their loved one's personality and unique spirit gradually die. This grief is often not recognized by other relatives, friends, and acquaintances because the onset is insidious, and the victim is still physically present. Depression is common in families, for the patient's condition only grows worse, never better.

Alzheimer's sufferers, in the early stages, also mourn the loss of their ability to think and react in appropriate ways. "And they are extremely intuitive and sensitive. It's like they're given an added sense. They mirror our feelings," says Jo Lindquist, co-founder of the Quad Cities Alzheimer's Disease Support Group and executive director of the local Quad Cities

---

[3]News Release: "Protein A–68 in Alzheimer's Disease," Alzheimer's Disease and Related Disorders Association, Inc. (November 10, 1986).

Alzheimer's Disease and Related Disorders Association (ADRDA). She works to find ways of reaching and bringing some pleasure to Alzheimer's sufferers. In her support group comprised of participants in various stages of the disease, she finds that one woman comes alive when dancing, for another it is listening to hymns, for another it is nursery rhymes. Most enjoy listening to the lively music popular during their youth. Art therapy is used also.

British geriatricians Isaacs and Gray claim that "at the core of every patient with brain failure there is an interest, a skill, an activity that can still be undertaken successfully that can give pleasure. Imagination and insight are required to find it."[4]

"Much of the agitation [of the Alzheimer's victim] is not a result of a disordered brain but of *hopelessness and helplessness*,"* claims Donna Cohen.

While Jo Lindquist works with Alzheimer's patients during the support group meetings held twice a month, trained staff listen to and meet with family members who are attempting to cope with day-to-day problems and frustrations of giving around-the-clock care. Members of the support group learn from one another and share a common bond of understanding.

"Sometimes total strangers treat my husband [with Alzheimer's] better than old friends do," complains one wife. "Our friends stay away; they just don't know what to say to my husband. It makes them too sad to see him like this."

Said another, "I get so angry. I can't even sit down and have quiet time for devotions. And then I feel guilty."

One wife admitted having to go outside the house so she could scream, giving vent to her anger and frustrations with her husband.

Community-Based Support Systems

To prevent burnout of family members, week-day adult day care centers are now springing up throughout the country. Cost for the patient is about $20 to $25 per day. In Day Center for Older Adults operated by Lutheran Social Services, one can observe a low-stimulus, safe environment with a regular routine, where Alzheimer's sufferers are cared for by staff members and volunteers who are compassionate, patient, and understanding. The facility is a modern one-level building formerly used as an elementary school (some churches are now providing space for adult day care centers). Using a holistic model, "participants" are treated with dignity, called by name, and receive lots of touching and warm hugs.

---

[4]Gray, B. and Isaacs, B. 1979. *Care of the Elderly Mentally Infirm*, p. 28. London: Tavistock Publications. Reprinted in, *A Better Life* by Coons, Metzelaar, Robinson & Spencer.
*Professor of Gerontology and Deputy Director, Gerontology Center School of Public health, University of Illinois at Chicago.

Their activities include simple tasks they can do with assistance (for those in early stages). The same staff members care for them every day to avoid added confusion. Adult day care can aid in postponing institutionalization in many cases.

Respite care, often provided by hospitals and nursing homes on a self-pay basis, is temporary (up to two weeks) custodial care which allows a spouse or family to take a weekend off or go on a family vacation.

A Gentle Approach Works

Because the person with Alzheimer's cannot process information or stimuli as he once did, caregivers must develop a whole new way of thinking and relating to that individual.

When working with Alzhiemer's patients:

DO:
Keep everything as simple as possible.
Expect the patient to ask the same questions repeatedly.
Give only simple tasks to perform.
Get some relief for yourself in your caretaking duties.
Hug the patient.
Remember he or she will follow you and want to know where you
    are.
Hold hands.
Be gentle.
Give instructions one at a time.
Ignore things which annoy you.
Remain calm and pleasant.
Get ample rest.
Keep the patient occupied (if possible) with simple chores.
Maintain your sense of humor.

DON'T:
Expect answers to your questions to be accurate.
Get irritated when the same questions are asked over and over.
Give instructions and then expect them to be carried out perfectly.
Fuss at the patient.
Assign too much responsibility.
Expect the patient to identify certain words, names, things, etc.
Take his or her behavior personally.
Scold or argue.
Try to do it all yourself.
Give choices—it is too confusing.
Get upset.

Raise your voice.[5]

Jo Lindquist, who worked five years in adult day care centers prior to becoming executive director of the ADRDA chapter, says when patients become agitated, a state known as "catastrophic reaction," she and her day care staff would ask five things: Is the patient hungry or thirsty, in pain or insulted, or in need of toileting? They would then ask one-word questions: Hungry? Thirsty? Pain? Angry? Toilet? Sometimes caring for those needs would break the cycle. "Other times, we would take the patient away from others to calm him, then hug and reassure him he was loved and cared for." Jo believes in the power of love. "Other times we would try to break the cycle by distracting them. Asking them to help move something would often work," said Jo.

Faith, a Source of Strength

The task of caring for a childlike adult year after year while watching the gradual erosion of personality and physical decline of a loved one is one of the most devastating experiences imaginable. Human strength alone hardly seems adequate to cope with demands and the cumulative results of what two authors have aptly called *The 36-Hour Day*.

"I used to ask, 'Why can't the Lord take Fred?' " Virginia admitted. "After I accepted his condition, I realized the Lord was giving me a lesson in patience, tolerance, and understanding."

Virginia's faith became a source of daily strength.

For the Christian whose faith has become a vital force in his or her life, suffering can be an occasion for a deeper fellowship with God and a more sympathetic understanding of humanity. The promises of God take on added meaning when the believer taps the boundless resources of God's love:

> Come to me, all who labor and are heavy-laden, and I will give you rest. Take my yoke upon you, and learn from me; for I am gentle and lowly in heart, and you will find rest for your souls. (Matt. 11:28–29, RSV)
>
> For I, the Lord your God, hold your right hand; it is I who say to you, "Fear not, I will help you." (Isa. 41:13, RSV)
>
> The eternal God is your dwelling place, and underneath are the everlasting arms. (Deut. 33:27, RSV)
>
> God is our refuge and strength, a very present help in trouble. Therefore we will not fear though the earth should change, though the

---

[5]Lisa P. Gwyther, A.C.S.W. *Care of Alzheimer's Patients: A Manual for Nursing Home Staff.* American Health Care Association & Alzheimer's Disease and Related Disorders Association, 1985, p. 103. Reprinted with permission from American Health Care Association, Washington, D.C.

mountains shake in the heart of the sea. . . . The Lord of hosts is with us; the God of Jacob is our refuge. (Ps. 46:1–2, 7, RSV)

My flesh and my heart fail; *but* God *is* the strength of my heart and my portion forever. (Ps. 73:26, KJV)

Advice to Offer Principal Caregivers

1. *Get an accurate diagnosis.* This can be done only by ruling out other conditions. There are some medical centers that do comprehensive testing in two to three days. Contact the national ADRDA to obtain a list of chapters. The ADRDA chapter in your region should be able to give you more information about the diagnostic center(s) in your area. Phone: (312) 853–3060.

2. *Once the diagnosis is confirmed, reach out and get as much help as possible.* Join a support group (start one if none exists); read the book, *The 36-Hour Day,* and write for a copy of *Understanding and Caring for the Person with Alzheimer's Disease* prepared by the Atlanta Area Chapter of ADRDA. It answers your questions about the disease, gives caring techniques and suggestions on how to deal with behavior problems such as wandering, sundowning, delusions and hallucinations, catastrophic reactions, and dealing with daily activities.

3. *Explain the disease to your relatives and friends.* Tell them you and your spouse or loved one need their understanding and continued love and support.

4. *Place an I.D. bracelet or tag engraved "memory impaired" on your loved one.* He or she may wander off and not remember the way home.

5. *Attain durable Power of Attorney as soon as possible.* Some states allow people while they are competent to sign Power of Attorney that will continue to operate in the event of incompetency. If the person is no longer competent, seek "Conservatorship" or "Guardianship for a Disabled Adult."

6. *Do not talk about the Alzheimer's sufferer as though he were not there.* People with this disease are sensitive and easily hurt.

7. *Find out what the person can do and encourage him or her to perform those simple tasks.* Accept the fact that many of the skills they once had are gone.

8. *Maintain a regular routine.* Patients function best in a familiar routine and calm environment. Put away clutter.

9. *Speak in short sentences.* Give simple commands one at a time.

10. *Keep activities childlike and simple.* Demonstrate by showing the patient correct methods of doing simple tasks such as combing hair or brushing teeth.

11. *Don't argue, scold, try to reason with, or accuse the person of lying.*

They lack understanding and perception of reality or right from wrong. Patience is essential.

12. *Practice reminiscence (remembering and discussing past events).* Discussing past events that focus on pleasant experiences and achievements is particularly helpful. This can promote the person's self-esteem. The technique called "reality orientation" is not effective with persons suffering severe memory loss, although reminders of time or place may be helpful in making some patients comfortable.[6]

13. *Vent your anger through physical activity, not on your loved one.* Scrub the floor, rake the yard, hoe the garden, whatever it takes to work off those feelings. You have a right to feel angry at the disease. Anger is not a sin; venting it on your spouse is. "Be angry but do not sin" (Eph. 4:26, RSV). If you do express anger with your loved one, forgive yourself and go on.

14. *Ask for assistance and temporary relief.* Make your needs known to relatives, friends, your pastor and members of the church. For safety reasons, give clear instructions to temporary caregivers. For example, tell them to lock doors, hide car keys, put knives out of reach, keep victim away from the stove, and never leave him or her alone.

15. *Try to get adequate rest and exercise.* Maintaining your health is important.

16. *Try to maintain your sense of humor.* It helps to be able to laugh about stressful situations.

17. *Give your loved one hugs, warmth, and affection.* Accept the fact that the disease makes them incapable of expressing their gratitude to you for your love and constant care.

18. *Live one day at a time, sometimes moment to moment.* "And as your days, so shall your strength be" (Deut. 33:25, RSV).

19. *Suggested devotional readings:* 1 Pet. 5:7; Ps. 31:3; 62:8; 55:22; Matt. 28:20; Heb. 13:5b; Luke 21:36; 2 Cor. 12:10; Gal. 5:22, 23; Col. 1:11; Rom. 8:26; Isa. 40:31; 43:1, 2; John 7:38.

Advice to Relatives and Friends of Caregivers

1. *Don't deny the problem; face it squarely.* Your unwillingness to accept the fact your friend or loved one has a severe dementing illness can make it more difficult for the principal caregiver. Inform yourself about the disease.

2. *Be there, listen to your friend or loved one who is responsible for the Alzheimer's victim's care.* "Sorrow which is never spoken is the heav-

---

[6]Carolyn J. M.S.W., Nancy Lyon-Morrison, M.Ed., and Eve B. Levine, M.S.W., *Understanding and Care for the Person with Alzheimer's Disease: A Practical Guide*, Atlanta ADRDA Chapter, 1985, p. 11.

iest load to bear."[7] Feelings once they are shared and validated will lessen. You help them most by sharing their grief.

3. *Offer to care for the patient.* Your loved one or friend needs a break from time to time. There is no need to fear caring for the victim if you heed the cautions the caregiver gives you.

4. *Invite them to your home.* The caregiver may no longer be able to take his or her spouse out for public dining, but may welcome an invitation to your home.

5. *Treat the victim with dignity and respect.*

6. *Be especially supportive when the patient is placed in the nursing home.* This is usually very painful for the principal caregivers. Be supportive of their decision. Remind them that their health is important, too.

7. *Ask about the Alzheimer's patient.* Though the person may be in terminal stages, a spouse will welcome your interest and concern.

Additional Reading

Holland, Gail Bernice. *For Sasha, with Love.* (The Anne Bashkiroff Story.) New York: Red Dembner Enterprises Corp., 1985.

Roach, Marion. *Another Name for Madness.* Boston: Houghton Mifflin, 1985. (A journalist writes about his mother.)

Seymour, Claire. *Precipice—Learning to Live with Alzheimer's Disease.* New York: Vantage Press, Inc., 1983. (Has a spiritual dimension.)

Mace, Nancy, and Peter Rabins, M.D. *The 36 Hour Day—A Family Guide to Caring for Persons with Alzheimer's Disease, Related Dementing Illnesses, and Memory Loss in Later Life.* Chicago: John Hopkins University Press, 1981. Available from ADRDA, 360 N. Michigan Ave., Chicago, Ill. 60601, 1981. $8.45.

Powell, Lenore S., Ed.D., and Katie Courtice. *Alzheimer's Disease—A Guide for Families.* Addison-Wesley Publishing Co., Reading, Mass. 08167, 1983.

Watt, Jim, and Ann Calder. *I Love You but You Drive Me Crazy.* Pforbez Publications, Ltd., 2133 Quebec St., Vancouver, B.C. V5T 2Z9.

For Children:

Guthrie, Donna. *Grandpa Doesn't Know It's Me.* Human Sciences Press, Inc., 72 Fifth Ave., New York, N.Y., 1986.

For Nursing Homes:

Coons, Dorothy H., Lena Melzelaar, Anne Robinson and Beth Spencer. *The Better Life* (Helping Members, Volunteers & Staff Improve the Qual-

---

[7]President Jerome Stone of ADRDA, Newsletter, Vol. 3, No. 2, Summer 1983.

ity of Life of Nursing Home Residents Suffering from Alzheimer's Disease and Related Disorders.) Columbus, Ohio: The Source, 1986.

French, Carolyn, M.S.W., Nancy Lyon-Morrison, M.Ed., and Eve B. Levine, M.S.W. *Understanding and Caring for the Person with Alzheimer's Disease*. 1985. Published by the Atlanta Area Chapter, ADRDA, 3320 Chestnut Drive, Atlanta, Ga. 30340, (404) 451–1300. Prices and ordering information available on request.

Feil, Naomi, ACSW. *Validation—The Feil Method*. (How to Help Disoriented Old-Old.) Available from: Edward Feil Productions, 4614 Prospect Avenue, Cleveland, Ohio 44103.

Gwyther, Lisa P. A.C.S.W. *Care of Alzheimer's Patients: A Manual for Nursing Home Staff*. American Health Care Assn. and the Alzheimer's Disease and Related Disorders Assn., 1985.

Ringland, Elinore, R.N. *Alzheimer's Disease: From Care to Caring*. (For professionals in long-term care institutions.) For more information, write: Healthcare, P.O. Box 4488, Rollingbay, Wash. 98061.

Videocassettes/Films

Someone I Once Knew, 16mm film or video demonstrating the impact of Alzheimer's disease on five patients and their families. Excellent for use with people unfamiliar with everyday situations of patients and families. 30 minutes. Rental: $85. Contact: Vicki Andrew, Simon & Schuster Communications, Tollway North, 198 Wilmot Rd., Deerfield, IL 60015.

Living with Alzheimer's—The MacNeil-Lehrer Report, video interview with Dr. Miriam Aronson and Dr. Peter Whitehouse. 30 minutes. Rental: $50. Contact: Corinne Wallace, The MacNeil-Lehrer Report, WNET/THIRTEEN, 356 W. 58th St., New York, NY 10019, (212) 560–3045.

Living with Grace, video, an in-depth case study of one family, emphasizing the positive sides of the situation when dealing with Alzheimer's. An excellent way to familiarize people with behavior of victims and management solutions. 28 minutes. Rental: $75. Contact: Donna Hill, University of Maryland, Video Services, Department of Physical Therapy, School of Medicine, University of Maryland, 32 South Greene Street, Baltimore, MD 21201, (301) 528–7720.

You Are Not Alone, video, focuses on range of issues including effects of Alzheimer's on caregivers, families and the nation. Helpful when dealing with legislatures or public officials. Also available is a set of four 3–5 minute trigger films, each with a discussion guide. Purchase: $75; trigger films, $60. Contact: Russ Neff, WITF-TV, Box 2954, Harrisburg, PA 17105, for more information.

Whispering Hope, documentary hosted by Jason Robards that includes moving family-victim profiles plus research findings. 52 minutes. Contact: Craig Braun, F.B.C. Productions, Inc., 36 East 61st St., New York, NY 10021.

Between Life and Death, video, contrasts the normal aged population with those with Alzheimer's disease, highlighting research, financial impact, case interviews and self-help. Contact: Sharon Ellison, Golden Gate Productions, KQED-TV, 500 Eighth St., San Francisco, CA 94103, (415) 533–2137.

NBC MONITOR—A Stranger in the House, video, award-winning overview of the disease with supporting patient vignettes. 16 minutes. Contact: John Dorbelak, Director of Sales Operations, NBC Enterprises, 30 Rockefeller Plaza, New York, NY 10020, (212) 644–2074.

Living in a Nightmare, video, follows two patients and their families through their daily lives: one in nursing home, one in own home. Good for understanding the patient and family. Contact: Larry Alt, Program Director, WXYZ-TV, P.O. Box 789, Southfield, MI 48037, (313) 827–9304.

Glass Curtain, video, personal account of a daughter attempting to cope with her mother, who has Alzheimer's. Emphasizes the family and caregiving. 30 minutes. Rental: $50. Contact: Doris Chase Concepts, 222 West 23rd St., New York, NY 10010, (212) 929–7285.

Do You Remember Love? A two-hour dramatic special starring Joanne Woodward as Barbara Wyatt-Hollis, a 50-year-old college professor and poet who is stricken at the height of her career. For rights and permissions information, write: Jame Thompson, DBA Productions, 3211 Cahuenga Boulevard, Hollywood, CA 90068.

Caring: Families Coping with Alzheimer's Disease. Shows three patients at different degrees of impairment. Caregivers share feelings of love, disappointment, loneliness, frustration, fatigue, and even humor as they cope. Contact: ADRDA, 70 East Lake Street, Chicago, IL 60691.

Looking for Yesterday. On-camera demonstration of Validation versus Orientation Therapy. 29 minutes. Rental: $25 per day. For families, hospital and nursing home staff and students of Aging. Can be ordered from: Edward Feil Productions, 4614 Prospect Avenue, Cleveland, OH 44103, (216) 881–0040.

National Organization

Alzheimer's Disease and Related Disorders Association, Inc.
70 East Lake Street
Chicago, IL 60601
(312) 853–3060
Presently has 68 chapters in various states and publishes a newsletter.

◇ **20** ◇

WHEN DEATH COMES AS A FRIEND

Nursing Home Placement, Death as Release, Life's Full Cycle

Mary Lou Killian's father was seventy-one when he came to live with her family. It wasn't always easy for her husband or their six children having another authority figure around the house. But Mary Lou was an only child, and her father had glaucoma and was going blind. There was no one else to care for him. His wife had died years ago. Mary Lou's father eventually lost the sight in both eyes.

He had few friends since he had come to live with his daughter; his lifelong friends were all in Cleveland. His blindness prevented him from leaving the house and making new acquaintances, so Mary Lou's family was his sole support system.

Mary Lou was torn between her family's needs and those of her father. Her teenagers couldn't have their friends over for parties. A party would last too long and be too noisy, and her father couldn't stand the commotion.

As his health deteriorated, her father demanded more and more of her time, leaving little time for her husband or children. Gradually, the children grew to resent his constant demands. Mary Lou seldom had a full night's sleep. Her father was restless and repeatedly called to her during the night. Though the children loved their grandfather, it was difficult for the family to lead a normal life while caring for a blind, ailing man nearing eighty-six.

One night Mary Lou found her father in excruciating pain. The emergency room physician admitted him to the hospital. He was diagnosed as having a tumor in the bladder, and surgery was advised. Following surgery, Mary Lou faced the fact that she would not be able to give her father the around-the-clock care he would require. He no longer had bladder or bowel control. Her half-time job, plus the added stress it would add to their homelife, forced her to consider placing her father in a nursing

236

home while he recovered. The doctor felt it would be a temporary arrangement.

"We'll do what we have to do," her father told her.

But Mary Lou agonized over the decision to place her father in the nursing home. It was the hardest decision she had ever made in her entire life. As an only child, she alone faced the decision; at times, she wanted to scream. She felt as if she had failed her father. He had lovingly cared for her mother when she was dying of cancer; now it was impossible for Mary Lou to do the same for him.

"When my father entered the nursing home, his life was taken over by their schedule. He was put to bed by 7:30 p.m., so he could no longer listen to evening ball games. Since he was from out-of-state, there were no friends with whom he could reminisce. And he was in a room with three other patients, so he no longer had any privacy. The thing that kept him going was believing that he would get to come home," said Mary Lou.

As weeks turned into months, his condition did not improve. It became apparent to Mary Lou that her father would not be able to return to their home. He required care twenty-four hours a day. His personality had also changed during those months. The strong man she had always known was now weak and helpless, and sometimes not lucid. His medications caused hallucinations and his granddaughter had been frightened by his behavior during a visit to the nursing home.

Finally, the day came when the family had to tell him they would not be able to bring him home. "From that point on, my father gave up. He died a month after we told him," said Mary Lou.

"It was hard for me to say to myself, 'I have a life of my own to live,' but I found you have to evaluate just how much of yourself you can give to caring for an aging parent. My family's needs were equally important.

"I found it was easier to cope with his death—for it came as a release from suffering—than it was to put him in the nursing home. I felt I had let him down. I know I didn't, because I cared for him for fifteen years, but my emotions tell me otherwise," she adds.

Mary Lou found herself in a position that is now termed the "sandwich generation," a family caught between responsibilities to children and aging parents. This trend is likely to continue because people are living longer due to advances in medical technology, and, couples are having their families later in life.

When Months Turn into Years

Tommy and Tyyne (pronounced Toon-ēē) Thompson both had aging mothers. Tom's mother, Mary, had reared seven sons, two of whom lived in the same community as their mother. Tyyne's mother was Finnish, spoke no English, and lived with Tyyne and her sister after their father died.

When Mary Thompson had her first stroke at age seventy-nine, Tom was convinced he and his brother could take care of her themselves. Tom would never put *his* mother in a nursing home. But three weeks of continuous care convinced them otherwise. Mary had minimal paralysis but was confused, restless, and called out for someone night and day. Tom lost twenty-five pounds and was worn out; so was his brother. A short time later, Tom had a heart attack, and since then has had two heart bypass surgeries. Mary Thompson's doctor felt that her time was limited—six months at the most, he told the family.

They chose a nursing home close by, one in which they had observed the individual attention and loving care given to patients. Each evening, Tom and his brother took turns feeding Mary, walking with her, giving her back massages and putting her to bed. Often, Tom would bring letters and cards and read them to his mother (many times the same ones over and over again) so she knew she was loved and remembered.

Tom and Tyyne became welcome visitors in the nursing home, for their warmth and caring spirits soon endeared them to other residents who seldom had visitors.

Tom admits it took three years before he could admit to himself that they had done the right thing by putting his mother in the nursing home. "I felt so guilty. My mother had done so much for us, and I thought I should be able to do as much for her," said Tom.

Six months turned into *twelve years*. The cost of her care consumed his mother's savings and Tom's. Eventually, the only option open to the family was applying for state aid.

During the twelve years, three of her sons died, and Mary had to be told. It seemed "out of order" for her children to die while she was still alive.

A fall finally precipitated Mary's demise. Tom stood by her bedside during her final hours. Both knew death was imminent. "If only I could rest," she told him.

"Soon, Mom, you'll rest," Tom said, referring to eternal rest, as they exchanged knowing glances.

Mary Thompson had lived life's full cycle, leaving behind her a legacy of children and grandchildren that remember her kind and loving spirit. She died at age ninety-one.

Tyyne's mother died in her sleep at the age of ninety-seven at home. Her family was thankful she avoided nursing home placement; this would have been a critical problem because of the language barrier.

Today, Tom and Tyyne care for another aged nursing home resident, a former neighbor. Every Monday night, they take her out to a restaurant. They volunteer their services to a local hospital that sponsors meals once a month for senior citizens. "We've always been around older people and we enjoy them," said the Thompsons.

The Presence of a Caring Friend

Geri Holè's mother was fifty-eight when she had her first stroke. In a period of four years, she had seven more. Geri witnessed her mother change from an attractive, young-looking, outgoing woman to the bent, incoherent figure of an old woman who swung one arm aimlessly, dragged one foot behind her, and slobbered incessantly. Her speech was slurred, her writing illegible. Geri was aware of how proud her mother had once been of her penmanship; now each time she attempted to sign her name, it was a painful reminder to her of all her losses. Her mother had fought to come back after each stroke until, finally, she realized she would never be the same as before. "If I can't get well, I'm ready to die," she told her daughter. Her biggest fear was becoming totally dependent.

A few weeks before her mother's death, Geri agonized over whether she should take a promotion out-of-state. Her father felt she should advance her career and accept the position; her mother did not want her to leave. Five days after Geri moved, her mother died.

Geri's immediate reaction was one of guilt. Had her leaving hastened her mother's death? Anticipating her feelings, the family doctor called.

"I don't want you to blame yourself for your mother's death, Geri," he began. His reassurances did much to ease her mind.

The day of the funeral, Geri and her father were surrounded by caring friends with whom they shared many happy memories. Reliving those times was comforting. By the end of the day, Geri was exhausted, but her mind was filled with thoughts of the day's events. She was thankful her mother's suffering had ended. As friends left and the house stilled, a wave of sadness swept over Geri and she felt her mother's absence. Sensing her need, a friend, Jeannie Oleson, lingered behind.

"Jeannie sat on the piano bench while I tried to relax on the couch. We sat in silence for a long time. Finally, when I yawned and she could see I was relaxed enough to get some sleep, she got up and said, 'I think I can go home now.' I will never forget what a comfort her quiet presence meant to me," said Geri.

Aging—A Season of Losses

Aging is a natural process beginning the day we are born. Each person ages differently—some slowly, some rapidly when precipitated by debilitating illnesses. Nonetheless, it is a process that inevitably each person faces. Few of us, however, are prepared for the losses aging brings.

Usually, the gradual loss of visual acuity begins mid-life. For some, the senses of hearing, taste and smell also diminish. At retirement, the loss of income, productive work and meaningful activities may greatly alter one's lifestyle and attitude toward living. For those who have planned for these years, the reverse can be true—retirement can become the period of life when they are free to do what they have longed for such as travel, write a book, or plunge full time into a favorite hobby.

In later years, the losses multiply and accelerate. The aging person eventually may lose his familiar surroundings and home, all his possessions, life's savings for costly medical care as health diminishes, and a sense of independence. Friends, a spouse, or children die, and his support systems dwindle.

Eventually, the roles reverse and the child becomes the parent to the aging person. When this happens, the parent may also lose the right to make decisions concerning his or her own life.

Some of these losses engender "mini-deaths" and, as such, are mourned, though sometimes imperceptibly to loved ones.

As depressing as the thought of these losses may be, an interesting phenomenon is happening as our society grows older. As Sylvia Herz told an American Psychological Association symposium on aging last year, the activities and attitudes of a 70-year-old today "are equivalent to those of a 50-year-old's a decade or two ago."[1] Most of us think of ourselves as being 20 years younger than we really are. A poem a friend wrote once about aging describes the dilemma of spirit versus body:

> I am young and beautiful
> > and full of life and hope and high ideals
> > and I will do wonderful things.
> But first, someone must rescue me.
> > I am being held prisoner in an old, disintegrating body.[2]
> > > —Marjorie Hintze

Preparing for the Inevitable

Modern science and technology have done much to change society and our individual lives. At the turn of the century, the average lifespan was 50 years of age. Today, life expectancy for women is age 78.5; for men, age 71. By the year 2080, the average life expectancy is predicted to be 85.2 for women and 76.7 for men.[3]

---

[1]Jack C. Horn and Jeff Meer, "The Vintage Years," *Psychology Today*, May 1987, p. 77.
[2]Used by permission.
[3]Middle Mortality Assumption taken from *Projections of the Population of the United States, by Age, Sex, and Race: 1983–2080*. U.S. Department of Commerce, U.S. Bureau of the Census, Series P–25, No. 952, p. 157.

Today, we are faced with ethical questions concerning the prolongation of life.

Aging parents can do much to prepare their children for those difficult decisions by discussing their wishes about their own death, the disposal of possessions, prearranging their own funeral, and making certain legal matters are in order while mental capacities are sound.

John Sherrill's book *Mother's Song* poignantly tells of the weight of the decision upon him and his family to carry through with his mother's wishes. Years before, she had discussed and given to each of her children a copy of the Living Will she had signed and had witnessed.

It read:

To Whom It May Concern:

> In the event that my mental condition has deteriorated to the point of mental incapacity, and that in the opinion of a qualified doctor of medicine, there is no probability of return of these mental faculties, I request that my attending physician not initiate but discontinue all supportive and palliative measures for prolonging life.[4]

When the day finally came when the Sherill family had to make the painful decision to remove life-sustaining fluids, allowing the mother to succumb to a gentle death from pneumonia, the decision was made easier by everyone's knowing her wishes.

During our years in the ministry, my husband and I have witnessed families, who, up to the time of the death of a parent, were on good terms. Disputes that arose over nursing home placement, possessions and estate, funeral plans made without consulting other siblings, or one child being expected to bear nursing home or funeral expenses that should be shared equally, have literally torn families apart.

Though most of us dislike talking about our own death, the wise parent will discuss these things with the family, knowing full well that for each of us death is inevitable.

If and When You Must Select a Nursing Home

Aging parents should be allowed and encouraged to retain their independence as long as possible. Many of the home health care services and adult day care centers provided today make that possible. The time for providing assistance comes when it is no longer safe for the aged parent to live alone. Sometimes a live-in companion is the answer if staying with adult children is impossible.

Nursing home placement becomes necessary when around-the-clock nursing care is required, when the person becomes incontinent and/or

---

[4]John Sherrill, *Mother's Song*, (Lincoln, Va.: Chosen Books, 1982), p. 37.

the spouse of family can no longer provide the care required, when the presence of the aged parent would create unbearable stress on marriage and family life, or when the aged person has no family to care for him or her.

The aging parent may feel as though the children want to rid themselves of the parent and feel dejected when placed in a nursing home. But not always—often, parents do not want to be a burden to their children.

Charlotte Holm, R.N., director of nurses at a nursing home facility in Wisconsin, says that many patients adjust quite well. "Some don't mind going to the nursing home because they have friends there. Some find it hard to give up all their possessions; for others, *things* no longer matter to them."

She advises, "It's wise to visit several nursing homes before you make a decision as to which home is best for your parent. It's also important to remember that nursing home placement isn't always permanent. Many patients need rehabilitation, and after recovery, can return to their homes. If that is the case, then you will want to select a facility that has a trained physical therapist.

"The parent should be included in the decision-making process if at all possible," Holm adds. "On one occasion a family told the aged father they were taking him for a ride, but instead brought him to the nursing home. Their reasoning was that he would have less time to worry about it. The man was devastated and angry. He had every right to be angry. That's how *not* to admit an elderly infirm person to a nursing home."*

Here are some additional guidelines to follow in selecting a nursing home:

1. *Look for personnel at as many levels of care as possible, and speak with them.* If they are friendly and helpful before you place someone, they are likely to have those characteristics most of the time. Pleasant caregiving personnel are essential to the success of the experience; one can do better without some of the frills and expensive decor.

2. *Check on the state of cleanliness in the rooms and general areas.* Do this more than once and at different times of the day. Understandably, odors can arise at certain times, but this should not be a general condition.

3. *Notice the grooming of residents.* If hair, nails, and clothes are reasonably clean, it is a very good sign that individual attention is being given on a regular basis.

4. *Look for pleasant, well-lighted, well-ventilated environments.*

5. *Arrive at mealtime.* See whether the food is appetizing. Ask the

---

*Private interview July 19, 1986.

residents if they like what they are eating. (Remember, though, that criticism of institutional food is a survival tactic.) Check to see how assistance in eating is provided for those who need it, and how soon they are helped.

6. *Check the activity program schedule, which should be posted.* Even though you feel your loved one does not need that kind of program, you can estimate the attention to psychosocial needs by the variety and time-plan of the activity program available.

7. *Results of the most recent Health Department inspection are supposed to be posted in an accessible place.* The number of citations is sometimes a sign of the kind of performance of a facility, but the *content* of the citations is generally more informative. Do this as unobtrusively as possible. Too much checking makes staff cautious about accepting a patient who is related to the questioner.[5]

After nursing home placement, Sister Patricia Murphy, author of *Healing with Time and Love*, reminds families to remember:

• Your loved one remains much the same person as before admission, with the same needs, likes and dislikes.

• There will be a need for adjustment time. There will be a certain amount of anger, resentment, fear, and insecurity with which the loved one will have to deal.

• You need time to adjust to this situation. You will have unfinished feelings that will affect the quality and frequency of your visits. Give yourself time. If there is a social service person at the home, be sure to get in touch so that you may discuss these feelings.

• Although your loved one will need the reassurance of your visits, too frequent and too lengthy visits can harm the patient's capacity to adapt to the situation, to find friends, or to reflect on what is taking place.

• You are permitted, as space allows, to bring a few of the patient's personal effects.

• You may be able to secure permission to take your loved one out of the facility. Shopping for little necessities keeps one in touch with the world and gives a feeling of being in charge.

• You can assist in the care of your loved one. However, be aware that if you do this on a regular basis, the staff may come to expect it, and you may find them neglecting the tasks you usually do when you are absent.

• Residents in long term facilities have *human rights* as well has *special rights* demanded by the transaction of trust and the payment of fees.

---

[5]Sister Patricia Murphy, O.L.V.M., *Healing with Time and Love* (Lexington Books, D.C. Heath and Company, Copyright 1979, D.C. Heath and Company), pp. 14, 15. Used by permission.

These rights are protected by state Departments of Health (see each state's administrative code for specifics).[6]

Faith—The Most Precious of All

On one occasion, my husband instructed a group of elderly members at their monthly meeting to write down the five things most precious to them. For some, those things were a home, a spouse, children. "Now," he said, "due to circumstances beyond your control, you must give up three of those things. Then he instructed, "Now give up one more." Some of those persons have already experienced many losses. The answer— the single most important precious thing—that emerged unanimously was their faith. "My faith is the most precious of all that I have," they agreed.

Of all believers in the world, the Christian is indeed the most fortunate! The Christian faith gives us a hope that is unique. It gives meaning to suffering, victory over death, and the promise of life beyond the grave.

One Easter Sunday morning while I was in nurses' training, a man well into his eighties lay dying. He would not respond to questioning, yet from his lips, in faint whispers came the words of a familiar hymn. His eyes were fixed on a place beyond that of my vision or comprehension. He balanced on the threshold between life and death. A few hours later he died. I have never forgotten that special Resurrection Sunday. I had witnessed a man who fought the good fight of faith and who died giving expression to a faith that had sustained him to the last moments of his earthly existence. For him, too, faith was the single most precious of all gifts!

Usually, our feelings about the death of elderly persons who have lived a full and happy life are far different than our response when someone is struck down in the prime of life. There is grief and a void that we feel as we miss the loved one's presence, but their death seems just and fair. When the full cycle of life has been completed, and the aged person welcomes death as a friend, death has come as a release from earthly cares.

There can be lingering guilt, however, when a parent dies alone. After my father died in 1974, I was bothered for quite some time by the fact that he died alone. My husband and I had driven ten hours to reach the hospital. When we arrived, it was easy to see my mother was distraught. Dad had pulled out his catheter, so the doctor had ordered hand restraints, and this troubled him greatly. Thinking that Mother needed rest after a most trying day at his bedside, we prayed with my father, and then left the hospital. "We'll see you in the morning, Dad," I said as we left his room. Five hours after we left him, my father died. I found myself thinking

---

[6]Ibid., pp. 15–19.

"If only I had stayed, held his hand, talked to him, made him comfortable, been with him! If only I had asked to have the restraints and the tubes removed! But that is hindsight.

The only means that I have found to work through those feelings is to confess them to God and ask forgiveness. Forgiving ourselves is always hard and takes time.

Advice to Offer

The Aging Parent:

1. *Discuss your death with adult children.* Sign and have witnessed a Living Will if you feel strongly that you want to die in dignity without resuscitation or extraordinary life-sustaining measures being taken. Give a copy to your doctor and each of your children.
2. *Settle legacies with each of your children before you die.* Discussing "who gets what" may do much to prevent any hard feelings after your death. Estate planning and an up-to-date will are essential.
3. *Pre-plan your funeral and burial.* These decisions best express your desires and spare your children those painful decisions once you are deceased.
4. *Tell your children how they can minister to you during your final hours.* Would you want them to read familiar scriptures to you? Would you want to hear taped sacred music? Is it important for you to have Communion one last time? The body retains the sense of hearing even though the person may appear to be unconscious.
5. *Suggested devotional reading:* Job 5:26; Ps. 90:1–6, 9, 10; Eccles. 3:1–2; 7:1; 2 Cor. 5:1–8.

The Adult Child:

1. *Be open to your parents' discussing death with you.* Older persons have often come to terms with their own death, but find others unwilling to listen. Ask questions so you will know what his or her wishes are if the parent does not volunteer this information.
2. *Tell your parents the things that are in your heart; don't wait until it is too late.* Most children feel a deep sense of appreciation to their parents. It is important to express those feelings while they are alive; failing to do so can lead to remorse for not having done so. Stormy child-parent relationships can sometimes be reconciled, allowing the parent to die in peace and the child to feel loved by that parent perhaps for the first time in his or her life.
3. *Find out where important documents are kept.* It may be up to you to

assume responsibility for your parent(s) legal affairs, including Power of Attorney.

4. *Encourage your parent(s) to remain independent as long as possible.* Explore the options of care available in the home for your parent(s), such as Meals on Wheels, home health care, adult day care centers, and so on. Call your local agency on aging, the social services department in a local hospital, or visiting nurse association to explore what services are available in the community.

5. *Don't take away your parent's right to participate in decision-making unless absolutely necessary.* Assuming this right robs the parent of a sense of independence and alters the course of life dramatically.

6. *Don't forget your parent's spiritual needs.* Large-print Bibles and devotional materials, Scripture on cassette tapes, or radios with earphones can be a means for your parents to continue to nurture their own spiritual faith.

7. *If you, as the adult child living closest, have been designated "caretaker," don't make important decisions alone without consulting other siblings.* Joint decisions usually result in healthier family relationships. The adult sibling left out of such decisions often feels angry, guilty or unimportant. Keep the lines of communication open; don't keep secrets.

8. *Keep other siblings informed.* The adult child living closest often sees the need to do something for and with the parent(s) living alone. Therefore, siblings living out-of-town have an obligation to listen to and accept the word of those in a position to observe what is really happening. Denying the problem will not cause it to go away.

9. *Inform other siblings as soon as possible of a life-threatening crisis.* Most adult children need to say goodbye to a parent in their own special way. Not being informed of a crisis can later cause resentment. If death occurs suddenly, inform siblings immediately—don't delay. Some want to see and be with the body before it is picked up by the funeral home.

10. *Know that it's common to feel guilty if your parent died alone.*

If You Are a Friend of the Family:

1. *Be supportive of your friend's difficult decisions regarding a parent's welfare, assuming of course, the adult child is caring and responsive to the parent's need.* Saying things like, "Well, I would never do that to *my* parent," can only add to their guilt.

2. *Offer practical assistance.* If your friend feels compelled to feed or visit an aged parent in a nursing home, offer to go in his or her place or go along on occasion.

3. *Be a good listener.* Caring for aging parents can be trying for a family.

Adult children need friends with whom they can talk about these frustrations.

4. *Help your friend sort out irrational guilt feelings.* Some adult children feel they have not done enough for their parents. By pointing out the ways they did assist, you can help your friend get some grasp of reality.

Additional Reading

Bayless, Pamela J. *Caring for Dependent Parents.* New York: The Research Institute of America, 1985. Address: 589 Fifth Avenue, New York, N.Y. 10017. Explains legal aspects and types of care available for the aged parent.

Burger, Sarah Greene, and Martha D. 'Erasmo. *Living in a Nursing Home, a Complete Guide for Residents, Their Families and Friends.* New York: Ballantine Books, 1976.

Grollman, Earl A. and Sharon H. *Caring for Your Aged Parents.* Boston: Beacon Press, 1978.

Grollman, Earl A. *When Your Loved One Is Dying.* Boston: Beacon Press, 1980.

_____. *Living When a Loved One Has Died.* Boston: Beacon Press, 1977.

Hickman, Martha Whitmore. *Waiting & Loving.* Thoughts Occasioned by the Illness and Death of a Parent. Nashville, Tenn.: The Upper Room, 1984.

Manning, Doug. *The Nursing Home Dilemma.* How to Make One of Love's Toughest Decisions. San Francisco: Harper & Row Publishers, 1985.

Murphy, Sister Patricia. *Healing with Time and Love: A Guide For Visiting the Elderly.* Lexington, Ma.: D.C. Heath and Company, 1979.

Rushford, Patricia H. *To Help, Hope, & Cope Book for People with Aging Parents.* Old Tappan, N.J.: Fleming H. Revell Company, 1985.

Sherrill, John. *Mother's Song.* A Family Learns the Promise of "A Time to Die." Lincoln, Va.: Chosen Books, 1982.

For a free copy of a *Living Will*, send a self-addressed stamped envelope to Chosen Books, Lincoln, VA 22078.

◇ **21** ◇

OUR HOPE IS HEAVEN

Our Hopes and God's Promises

Frank and Judy Rodts talked of heaven with their eight-year-old son Justin as he lay dying in their arms.

"God is here to take you to heaven, Justin. It's all right. It is going to be very beautiful there, and some day we'll all be together again," his parents told him. Although Frank and Judy questioned why God had not healed their son of leukemia, they never questioned God's promise that Justin would go to heaven (Chapter 8).

Bob and Nancy Carlson's daughter, Karina, has an inoperable cancer. Nancy says, "You have to believe in heaven, because if you don't, what do you have? What do you have to live for?" (Chapter 8).

When Lowell, Jeannie, and Shawn Apple—a vital, young Christian family—died as the result of an auto accident, relatives placed a gravestone on the three graves which says "Together Forever" (Chapter 16).

A second grade class sent Charlotte Graeber pictures the children had drawn after her husband's plane crashed killing him. One drawing depicted a plane with wings heading for a cloud marked "The Better Place," meaning heaven (Chapter 16).

Dora Larson found comfort in believing that her ten-year-old murdered daughter instantly went to heaven (Chapter 6).

Almost consistently through the interviews with persons of varying religious backgrounds ran a common thread: belief in heaven.

Belief in Heaven

According to a recent random survey done by *USA WEEKEND*, 80 percent of adults surveyed believe in heaven, and 96 percent believe in God.[1] Several years ago, the Gallup Poll did the most comprehensive study ever done in the area of religion. In the national survey, these facts came to

---

[1]Jean Becker, "We Believe—and We Believe We're Going to Heaven," *USA WEEKEND* (Dec. 19–21, 1986), p. 4.

light: 90 percent of Americans surveyed affirm their belief in life after death, and 95 percent believe in the existence of a God. But only about two-thirds of Americans believe in a personal God who watches over, helps and judges people—the God of biblical revelation. The belief in God and heaven permeates our culture, more in America than in West European countries.[2]

For thousands of years, the destiny of the human soul after death has occupied the minds of both the learned and the common person. In the Old Testament, Job raised the question: "If a man dies, will he live again?" (Job 14:14, NIV).

For the Christian, that question was answered 2,000 years ago through the death and resurrection of Jesus Christ.

Common Concerns

Naturally, intense suffering or the threat of death—one's own or the life of a loved one—raises questions about the fear of dying, what happens to the human body, separation from loved ones, and the place called heaven.

We all know that death is a painful reality and we view it as the final enemy. Death is disruptive, final, cruel, and agonizing for loved ones left behind. But it is a door through which all of us must pass. No one escapes death. "What man can live and not see death or save himself from the power of the grave?" asks the Psalmist (89:48, NIV).

The Christian, however, can view death with hope. The Christian views death as a triumphant passage into a fuller, more glorious life. Death is the door to eternity.

As Oliver Cromwell, Lord Protector of England in the 16th century, lay dying, he turned to his weeping friends and said, "Is there no one who will praise the Lord?" He had no feeling of misfortune concerning his death. For him, life beyond death was a certainty. In one of his books, the last chapter was entitled "Death." The chapter contained three words: "To Be Continued."

Christ's teachings and the Scriptures give us answers to these common concerns about the body, dying, and heaven. God's promises have brought comfort and meaning to believers down through the centuries. Martyrs have died praising God, knowing suffering and death was not the end, certain in their belief that heaven awaited them. Prisoners in concentration camps—like Corrie ten Boom—have witnessed to God in the depths of hell. They are strengthened by their beliefs in Jesus Christ and His resurrected presence. Convicted killers on death row have repented of their

---

[2]"Despite Social Upheaval Religion Holds Steady," *Religion in America: 50 Years*, *The Argus* (Oct. 24, 1985).

wrong-doing and prepared their hearts for heaven. Grieving parents have stood by the graveside of a precious daughter or son and taken comfort in knowing that God would care for their child, and they would someday see her or him again. And for those who have lived godly lives, the fear of dying gives way to a joyful confidence in knowing that death is not an end but a new beginning. "Death is swallowed up in victory" (1 Cor. 15:54, TLB).

An unknown poet has compared this mystery to birth:

When God sends forth a spotless soul
    To learn the ways of earth,
A MOTHER'S LOVE is waiting here;
    We call this wonder BIRTH.

When God calls home a tired soul,
    And stills a fitful breath,
LOVE DIVINE is waiting there,
    This, too, is BIRTH, not death.[3]

The Apostle Peter spoke of this new birth:

Praise be to the God and Father of our Lord Jesus Christ, who in his great mercy gave us new birth into a living hope by the resurrection of Jesus Christ from the dead! (1 Pet. 1:3, NEB)

New Bodies in Heaven

Paul E. Billheimer in *Destined for the Throne* sheds light on our understanding of the spirit in relationship to the natural body:

When the spirit leaves the body, the body disintegrates. It loses its structure because it is dependent upon the spirit for its organization as reality. The spirit has independent reality. The body has only relative reality. . . . In other words, your spirit is the real "you," the real person.[4]

According to Ecclesiastes, when we die, "the dust returns to the ground it came from, and the spirit returns to God who gave it" (Eccles. 12:7, NIV). The natural body dies; the spirit lives on.

We are assured that, for those who know the Lord, when the spirit is separated from the body, it is immediately at home with God. Paul said to be absent from the body is to be present with the Lord (2 Cor. 5:8).

Much of the agony—both physical and spiritual—in this world is associated with the pain we experience while housed in our earthly bodies. How devastating it is to watch the once-healthy body of a small child

[3]Herbert H. Wernecke, *When Loved Ones Are Called Home.* (Grand Rapids: Baker Book House, 1950). Used by permission.
[4]Paul E. Billheimer, *Destined for the Throne*, (Minneapolis: Bethany House Publishers, 1975). Used by permission of Christian Literature Crusade, Fort Washington.

sicken and die, or the elderly, infirm parent experience excruciating pain day after day.

Then our search of the Scriptures leads us to the promises of God and the words of the Apostle Paul as he describes the new body we can expect in heaven:

> Our earthly bodies which die and decay are different from the bodies we shall have when we come back to life again, for they will never die. The bodies we have now embarrass us, for they become sick and die. . . . Yes, they are weak, dying bodies now, but when we live again, they will be full of strength. . . . Every human being has a body just like Adam's, made of dust, but all who become Christ's will have the same kind of body as his—a body from heaven (1 Cor. 15:43, 44, 48, TLB).

The new resurrection body of the believer will be like Christ's. It will be real, recognizable, and indestructible, as well as glorious, powerful, and heavenly.

"We shall be like him" (1 John 3:2, NIV). And "just as we have borne the likeness of the earthly man, so shall we bear the likeness of the man from heaven" (1 Cor. 15:49, NIV), said Paul.

"For we know that if the earthly tent we live in is destroyed, we have a building from God, a house not made with hands, eternal in the heavens" (2 Cor. 5:1, RSV).

The prospect of a new body has special meaning for believers who have endured great suffering or have struggled with impaired, weak, imperfect bodies.

Some years ago, I interviewed a young man who defied death and lived after touching a high voltage wire while working as a lineman for a power company; 7,620 volts of electricity surged through his body for one to two minutes. As a result of that accident, both of Austin Henry's legs had to be amputated; one arm, though saved from amputation, is nearly useless. Despite his physical limitations, Austin has resumed working at the power company, and owns and manages a farm. Austin's attitude, in part, reflects his deep faith and his belief that this body is temporary. "Life is short, and this [body] is an inconvenience, but someday in heaven, I'll have a new body," said Austin.

No More Sorrow, No More Tears

Life itself is a gift from God, and as such, most people value life. But our lives are subject to earthly concerns that sometimes are almost more than the soul can bear. Some of the personal experiences in this book may have seemed unimaginable and represent "the worst thing" that can happen to an individual or family.

We live in a world filled with dangers, surrounded by evil influences and powers that would rob us of our very souls if we allowed them. Sickness, tragedy, and heartache abound. Some lives are filled with constant strife. I often think of the poor nations of this world, where people live in famine and poverty, where every waking hour must be spent trying to secure enough food just to survive.

But how different heaven will be!

The Book of Revelation tells us that in heaven, there will be no more sorrow, no more tears. John recorded these truths as they were revealed to him:

> He will wipe every tear from their eyes, and death shall be no more, neither shall there be mourning nor crying nor pain any more, for the former things have passed away. (Rev. 21:4, RSV)

In heaven there will be no more poverty, no more failure, no more oppression, no more death, no more of this world's conflicts with money or concerns about keeping a roof over our heads or food on the table. A new, different, glorious life awaits. Is it any wonder that the Apostle Paul, as he explained these mysteries to the people in Corinth, reminded them of what had been written: "O death, where is thy victory? O death, where is thy sting?" (1 Cor. 15:55, RSV).

Is it no wonder that God's promise of "no more sorrow, no more tears" and the promise of heaven is comforting to those who must bury their dead?

Together Forever?

Much of the pain associated with the fear of death, and death itself, is separation from loved ones. Don Baker, in his booklet *Heaven*, says there will be three surprises in heaven. We will be surprised

to find some we did not expect
to not find some we did expect, and
to find ourselves in heaven.

Baker goes on to say:

> The society of Heaven will be select. There are many kinds of aristocracy in this world but the aristocracy of Heaven will be one of holiness. The humblest sinner who repents will be an aristocrat there. The humblest sinner who, while in this life, trusts in Jesus Christ will be an exalted member of the Heavenly Family there.
> The Eternal City is for those who have made reservations here, for those who have trusted in Jesus Christ, God's Son. Heaven is a prepared place for a prepared people, and preparation is made in the

here and now of everyday life. Its residents . . . are the redeemed of all ages.[5]

Another common concern related to dying is the threat of *eternal* separation from loved ones. These concerns were expressed in a letter a young woman wrote to her father who was dying of cancer:

> It pains me to see you like this. I worry most, not about your dying—which hurts me so much—but about your peace and happiness after you're gone. Daddy, we want to meet you in heaven someday, so please talk to God. Ask Jesus into your heart. After all, what else do you have? . . . God loves each and every one of us. All you have to do is reach out to Him. I did. He sure made life much better for me, and I'm happier inside and out.

The Apostle Paul wrote to his friends in the church at Rome, "If you confess with your mouth, 'Jesus is Lord,' and believe in your heart that God raised him from the dead, you will be saved" (Rom. 10:9, NIV).

Jesus said, "I am the way and the truth and the life. No one comes to the Father except through me" (John 14:6 NIV). "I am the door. If anyone enters by Me, he will be saved" (John 10:9, NKJV).

"All that the Father gives me will come to me; and him who comes to me I will not cast out . . . For this is the will of my Father, that every one who sees the Son and believes in him should have eternal life" (John 6:37, 40, RSV).

One cannot disregard the biblical evidence that one day, there will be a reckoning for what we do and how we live our lives. "And just as it is appointed for men to die once, and after that comes judgment . . ." (Heb. 9:27, RSV).*

But the Apostle Paul reaffirms God's plan: "For God has not chosen to pour out his anger upon us, but to save us through our Lord Jesus Christ; he died for us so that we can live with him forever . . ." (1 Thess. 5:9, 10; see also 4:16–17, TLB).

For each of us who claim Christ as Lord, belief in the resurrection is essential. Hans Küng explains:

> I cannot stop halfway with my unconditional trust, but must follow the road consistently to its end. . . . I have a reasonable confidence that the almighty Creator, who calls us from not-being into being, can also call us from death into life. . . . I am confident in the Creator and Conserver of the cosmos . . . that he has the last word as he had the first; that he is the God of the end as well as the God of the beginning: Alpha and Omega. Anyone who so believes seriously in the eternally

---

[5]Don Baker, *Heaven*: A Glimpse of Your Future Home (Portland, Ore.: Multnomah Press, 1983). Used by permission.
*For more about judgment, read 2 Thess. 1:7–9; 4:16–17.

living God, who believes then also in God's eternal life, believes in *his own*—in man's—eternal life.[6]

Yes, God has prepared a place called heaven of incredible beauty where we will be with "the redeemed of all ages," our loved ones, the Lord Jesus Christ, and God himself. When Jesus prayed, He said, "Thy kingdom come, thy will be done on earth as it is in heaven." The word "kingdom" conveys a communal image—a realm of relationships. Emil Brunner so aptly says it, " 'It is life *with* God, *in* God, *from* God; life in perfect fellowship.' Therefore it is a life in love, it is love itself."[7]

Much Is Still a Mystery

We know only in part what God has prepared for us. Much remains a mystery. Yet, we do not hesitate, for we know who holds the future.

> I know not how that Bethlehem's Babe
> Could in the Godhead be;
> I only know the Manger Child
> Has brought God's life to me.
>
> I know not how that Calvary's cross
> A world from sin could free;
> I only know its matchless love
> Has brought God's love to me.
>
> I know not how that Joseph's tomb
> Could solve death's mystery;
> I only know a living Christ,
> Our immortality.[8]

Additional Reading

Baker, Don. *Heaven:* A Glimpse of Your Future Home. Portland: Multnomah Press, 1983. (Booklet)

Ball, Charles Ferguson. *Heaven.* What You Can Know for Sure About Life After Death. Wheaton, Ill.: Victor Books, 1980.

Bayly, Joseph. *Heaven.* Elgin Ill.: David C. Cook Publishing Co., 1977. (Booklet)

Billheimer, Paul E. *Destined for the Throne.* Minneapolis: Bethany House Publishers, 1975.

---

[6]Hans Küng, *Eternal Life?* Life After Death as a Medical, Philosophical, and Theological Problem (Garden City, N.Y.: Doubleday & Company, Inc., 1985), p. 114. Used by permission.

[7]Emil Brunner, *Our Faith* (London: SCM Press LTD, 1949), p. 121.

[8]Harry Webb Farrington, "I Know Not How That Bethlehem's Babe," *The Hymnal* (St. Louis, Mo.: Eden Publishing House, 1941), p. 241.

Brunner, Emil. *Our Faith.* London: SCM Press Ltd., 1936.

Carlson, Neal. *To Die Is Gain.* Grand Rapids: Baker Book House, 1974. (Booklet)

Gutzke, Manford G. *Fear Not.* A Christian View of Death. Grand Rapids, Mich.: Baker Book House, 1974.

Hill, Brennan. *The Near-Death Experience: A Christian Approach.* Dubuque, Iowa: Wm. C. Brown Company Publishers, 1981.

Matson, Archie. *Afterlife: Reports from the Threshold of Death.* New York: Harper & Row Publishers, 1977.

Moody, D.L. *Heaven.* How to Get There. Springdale, Pa.: Whitaker House, 1982.

Morey, Dr. Robert A. *Death and the Afterlife.* Minneapolis: Bethany House Publishers, 1984. (An extensive examination of the biblical language related to human destiny beyond death.)

Page, Allen F. *Life After Death.* Nashville: Abingdon Press, 1987.

Rawlings, Maurice, M.D. *Beyond Death's Door.* Nashville, Tenn.: Thomas Nelson Publishers, 1978.

Toynbee, Arnold. *Life After Death.* New York: McGraw, 1976.

◊　　◊

SUMMARY

The Nature of Grief, Do's and Don'ts

No one can get through life without loss and grief.

Grief is a *God-given* natural, healthy, self-corrective process. It is an ongoing, continuous, highly fluid process whereby an individual can separate from someone or something that has been lost.[1]

The grieving person may experience numbness, disbelief, denial, anger or rage, confusion, depression, guilt, fear—and vacillate from one moment to the next. Grief comes in waves. The grieving person is feeling-oriented.

Each individual responds to grief differently. Responses vary with each individual according to temperament, background, emotional and physical health, age, the maturity of one's faith, and past losses, as well as a host of other reasons. A current loss can trigger unresolved losses from the past.

Intense grief can produce physical symptoms. The grieving person may experience the following: fatigue; shortness of breath; dizziness; palpitations; frequent, ongoing feelings of numbness, irritability and restlessness; headaches and diarrhea; appetite loss; insomnia; and inability to organize daily activities. The person may be filled with self-blame, preoccupation with the image of the deceased; guilt, with feelings of not having done enough for the deceased; and hostility toward the physicians and other medical professionals who attended the deceased.[2]

It is healthier to express emotions than to repress them. Repression is the means by which intolerable memories are kept out of the consciousness. Unfortunately, crying is often seen as a sign of weakness, especially for men. It should be understood that tears are a way of cleansing inner wounds. Because grief is unique to every individual, observers

---

[1]Kenneth Moses, Ph.D., President, Resource Network, Inc., Evanston, Ill. Lecture at Western Illinois University, Macomb, Ill. 1980.

[2]William R. Dubin and Jeffrey R. Samofft. "Sudden Unexpected Death: Intervention with Survivors." *Annals of Emergency Medicine* (January 1986), p. 100/55.

should understand that some persons will cry profusely, while others may not cry at all.

Anger is a common response to loss. Someone important has been taken away; life for the grieving person will never be the same.

Guilt is a normal and common reaction as well. No one succeeds in being good and loving all the time. Usually there is a sense of unfinished business and "if only" regrets. Some guilt is neurotic or irrational. Self-blame and guilt can become overwhelming and destructive if prolonged. Friends or trained professionals can aid in helping the grieving person sort out these feelings. True guilt will need to be dealt with through the act of repentance, confession, and asking God's forgiveness.

It has been said grief has a beginning, a middle, an end. Healing is a process that takes time and is unique to each person. Pain must be faced before it can be healed. The grieving person will review memories of the deceased and only gradually confront each one with the realization that it no longer corresponds to something real. The whole sequence is re-peated over and over. The specific psychological task of this process is to break the emotional tie one has with the deceased so he or she can reinvest attachment and emotional energy to living people.[3]

But time doesn't necessarily heal all wounds. There is no time limit to grief. The problems with grieving are social; it is done in the context of relationships.[4] When the grieving person has not been given permission to grieve, or for other reasons the grieving person is not moving through the grief process, he or she may "get stuck" in one of the stages of grief for a prolonged period of time. At that point, it would be wise for the individual to seek counseling with a trained professional.

A life-shattering loss can shake the bereaved's beliefs about God, but it can also become a time for getting to know God better. Sorrow has a refining influence on the soul, and it can help an individual put priorities in their proper perspective and clarify values. Grief can be the occasion for growth, depending on how an individual chooses to respond. The individual who has a deep, abiding faith and trust in God comes through the experience stronger and is usually motivated to reach out to others going through similar tragedies.

Some Do's and Don'ts for Caregivers

As a caregiver to someone who has experienced the death of a loved one, you will want to remember the following Do's and Don'ts.

---

[3]Ibid., p. 54/99.
[4]Kenneth Moses, Ph.D.

DO:

- Acknowledge the loss with a call, card, or letter (letters can be read and reread). By writing a letter you are "offering handwritten hugs where human arms cannot reach." If possible, go to visitation or attend the funeral. Your presence means you care.
- Simply say, "I'm so sorry" or "Words fail me" or "I share a bit of your grief."
- Remember, a sympathizing tear, a warm embrace, an arm around the shoulder, a squeeze of the hand convey your sympathy. Words aren't always necessary.
- Give the mourner permission to grieve.
- *Listen* nonjudgmentally to the grieving person's thoughts and feelings.
- Allow the grieving person to talk about the deceased loved one.
- Ask open-ended questions like "What happened?" Open-ended questions invite the grieving person to express him- or herself.
- Tell them you'll remember them in your prayers.
- Offer practical assistance.
- Share a pleasant memory or words of admiration for the deceased with the grieving person.
- Remember them on the painful holidays, especially the "firsts."
- Remember that grief is long-lasting.
- Remember that you are a vital part of the grieving person's support system. Never underestimate your role as a caregiver.
- Remember that usually the most difficult time is seven to nine months after the death.
- Remember to extend condolences to forgotten mourners: grandparents, siblings, stepchildren, aunts and uncles, cousins, friends—anyone who was especially close.
- Remember that nothing you can say will stop the grieving person's pain.

DON'T:

- Avoid the grieving person because you don't know what to say.
- Say, "Don't cry" or "Be brave." This may cause the grieving person to repress sad feelings.
- Use clichés, trite statements, or euphemisms. Avoid statements such as "He's at rest," "Be glad it's over . . ." "Time heals all wounds" or "The Lord knows best."
- Be afraid of tears. Grieving persons seldom forget those with whom they've shed tears.
- Say, "I know how you feel." Each person's grief is unique, and no one can totally understand another's grief.
- Make statements or ask questions that induce guilt or affix blame. There

is always some unfinished business and guilt associated with the death of a loved one.

• Change the subject when the grieving person talks about his or her loved one.
• Tell the grieving person his or her loss is God's will. Most grieving persons are troubled by that statement, but are too polite to say so. Avoid any of the following statements:

> Sooner or later He is going to get you.
> He will get you in the end.
> God had numbered his days, and when they ran out, God took him.
> I don't understand why he had to die, but God doesn't make mistakes.
> God must have needed another bud for his rose garden.
> You never know when the Lord's going to snatch you from this world, do you?
> God knows best. He won't put any more on you than you can bear.[5]

• Try to answer the question, *Why?*
• Discount the loss of a baby or child by reminding grieving parents they can have other children or be glad they have other children.
• Attempt to minimize the loss of a baby through miscarriage, still-birth, or early infant death. Parents experience the death of their dreams and hopes for the future embodied in their wished-for baby. The age makes little difference; their pain is just as great.
• Encourage the grieving person to "get over it" because of your discomfort with his or her depressed state.

---

[5]William G. Justice D. Min., *When Your Patient Dies*, Catholic Health Association, p. 25.

◊ Appendix A ◊

KNOWN CAUSES OF BIRTH DEFECTS

Dr. Heinz Berendes, head of the epidemiology and biometry branch of the National Institute of Child Health and Human Development—a division of the Department of Health and Human Services—and other scientists who study birth defects say that defects occur in one of three ways: as a result of either mutation (changes in the genetic material of the sperm or egg), or chromosomal anomaly (an abnormality in the number or structure of the chromosomes that "carry" the genes), or a mother's exposure to a teratogen. A teratogen is an agent that the mother comes into contact with or ingests—such as a drug or chemical—that breaks through the placental barrier to assault the fetus; radiation is also an agent that can pass directly through the mother's body to the fetus. Estimates vary over what portion of birth defects is caused by what agent. Dr. James Wilson, widely considered the dean of American teratologists, in 1973 estimated that mutations or chromosomal aberrations account for 25 percent of all malformations, and another 5 to 8 percent are caused by known teratogens (including natural agents such as viruses). For the remaining 65 to 70 percent of all birth defects, the cause is indeterminable.[1]

---

[1]Christopher Norwood, "Terata," *Mother Jones* (January 1985), p. 16. Used by permission.

◊ Appendix B ◊

FACTS ABOUT MISCARRIAGE

"There is a tendency to minimize the impact of a miscarriage," says Dr. Anthony Labrum, associate professor of obstetrics, gynecology and psychiatry at the Rochester's School of Medicine. Dr. Labrum coauthored a study about the emotional aftereffects of miscarriage. Even doctors, Labrum says, say things like "you'll get over it" and "it happens to a lot of women."

Facts about miscarriage prove much more helpful than platitudes that devalue or discount that baby's importance to a mother.

Dr. Sheldon Cherry, associate clinical professor of obstetrics and gynecology at New York's Mount Sinai Hospital, reports that the majority of miscarriages—an estimated one-half to two-thirds—are due to chromosomal abnormalities in the fetus. Because the fetus itself is defective, it is unable to grow and is ejected by the uterus, explains Dr. Cherry in *For Women of All Ages*.

The remainder of miscarriages stem from deficiencies in the maternal environment. These include hormonal imbalances in the mother, congenital abnormalities in the uterus, the presence of a virus, or less commonly, fibroid tumors in the uterus. Such problems, given increasingly sophisticated gynecological techniques, rarely mean that a woman will never have a full-term pregnancy. Quite the contrary, the large majority of women who have miscarriages subsequently go on to enjoy healthy pregnancies and deliveries, Dr. Cherry reports.

New research is uncovering new findings. Dr. Dorothy Warburton, director of New York City's Columbia Presbyterian Hospital cytogenetics laboratory, says that as few as two or more alcoholic beverages a week can double the chances for miscarriage, and a daily drink appears to be associated with a tripling in the risk of spontaneous miscarriage. Other findings include the correlation between smoking and miscarriage—a higher chance of miscarriage. And the risk of miscarriage increases with maternal age, especially after age thirty-five.[1]

---

[1]Janice Billingsley, "The Child Who Never Arrived: A New Look at Miscarriage," *Ladies Home Journal* (July 1979), p. 32.

As many as one out of five or six pregnancies ends in miscarriage, most occurring during the first three months.

Nearly one million families lose a child through stillbirth, miscarriage or infant death each year in the United States.[2]

---

[2]Donna Moriarty, "The Right to Mourn," *MS Magazine* (November 1982), p. 79.

◇ Appendix C ◇

FACTS ABOUT CHILD MOLESTERS

A sex offender who assaults an adult is four times more likely to receive a prison term than one who attacks a child.

Of all those assaulting children, 1 in 100 is apprehended.

Of all those apprehended, 1 of 10 is convicted.

Of all those convicted, 60 percent are released on probation and serve no sentence; 26 percent are sent to state mental hospitals for treatment; 14 percent are sentenced to prison.

The average time spent in mental health facilities by a convicted molester is eighteen months.

The average time spent in prison by a convicted molester is forty-one months.

The statistics above result in a national average of each molester only serving 15.09 minutes in jail.[1]

Children under fifteen years old accounted for one of every twenty-five homicide victims in the United States in 1980.[2]

---

[1]Taken from the brochure, "In Defense of Children," produced in cooperation with Societies League Against Molestation (SLAM) and the Help Find Johnny Gosch group of West Des Moines, Iowa.

[2]Federal Bureau of Investigation, Crime in the United States: *Uniform Crime Report for the United States*, Washington, D.C., U.S. Department of Justice, 1980.

BIBLIOGRAPHY

Anthony, Sylvia. *The Discovery of Death in Childhood and After*. Middlesex, Eng.: Penguin Books, 1973.

Arms, Suzanne. *To Love and Let Go*. New York: Alfred A. Knopf, 1983.

Bakoe, Susan Craig. "Rape—A Couple's Tragedy." *Quad-City Times Sunday Woman*, October 21, 1984.

Baldwin, Stanley C. *Bruised But Not Broken*. Portland, Ore.: Multnomah Press, 1985.

Bayless, Pamela J. *Caring for Dependent Parents*. New York: The Research Institute of America, 1985.

Behnham, Arliss R. *The Long Way Back*. Grand Rapids: Baker Book House, 1977.

Ball, Charles F. *Heaven—What You Can Know for Sure About Life After Death*. Wheaton, Ill.: Victor Books, 1980.

Barker, Peggy. *What Happened When Grandma Died*. St. Louis: Concordia Publishing Company, 1984.

Bayly, Joseph. *Heaven*. Elgin, Ill.: David C. Cook Publishing Co., 1977.

Bermudes, Dr. Robert W. *Conquering Cancer*. Lima, Ohio: C.C.S. Publishing Company, Inc., 1983.

Biebel, David B. *Jonathan, You Left Too Soon*. Nashville: Thomas Nelson Publishers, 1981.

Biegert, John E. *When Death Has Touched Your Life*. New York: The Pilgrim Press, 1981.

Billheimer, Paul E. *Destined for the Throne*. Minneapolis: Bethany House Publishers, 1975.

Bishop, Joseph P. *The Eye of the Storm*. Minneapolis: Bethany House Publishers, 1976, 1982.

Blackburn, Bill. *What You Should Know About Suicide*. Waco, Tex.: Word Books, Publishers, 1982.

Bloom, Lois A. *Mourning, After Suicide*. New York: The Pilgrim Press, 1982.

Boom, Corrie ten, and Jamie Buckingham. *Tramp for the Lord*. Old Tappan, N.J.: Christian Literature Crusade and Fleming H. Revell Company, 1974; Corrie ten Boom. *Each New Day*. Minneapolis: World Wide Publications, 1977.

Brandt, Leslie. *Why Did This Happen to Me?* St. Louis: Concordia Publishing House, 1977.

Brite, Mary. *Triumph Over Tears—How to Help a Widow.* Nashville: Thomas Nelson Publishers, 1979.

Brown, Robert McAfee, edited. *The Essential Reinhold Niebuhr.* New Haven: Yale University Press, 1986. (Selected Essays and Addresses)

Cain, Albert C. *Survivors of Suicide.* Springfield, Ill.: Charles C. Thomas Publishers, 1972.

Caine, Lynn. *Widow.* New York: William Morrow & Company, Inc., 1974.

Carpenter, Jan. *Turning Sorrow into Song.* Minneapolis: World Wide Publications, 1986.

Cato, Sid. *Healing Life's Great Hurts.* Chicago: Chicago Review Press, 1973.

Cohen, D., Eisdorfer, C. *Family Handbook on Alzheimer's Disease.* New York: W.H. Freeman, 1983.

Coffin, William Sloane. *The Courage to Love.* San Francisco, Calif.: Harper & Row, Publishers, 1982.

Cole, C. Donald. *Abraham, God's Man of Faith.* Chicago: The Moody Bible Institute, 1977.

Colgrove, Melba, Ph.D., Harold H. Bloomfield, M.D., Peter McWilliams. *How to Survive the Loss of a Love.* New York: Bantam Books, 1976.

Cousins, Norman. *Anatomy of an Illness.* New York: Bantam Books, 1979.

Cox-Gedmark, Jan. *Coping with Physical Disability.* Philadelphia: The Westminster Press, 1980.

Davidson, Glen W. *Living with Dying.* Minneapolis: Augsburg Publishing House, 1975.

———. *Understanding Death of a Wished-For Child.* Springfield, Ill.: OGR Services Corporation, 1979.

———. *Understanding Mourning.* Minneapolis: Augsburg Publishing House, 1984.

Decker, Bea. *After the Flowers Have Gone.* Grand Rapids: Zondervan Publishing House, 1973.

"Divorced Parents Stay Angry," *The Argus* (AP). Rock Island, Ill., October 24, 1986, p. 14.

Dobihal, Edward F., Jr., Charles William Stewart. *When a Friend Is Dying.* Nashville: Abingdon Press, 1984.

Dougan, Terrell, Lyn Isbell, and Patricia Vyas. *We Have Been There.* Nashville: Abingdon Press, 1984.

Erickson, Kenneth A. *Please, Lord, Untie My Tongue...* St. Louis: Concordia Publishing House, 1983.

Evely, Louis. *In the Face of Death.* New York: The Seabury Press, Inc., 1979.

Finkel, Maurice. *Fresh Hope With New Cancer Treatments.* Englewood Cliffs, N.J.: Prentice-Hall, Inc., 1984.

Ford, Leighton. *Sandy—A Heart for God.* Downers Grove, Ill.: InterVarsity Press, 1985.

Flynn, Leslie and Bernice. *God's Will: You Can Know It.* Wheaton, Ill.: Victor Books, 1979.

Fordham, Kate. *No Pit Too Deep. A Diary of Divorce.* Tring Herts, England: Lion Publishing, 1982.

Freeman, James Dillett. "Prayer for Protection." Unity School of Christianity.

Gardner, Richard A., M.D. *The Boys and Girls Book About Divorce.* New York: Bantam Book, 1970.

Garton, Jean Staker. *Who Broke the Baby?* Minneapolis: Bethany House Publishers, 1979.

Gerberding, Dr. Kieth. *Why Is There Evil When God Is Good?* Lima, Ohio: Fairway Press, 1983.

Grollman, Earl A. *What Helped Me When My Loved One Died.* Boston: Beacon Press, 1981.

————. *Concerning Death: A Practical Guide for the Living.* Boston: Beacon Press, 1974.

————, and Sharon H. Grollman. *Caring for Your Aged Parents.* Boston: Beacon Press, 1978.

Hanes, Mari, with Jack Hayford. *Beyond Heartache.* Wheaton, Ill.: Tyndale House Publishers, Inc., 1984.

Hendin, David. *Death as a Fact of Life.* New York: W.W. Norton & Company, 1984.

Henry, Iona, with Frank S. Mead. *Triumph over Tragedy.* Westwood, N.J.: Fleming H. Revell Company, 1957.

Hewett, John H. *After Suicide.* Philadelphia: The Westminster Press, 1980.

Hick, John H. *Death and Eternal Life.* San Francisco: Harper & Row, Publishers, 1976.

Hickman, Martha Whitmore. *I Will Not Leave You Desolate, Some Thoughts for Grieving Parents.* Nashville: The Upper Room, 1982.

————. *Waiting and Loving—Thoughts Occasioned by the Illness and Death of a Parent.* Nashville, Tenn.: The Upper Room, 1984.

Hill, Brennan, Ph.D. *The Near-Death Experience: A Christian Approach.* Dubuque, Iowa: Wm. C. Brown Company, Publishers, 1981.

Holmes, Marjorie. *To Help You Through the Hurting.* New York: Bantam Books, 1983.

Jackson, Edgar N. *The Many Faces of Grief.* Nashville: Abingdon Press, 1972, 1973, 1974, 1975, 1976, 1977.

Jensen, Irving L. *Job—A Self-Study Guide.* Chicago, Ill.: The Moody Bible Institute, 1975.

Johnson, Paul A., as told to Larry Richards. *Whom Can I Turn To?* Portland, Ore.: Multnomah Press.

Jones, Jean Gannon. *Time Out for Grief.* Huntington, Ind.: Our Sunday Visitor, Inc., 1979, 1982.

Justice, William G., Jr. D. Min. *When Your Patient Dies.* Catholic Health Association, p. 25.

Kane, Thomas A. *The Healing Touch of Affirmation.* Whitinsville, Miss.: Affirmation Books, 1976.

Keller, Helen. *My Religion.* New York: Pyramid Book by Doubleday & Co., Inc., 1927.

Kohn, Williard K., and Jane Burgess Kohn. *The Widower.* Boston: Beacon Press, 1978.

Kopp, Ruth, M.D., with Stephen Sorenson. *When Someone You Love Is Dying— A Handbook for Counselors and Those Who Care.* Grand Rapids: Zondervan Publishing House, 1980.

Kopp, R. *Where Has Grandpa Gone?* Grand Rapids: Zondervan Publishing House, 1983.

Kreis, Bernadine, and Alice Pattie. *Up From Grief—Patterns of Recovery.* Minneapolis: The Seabury Press, 1969.

Kubler-Ross, Elisabeth. *Death—The Final Stage of Growth.* Englewood Cliffs, N.J.: Prentice-Hall, Inc., 1975.

———. *Questions and Answers on Death and Dying.* New York: The Macmillan Publishing Co., 1974.

Kuhlman, Kathryn. *A Glimpse into Glory.* Plainfield, N.J.: Logos International, 1979.

Kushner, Harold S. *When Bad Things Happen to Good People.* New York: Schocken Books, 1981.

Kung, Hans. *Eternal Life—Life After Death as a Medical, Philosophical and Theological Problem.* Garden City, N.Y.: Image Books, 1985.

Laney, J. Carl. *The Divorce Myth.* Minneapolis: Bethany House Publishers, 1985.

Lee, Felicia. "Grown Children Also Stung by Trauma of Divorce." *USA Today*, April 19, 1984.

Leraux, Charles. "The Silent Epidemic." *Chicago Tribune*, 1981. (First of three-part series)

LeShan, Eda. *Learning to Say Good-By.* New York: The Macmillan Publishing Co., 1976.

Lewis, C.S. *A Grief Observed.* New York: Bantam Books, 1961, 1976.

———. *The Problem of Pain.* New York: The Macmillan Publishing Co., 1962.

Liebman, Joshua Loth. *Peace of Mind.* New York: Simon and Schuster, Inc., 1946.

Linburg, James. *Psalms for Sojourners.* Minneapolis: Augsburg Publishing House, 1986.

Linn, Dennis, Matthew Linn. *Healing Life's Hurts.* New York: Paulist Press, 1978.

Manning, Doug. *Comforting Those Who Grieve—A Guide for Helping Others.* San Francisco: Harper & Row, Publishers, 1985.

———. *Don't Take My Grief Away—What to Do When You Lose a Loved One.* San Francisco: Harper & Row, Publishers, 1984.

Mannion, Michael T. *Abortion & Healing: A Cry to be Whole.* Kansas City, Mo.: Sheed & Ward, 1986.

Marshall, Catherine. *To Live Again.* New York: McGraw-Hill, 1957.

McBride, Michele. *The Fire That Will Not Die.* Palm Springs, Calif.: ETC Publications, 1979.

McDonald, H.D. *The God Who Responds.* Minneapolis: Bethany House Publishers, 1986.

MacNutt, Francis, O.P. *The Power to Heal.* Notre Dame, Ind.: Ave Maria Press, 1977.

Mace, Nancy L., and Peter V. Rabins. *The 36-Hour Day: A Family Guide to Caring for Persons with Alzheimer's Disease.* Johns Hopkins University Press, 1981.

Malz, Betty. *My Glimpse of Eternity.* Old Tappan, N.J.: Fleming H. Revell Company, 1977.

Means, James E. *A Tearful Celebration.* Portland, Ore.: Multnomah Press, 1985.

Mehl, Duane. *At Peace with Failure.* Minneapolis: Augsburg Publishing House, 1984.

Melton, David. *Promises to Keep: A Handbook for Parents of Learning Disabled, Handicapped, and Brain-Injured Children.* Englewood Cliffs, N.J.: Prentice-Hall, Inc., 1962.

Mitchell, Kenneth R., and Herbert Anderson. *All Our Losses, All Our Griefs—Resources for Pastoral Care.* Philadelphia: The Westminster Press, 1983.

Moody, D.L. *Heaven—How to Get There.* Springdale, Pa.: Whitaker House, 1982.

Moody, Raymond A., Jr., M.D. *Life After Life and Reflections on Life After Life.* Convington, Ga.: Mockingbird Books, 1975.

Morey, Dr. Robert A. *Death and the Afterlife.* Minneapolis: Bethany House Publishers, 1985.

Morra, Marion, and Eva Potts. *Choices.* New York: Avon, 1980.

Moses, Kenneth, Ph.D., President, Resource Networks, Inc. Evanston, Ill. Lecture at Western Illinois University Macomb, Ill., 1980.

Moster, Mary Beth. *Living with Cancer.* Wheaton, Ill.: Tyndale House Publishers Inc., 1979.

Murphy, Sister Patricia, O.L.V.M. *Healing with Time and Love: A Guide for Visiting the Elderly.* Lexington, Mass.: D.C. Heath and Company, 1979.

Neal, Emily Gardiner. *In the Midst of Life.* New York: Hawthorn Books, Inc., 1963.

Nolen, William A., M.D. *Surgeon's Book of Hope.* New York: Coward, McCann & Geoghegan, 1980.

Noyer, Joan, and Norma MacNeil. *Your Child Can Win.* New York: William Morrow & Company, Inc., 1983.

Nouwen, Henri J.M. *The Wounded Healer.* Garden City, N.Y.: Image Books, 1972.

Nye, Miriam Baker. *But I Never Thought He'd Die.* Philadelphia: The Westminster Press, 1978.

Nystrom, Carolyn. *What Happens When We Die.* Chicago: Moody Press, 1981.

Oates, Wayne E. *Your Particular Grief.* Philadelphia: The Westminster Press, 1981.

Overly, Fay L. *Missing.* Denver, Colo.: Accent Publications, Inc., 1985.

Perske, Robert. *Show Me No Mercy.* Nashville: Abingdon Press, 1984.

Peters, Dan and Steve, with Cher Merrill. *Why Knock Rock?* Minneapolis: Bethany House Publishers, 1985.

Petri, Darlene. *The Hurt and Healing of Divorce.* Elgin, Ill.: David C. Cook Publishing Co., 1976.

Price, Eugenia. *Getting Through the Night.* New York: Ballantine Books, 1982.

————. *What Is God Like?* Grand Rapids: Zondervan Publishing House, 1960.

"Protein A-68 in Alzheimer's Disease," Alzheimer's Disease and Related Disorders Association, Inc., November 10, 1986.

Quad Cities Rape/Sexual Assault Counseling Center for Rock Island and Scott County. Brochure. Used by permission.

Ramsey, Dr. Donald W., and Rene Noorbergen. *Living with Loss.* (A Dramatic New Breakthrough in Grief Therapy.) New York: William Morrow and Company, Inc., 1981.

Rando, Therese A. *Grief, Dying, and Death.* Champaign, Ill.: Research Press Company, 1984.

Rank, Maureen. *Free to Grieve.* Minneapolis: Bethany House Publishers, 1985.

Raphael, Beverley. *The Anatomy of Bereavement.* New York: Basic Books, Inc., 1983.

Reed, Elizabeth L. *Helping Children with the Mystery of Death.* Nashville: Abingdon Press, 1970.

Rice, Richard. *God's Foreknowledge and Man's Free Will.* Minneapolis: Bethany House Publishers, 1985.

Robertson, John M. *Here I Am, God; Where Are You? Prayers and Promises for Hospital Patients.* Wheaton, Ill.: Tyndale House Publishers, 1984.

Robinson, Haddon W. *Grief.* Grand Rapids: Zondervan Publishing House, 1974.

Ross, Eleanora. *After Suicide: A Ray of Hope.* Iowa City: Ray of Hope, Inc., 1986.

Rudolph, Marguerita. *Should the Children Know?* New York: Schocken Books, 1978.

Russell, Philippa. *The Wheelchair Child: How Handicapped Children Can Enjoy Life to Its Fullest.* Englewood Cliffs, N.J.: Prentice-Hall, Inc., 1984.

Ryan, Juanita, R. *Standing By.* Wheaton, Ill.: Tyndale House Publishers, 1984.

Salsbury, Kathryn, and Eleanor Johnson. *The Indispensable Cancer Handbook.* New York: Seaview Books, 1981.

Schick, Edwin A. *Revelation.* Philadelphia: Fortress Press, 1977.

Schwarzbauer, Reverend Engelbert. *The Agony and the Grandeur of Death.* Collegeville, Minn.: The Liturgical Press, 1976.

Schwiebert, Pat, and Paul Kirk. *When Hello Means Goodbye.* University of Oregon Health Sciences Center, 3181 S.W. Sam Jackson Park Road, Portland, Ore., 1981.

Sharkey, Frances, M.D. *A Parting Gift.* New York: Bantam Books, 1982.

Shennan, Victoria. *Improving the Personal Health and Daily Life of the Mentally Handicapped.* Englewood Cliffs, N.J.: Prentice-Hall, Inc., 1984.

Shepard, Martin, M.D. *Someone You Love Is Dying: A Guide for Helping and Coping.* New York: Harmony Books, 1975.

Siegel, Anita. *The Sky Is Bluer Now—Thoughts About Cancer and Living.* The Self-Help Center, Evanston, Ill.

Simundson, Daniel J. *Where Is God in My Suffering?* Minneapolis: Augsburg Publishing House, 1983.

————. *Faith Under Fire—Biblical Interpretations of Suffering.* Minneapolis: Augsburg Publishing House, 1980.

Skoglund, Elizabeth. *Coping.* Ventura, Calif.: Regal Books Division, G/L Publications, 1971.

Smedes, Lewis B. *How Can It Be All Right When Everything Is All Wrong?* San Francisco: Harper & Row, Publishers, 1982.

Sorosky, Arthur D., M.D., Annette Baran, M.S.W., and Reuben Pannor, M.S.W. *The Adoption Triangle.* Garden City, N.Y.: Anchor Press/Doubelday, 1978.

Stearns, Ann Kaiser. *Living Through Personal Crisis.* Chicago: The Thomas More Press, 1984.

Steel, Valetta, with Ed Erny. *Thrice Through the Valley.* Wheaton, Ill.: Tyndale House Publishers, 1986.

Stevenson, Nancy Comey, and Cary Highley Straffon. *When Your Child Dies: Finding the Meaning in Mourning.* Lakewood, Ohio: Theo Publishing Co., 1981.

Stowell, Joseph M. *Through the Fire.* Wheaton, Ill.: Victor Books, 1985.

Sullender, R. Scott. *Grief and Growth—Pastoral Resources for Emotional and Spiritual Growth.* New York: Paulist Press, 1985.

Sumrall, Lester. *You Can Conquer Grief Before It Conquers You.* Nashville: Thomas Nelson Publishers, 1981.

Tanner, Ira J. *Healing the Pain of Everyday Loss.* Minneapolis: Winston Press, 1976.

Tapscott, Betty. *Out of the Valley.* Nashville: Thomas Nelson Publishers, 1980.

Temes, Roberta. *Living with an Empty Chair.* New York: Irvington Publishers, Inc., 1977.

Tormey, John C. *Life Beyond Death—Reflections on Dying and Afterlife.* Liguori, Mo.: Liguori Publications, 1981.

Towns, James F., Ph.D. *Growing Through Grief.* Anderson, Ind.: Warner Press, Inc., 1984.

Tuttle, Robert G. *Help Me, God! It's Hard to Cope.* Lima, Ohio: C.S.S. Publishing Company, 1984.

Vail, Elaine. *A Personal Guide to Living with Loss.* New York: John Wiley & Sons, 1982.

Veninga, Robert. *A Gift of Hope—How We Survive Our Tragedies.* Boston: Little, Brown & Company, 1985.

Vogel, Linda Jane. *Helping a Child Understand Death.* Philadelphia: Fortress Press, 1975.

Vredevelt, Pam W. *Empty Arms.* Portland, Ore.: Multnomah Press, 1984.

Weatherhead, Leslie D. *The Will of God.* Nashville: Abingdon Press, 1944, 1972.

Westburg, Granger. *Good Grief.* Philadelphia: Fortress Press, 1962, 1971.

Wiersbe, Warren W. *Why Us? When Bad Things Happen to God's People.* New Jersey: Fleming H. Revell Company, 1984.

Williams, Philip W. *When a Loved One Dies.* Minneapolis: Augsburg Publishing House, 1976.

Wolff, Pierre. *May I Hate God?* New York: Paulist Press, 1979.

Womach, Merrill and Virginia. *Tested by Fire.* Old Tappan, N.J.: Fleming H. Revell Company, 1976.

Wordon, J. William. *Grief Counseling and Grief Therapy—A Handbook for the Mental Health Practitioner.* New York: Springer Publishing Company, 1982.

Yancey, Philip. *Where Is God When It Hurts?* Grand Rapids: Zondervan Publishing House, 1977.

Zanca, Rev. Kenneth J. *Mourning: The Healing Journey.* Locust Valley, N.Y.: Living Flame Press, 1980.

Zigli, Barbara. "Pre-teen Boys Suffer Most from a Divorce." *USA Today.* April 18, 1984.

PUBLIC LECTURES

Auman, Lucia, S.W. "Coping with Transition." October 23, 1986. Davenport, Iowa.

Erickson, Beth, Ph.D. "Give Sorrow Words: Loss and Its Impact on Family and Individual Functioning." September 27, 28, 1985.

Feil, Naomi, M.S., A.C.S.W. "Validation Therapy Works!" (Regarding Alzheimer's Disease). Davenport, Iowa, October 31, 1986.

Frank, Rev. Dr. Robert L. "Coping with Loss-Grief." November 15–17, 1985. (Instructor in philosophy and thanatology at McHenry County College, Crystal Lake, Ill.)

Grollman, Earl A. "How to Talk with Children About Death," and on the Nature of Grief addressing clergy and health care professionals. February 11, 1987, LaGrange, Ill.

Hasley, Chaplain Ron. "The Mystery of Pain and Suffering." Rock Island, 1984. Director of Pastoral Care and Hospice, Lutheran Hospital, Moline, Ill.

Kubler-Ross, Elisabeth. "Death and Dying." Davenport, Iowa, 1975. Two-day seminar to health care personnel and clergy.

Lannie, Victoria Jean. "The Joy of Caring for the Dying." Franciscan Medical Center, Rock Island, Ill., 1984.

———. "Confronting Unexpected Death." Franciscan Medical Center, Rock Island, Ill., 1984. Nurse thanatologist consultant. Address to health care professionals and clergy.

Miller, Marv, Ph.D. "Suicide Prevention." Franciscan Medical Center, Rock Island, Ill. 1985. Address to health care professionals and clergy.

Mieszala, Pat, R.N. "Psychological Parameters of Burn Patient Care." Franciscan Medical Center, Rock Island, Ill. 1980.

Moses, Kenneth, Ph.D. "Grief Counseling and Mourning Theory." Western Illinois University, Macomb, Ill. 1980.

Skinner, Paul, Ph.D. "Communication: Listening and Non-verbal Behavior." Franciscan Medical Center, Rock Island, Ill. 1984.

PRIVATE INTERVIEWS WITH PROFESSIONALS

Auman, Lucia, M.S. "Counseling with Pregnant Women Regarding Alternatives." Staff Counselor, Maternal Health Center, Davenport, Iowa, October, 1986.

Doherty, Patrick, M.R.C. "Counseling the Disabled Patient." Rehabilitation counselor, Franciscan Medical Center Rehabilitation Center, Rock Island, 1980.

Cecile, Sister John. "Crisis Communication." Milan, Ill., 1984.

Gould, Father Eugene. "Crisis Communication." Milan, Ill., 1984.

Holm, Charlotte, R.N. "Nursing Home Placement." Director of Nursing, River View Terrace Nursing Home, Tomahawk, Wis., July 19, 1986.

Hughes, Mary Anne. "Healing Visions—Post-Abortion Counseling." President, National Youth Pro-Life Coalition, New York (per phone interview October 24, 1986).

Lindquist, Jo. "Caregiving for Alzheimer's Patients and Families." Executive Director, Quad Cities Chapter of the Alzheimer's Disease and Related Disorders Association, Inc., Davenport, Iowa, February 2, 1987.

McCormick-Pries, Chris, A.R.N.P. "Post-Suicide Counseling." Chairperson of Adolescent Suicide Prevention Task Force of Scott and Muscatine County, Iowa.

McEchron, W. David, Ph.D., P.C. "Abortion Counseling." Psychologist in private practice, Davenport, Iowa.

Miller, Jeri, R.N. "Communication with the Disfigured Burn Patient." Staff nurse, Franciscan Medical Center, Rock Island, Ill. 1984.

Paper, Carol, B.S.W. Executive Director of Hospice Care of Scott County, Iowa, September 25, 1985.

Thorn, Vicky, Coordinator, Project Rachel, Milwaukee, Wis. (per phone interview October 23, 1986).

Tyler-Jamison, Berlinda, M.S.W. Director of Victim Services, Quad Cities Assault Counseling Center, Rock Island, Ill., September 10, 1985.

Whitmer, Chaplain Marlin. "Communication with Widows and Widowers." Director of Pastoral Care, St. Lukes Hospital, Davenport, Iowa, 1985.